Go and Do Likewise

WILLIAM C. SPOHN

Go and Do Likewise

Jesus and Ethics

CONTINUUM NEW YORK

1999
The Continuum Publishing Company
370 Lexington Avenue
New York, NY 10017

All biblical citations are taken from the
New Revised Standard Version Bible, copyright 1989,
Division of Christian Education of the
National Council of the Churches of Christ
in the United States of America.

Printed in the United States of America

Library of Congress Cataloging-in-Publication Data

Spohn, William C.
    Go and do likewise : Jesus and ethics / William C. Spohn.
        p.   cm.
    Includes bibliographical references and index.
    ISBN 0-8264-1118-5
    1. Jesus Christ—Ethics.   2. Christian ethics.   I. Title.
BS2417.E8S67   1999
241—dc21   98-40778
                                                              CIP

For
Michael J. Buckley, S.J.,
and
James M. Gustafson

In Gratitude

Contents

Preface   ix

Introduction   1

PART 1
THE SOURCES

1 Ethics and the Word of God   9

   Discipleship and Ethics   10

   I. A Threefold Approach   12

   II. Scripture: An Engaged Reading   16

2 Virtues, Practices, and Discipleship   27

   I. Ethics of Virtue and Character   27

   II. Spirituality and Its Practices   33

   III. Practices: Linking Spirituality and Virtue   42

3 The Analogical Imagination   50

   I. The Bridge of Imagination   50

   II. Imagination in Christian Ethics   60

   III. The Kingdom of God: Metaphor and Analogy   66

PART 2

CHRISTIAN TRANSFORMATION

4 Perception 75
  I. God Has Begun to Reign 76
  II. Jesus and Compassionate Vision 87
  III. Virtue Ethics on Moral Perception 92

5 Correcting Perception 100
  I. Correcting Perception: Frames and Metaphors 101
  II. The Means of Grace: Practices That Sharpen Perception 112

6 Emotions and Dispositions 120
  I. Images That Tutor the Emotions 121
  II. Encounters with Jesus 127
    Encounter Stories and Dispositions 134
  III. The Practice of Meditation 136

7 Dispositions and Discernment 142
  I. From Stories to the Master Story 143
  II. The Practice of Discernment 152

8 Identity and the Lord's Supper 163
    Christian Identity 164
  I. The Table of Unity and Disunity 165
  II. Identity and Identification 169
  III. The Practice of Eucharist 175

Conclusion 185
Notes 189
Index of Scripture References 217
Index of Names 219
Index of Subjects 223

Preface

M Y FATHER LIKES TO INVOKE the old saw that "self-made men relieve the deity of an awesome responsibility." Books are no more self-made than people are. Books are written in private but are hardly solitary creations; friendships, classes, communities, and traditions stand behind the work. Two great mentors have blessed my life with their wisdom and friendship: Michael J. Buckley, S.J., and James M. Gustafson. They showed how fruitful is a life that combines love of learning and the desire for God.

My debt to the community and spirituality of the Society of Jesus should be evident on every page of this work. More friends, teachers, spiritual directors, and retreat directors have contributed to this work than can be named here. Roger Haight, S.J., got this project going by asking me to address the Catholic Theological Society of America convention in 1994 on the topic of Jesus and ethics. Frank Oveis of the Continuum Publishing Group heard that address, suggested that it could become a book, and worked patiently to bring it to reality. It is a grace to be asked to do things that we would never have volunteered to do.

I am particularly grateful to colleagues and students at the Jesuit School of Theology at Berkeley and the Department of Religious Studies at Santa Clara University. The administration at Santa Clara has provided encouragement and opportunity to complete this work, particularly from 1996 to 1998 through the Presidential Professorship of Ethics and the Common Good in the Markkula Center for Applied Ethics at the university.

I am grateful to the community of Holy Spirit Parish, Newman Hall, of Berkeley, California, where the Paulist Fathers lead a wonderfully diverse community to live the gospel on the campus and on the streets. I am grateful for a generous grant from "Leaders for a Just World," a program of the James Irvine

Foundation at Santa Clara University. It funded Grainne O'Leary's invaluable work as research assistant. Colleagues who are willing to read manuscript drafts will have a special place in the kingdom of God—seeing that they have already been through purgatory. The grant enabled a group of colleagues to come together for a consultation on this manuscript. They represented expertise in the three approaches that converge in this study, namely, New Testament studies, virtue ethics, and spirituality. Their suggestions considerably improved and streamlined the argument: Denise Carmody, Martin Cook, Jim Reites, S.J., J. David Pleins, and Barry Stenger of Santa Clara; Alberto Damingo, C.S.S.R., from Salamanca; John R. Donahue, S.J., Jim Bretzke, S.J., and Mark Ravizza, S.J., of the Jesuit School of Theology at Berkeley; Robert Smith and Martha Ellen Stortz of the Pacific Lutheran Theological Seminary, also of the Graduate Theological Union at Berkeley.

Special gratitude goes to Marty, who shared her insights on spiritual practices generously, believed that this book needed to be written, endured its production with good humor and unflagging support, and deserves more credit than words can convey.

Introduction

WHAT DOES JESUS HAVE TO DO with ethics? Whenever Christians seek to understand the fullness of Jesus Christ, they go back to Jesus of Nazareth.[1] We discover in the particular story of this historical figure the one who is often obscured by the abstractions of Christology. Contemporary Christologies "from below" insist on beginning from the specific stories of the Gospels. Recently, moral theologians are taking a similar turn to answer the question, What moral significance does Jesus have for Christians today?

There are two brief answers given by believers: "everything" and "not much." They hold down the two ends of the spectrum. This book will avoid these extremes, while making a constructive proposal that Jesus Christ is the paradigm for Christian moral life. On the one end, Jesus has "everything" to do with ethics. Certain evangelical and fundamentalist Christians hold that human beings are such thorough sinners that they cannot achieve moral insight on their own. They must turn to Jesus Christ and be converted in order to know what to do and become. Turning from the deceptions of worldly reason, they will find authoritative guidance in the New Testament, which contains the precise words and commands of Jesus of Nazareth, now reigning as Lord and Christ. Direct, uncontaminated access to God's wisdom, however, proves quite elusive. Witness the American "Christian Coalition," which has closely identified the message of Jesus with the conventional wisdom of middle-class conservatives.

The other extreme holds that Jesus has "not much" to do with ethics. Roman Catholics are more likely to say "not much" than "everything." Catholics have traditionally held that human nature has not fallen as far into darkness as the Protestant Reformers assumed. Although sin clouds reason and weakens the will, conscience and moral judgment still function. If God's designs for human

1

flourishing were utterly erased from our experience and reflection, we would no longer be human. For centuries, Catholic clergy trained on manuals of moral theology that mostly ignored Jesus Christ. Morality rested on natural law, which was the same for all persons, whether they knew Christ or not. Although this naturalist ethics rested on the belief in divine creation, it operated experientially through common practical reason without reference to the Gospels.

Some theologians respond to our question by stating that Jesus of Nazareth is irrelevant, peripheral, or too concrete to have any direct import for ethics. After Vatican II, moral theologians began to insert chapters on Christian discipleship in their treatises but relegated the influence of religious experience and symbols to the general background of morality.[2] At best, faith commitments provide motivational support to human obligations and values while leaving their contents untouched.[3]

Finally, there are others today who consider the figure of Jesus too narrowly particular to function in ethics. For some feminist theologians the maleness of Jesus underwrites patriarchal oppression and negates him as a source of liberating practice. Others who seek a universal religious morality object that the figure of Jesus is too Western, too dualistic, too historically concrete. I will propose an alternative view in which Jesus plays a normative role as the concrete universal of Christian ethics.[4] Through faithful imagination his story becomes paradigmatic for moral perception, disposition, and identity. Others want to subordinate the figure of Jesus to their particular agenda for moral action. Proponents of Christian "family values" and liberal Christians both invoke religious rhetoric to motivate congregations to political agendas that are unchallenged by the gospel.

As I understand Christian faith, Jesus Christ is confessed to be the definitive but not the exclusive revelation of God.[5] Theologically, this confession means that for Christians Jesus Christ is the one to whom the revelations of other traditions point. Morally, this confession means that Jesus Christ plays a normative role in Christians' moral reflection.[6] His story enables us to recognize *which* features of experience are significant, guides *how* we act, and forms *who* we are in the community of faith. The main constructive portion of the argument in this volume, chapters 4 through 8, moves progressively to deeper levels of moral experience. It begins with moral *perception* that notices the significant features of experience. Then it considers moral *dispositions*, which guide how Christians should be engaged and disposed to act. Finally, we move to *identity*, that is, who we are and seek to become. Obviously these three aspects of moral life interact. Our basic identity has great influence on what we perceive, and our main moral dispositions influence both what we see and who we think ourselves to be.

It should be clear that this will not be a discussion of how values and principles drawn from the story of Jesus can illumine or solve specific contemporary issues. It would take another volume to address that important task of Christian ethics.[7] An exclusive focus on moral issues, however, risks fragmenting life into a series of discrete decisions and isolating the moral agent from communities of wisdom and accountability. This book offers a discussion that is more a phenomenology of the Christian calling. It operates under the same conviction that shaped the work of H. Richard Niebuhr: behind questions of action lie interpretation and identity. Who we understand ourselves to be and how we interpret what is going on will determine what we think we ought to do.[8]

When Christian individuals and communities try to figure out what to do about racism, economic injustice, sexism, and environmental degradation, they should do so in reference to who they are called to be as disciples of Jesus Christ. How that calling functions as their moral guide is the subject of this book. Christian moral formation is not a technique to produce answers to every moral issue. It can only hope to bring the full resources of Christian tradition and community life into the discernment.

The first three chapters of the work make the case for the sources and method that will be employed. The story of Jesus shapes Christian ethics through the convergence of three sources: the New Testament, virtue ethics, and spirituality.

The first chapter focuses on the use of the New Testament. Scripture has more to offer the moral life than specific moral rules or general theological concepts like incarnation or "law and gospel" from which a theological ethics can be derived. The New Testament writings witness to the life of Jesus of Nazareth as the way that leads to life. That story should shape the dispositions and identity of Christians so that they live a distinctive life of discipleship together.

The second chapter treats the other two sources, virtue ethics and spirituality. Scripture seeks radical transformation of believers. Since virtue ethics attends to the full range of moral experience, from vision to character, it offers the most fruitful approach to this transformative text. Virtue theorists, however, say little about how virtuous habits are developed and vicious ones eliminated. I will argue that *spiritual practices* can supply the missing link between virtue ethics and the transformation of emotions and moral habits. Christian spirituality has developed specific practices of prayer, service, and worship that are meant to deepen engagement with God. Indirectly, these same practices train the imagination and reorient the emotions to produce a way of life consonant with sound morality and New Testament moral teaching. They in turn provide the normative considerations that keep Christian spiritual practices honest and fruitful.

The third chapter describes the *analogical imagination*. The imagination gives us access to Jesus as the concrete universal of Christian ethics, the paradigm that normatively guides Christian living. The imagination moves analogically from the classic patterns of his story to discover how to act faithfully in new situations. The basic command that Jesus gives at the end of the Good Samaritan story invites Christians to think analogically: "Go and do likewise" (Luke 10:37). The mandate is not "Go and do exactly the same" as the Samaritan. It is decidedly not "Go and do whatever you want." The term "likewise" implies that Christians should be faithful to the story of Jesus yet creative in applying it to their context. The New Testament provides the patterns that ground the analogical imagination: metaphorical frameworks (particularly the kingdom of God), parables and ecounters with Jesus, and the overall narrative pattern of the life, death, and resurrection of Jesus.

Chapters 4 and 5 address *moral perception*. They take up Jesus' challenge to see the world as he saw it, as the place where God's reign is breaking in. Since that vision bears little resemblance to the world shown on television news broadcasts, we will need to make some serious adjustments. What we notice depends on the lenses through which we see our world. Scripture's images and metaphors correct our vision so we see others in a special way: as "neighbor," "sister and brother," and "the one for whom Christ died." We are no longer competitors or strangers, but we share a common life that naturally brings forth compassionate and effective action. Conversion means discarding the old lenses of hostility, rivalry, and greed. Spiritual practices sharpen the new powers of perception. They help the Spirit's gift of new sight to expand and mature. The practices of asceticism and intercessory prayer train us to see "the world according to God."

The sixth and seventh chapters delve behind vision to the inner dynamics of the moral life, *dispositions*. These are the springs of the moral life, the character tendencies that make us ready to act in certain ways. Dispositions are based in emotions and our basic convictions and values. While metaphors help us perceive the world in new ways, the stories of scripture shape our emotions to act in ways appropriate to the gospel. The parables of Jesus confront business as usual with the dramatic reality of the reign of God. The parables were meant to evoke strong emotions—hope, fear, forbearance, courage, mercy, single-mindedness, prodigal generosity. Those emotions are not meant to be momentary sentiments, but steady qualities of character.

The stories of Jesus' encounters with people challenge our customary emotional scenarios. Every emotion contains a script that tells us how to act. Anger seeks to redress an injustice by restitution or revenge. Envy seeks to remove unfair advantage. The miracles and healing encounters of Jesus write a different script for Christians. The practice of meditating on the Psalms and the Gospel text help us change our usual scenarios. The Psalms evoke certain emotions and then channel them into relation with God. They shaped the emotions of Jesus, who knew them by heart.

Chapter 8 goes to the root of Christian life, individual and communal *identity*. I use the term "identity" to refer to the deliberate and mostly conscious sense of who we are. Identity emerges from identifications, that is, from the causes, convictions, and communities to which we commit ourselves. Committed Christian life coalesces around the overall profile of Jesus' life and destiny. The "full story" of Jesus becomes the paradigm for Christian life, which is primarily life in common. The individual participates in the life and destiny of Jesus by sharing the life of an actual body of disciples. No one can be a Christian alone. God's reign of justice and love in a universal community of reconciliation has to begin somewhere specific. Life in common and in service to the world is sustained by the practices of the Lord's table, forgiveness, and solidarity with the poor. Following Christ happens locally, not ideologically.

Finally, I must acknowledge that this book is written from the perspective of someone who attempts to live the Christian life and belongs to a particular communion, the Roman Catholic Church, while being shaped by the witness and writings of Christians of other communions. I hope that the commitment of faith forms my identity even more than being male, married, of Irish and German descent, Californian, and a professional academic in a Catholic, Jesuit university. My whole social location influences the tone of this book.

I do not write out of a "hermeneutics of suspicion" in addressing the New Testament and communities that try to be faithful to Jesus Christ. Others have already done that, and much of their writing continues to call the church back to living more authentically. Although I hope I have learned from these critics, I will be writing from a "hermeneutics of appreciation." No text can be adequately interpreted unless it is read with a certain amount of generosity that allows the reader to enter the world of the text. However, Christian life is primarily a matter not of entering a text and its world but of being welcomed into a mysterious and encompassing relation with God in Christ through the power of the Spirit. Scripture makes it clear that trusting faith and faithful practice are the only avenues "to know the Lord." There is a knowledge that comes only from participation, from living inside the circle of faith rather than outside it. I do not believe that the reign of God is coterminous with any or all Christian communities. Being a participant in a particular way of life has its limits, to be sure. It seems to me, however, that even an inconsistent participant understands a way of life better than the most fair-minded spectator. It is also true that we are far better known by our friends than by a prosecuting attorney.

PART 1

The Sources

CHAPTER 1

Ethics and the Word of God

WHEN I TOLD A NEW TESTAMENT SCHOLAR that I was writing a
book on Jesus and ethics, he asked, "Which Jesus?" His question was
only half in jest. Late-twentieth-century biblical studies has distinguished the
distinctive theological slants that the different evangelists and Paul took on the
story of Jesus. In this approach, any appeal to a single picture of Jesus runs the
risk of slighting other New Testament portraits that are equally valid. Other
friends who are theologians wondered, half in jest but fully in earnest, "What
does Jesus have to do with ethics?" Some worry about moralizing Christian
faith. Others balk at linking the Savior to the rational business of justifying acts
by appeal to principles. A community of faith might struggle to discern God's
invitation in "the signs of the times," but what does that have to do with invoking ethics, which they see to consist of abstract principles and arguments about
moral absolutes?

Although it will take at least an entire book to answer these questions, I
believe that the concerns of exegesis, theology, and ethics do not invalidate the
radical insight of faith. To be a Christian means to follow Jesus, to be his disciple in community with others who walk the same path. His call is to "follow
me," not to follow a set of concepts, a code of conduct, or an institution. I was
reminded of this recently while waiting for a postponed flight in a crowded airport lounge. A group of young Muslims in traditional robes surrounded an
aged teacher with long gray beard and staff in hand. He was seated, and they
were around him, some standing and some sitting on the floor in front of him,
hanging on his every word. At first it seemed a little bizarre to see such a tableau
in Los Angeles International Airport in 1995. As I continued to pass the time
by reading Marcus Borg's book on Jesus,[1] it dawned on me that this is what dis-

9

ciples did—they were sitting at the feet of their master in the ancient sign of respect and subordination. Jesus' disciples must have done the same thing on the hills of Galilee and the town squares of Judea.

After discussing the importance of ethics for discipleship, I will introduce the three sources to be used, namely, virtue ethics, spirituality, and scripture. Then I will sketch the role that scripture will play in this synthesis.

————————————————DISCIPLESHIP AND ETHICS————————————————

Discipleship necessarily involves ethical reflection and accountability. Disciples look to their masters for guidance, inspiration, and challenge. They become apprentices of someone who knows what they need to learn. If Christians are disciples of Jesus, that implies that his life and teachings are *normative* for them. This relation necessarily means that the disciple acknowledges the authority of the master, particularly when the master lives up to the message. The particular life and death of Jesus set the boundaries for Christians, direct their intentions, and shape the emotions and actions of individuals and communities.[2] That is to say, the life of Jesus functions as their "norm" or standard. Usually we think of moral norms as general statements, such as "equals should be treated equally." The norm for Christian life is more complex and more concrete than that. A main task of this book will be to show how a particular life can function as a moral paradigm that offers normative guidance for a way of life.

Jesus' life, depicted in the central story that unifies the writings of the New Testament, has a specific direction, a definable shape, and an undeniable urgency that continues to make the fundamental moral claim on Christians of every generation. Paul appeals to this standard when he urges the Philippians, "live your life in a manner worthy of the gospel of Christ" (1:27). The gospel is not the only norm, as shown by Paul's frequent appeals to human values, practical logic, common secular wisdom, and the like. In the New Testament and most Christian theologies, at a minimum, general human moral standards are also presumed to be normative. The life of Jesus as related in the Gospels, however, is the fundamental norm for Christian identity. When Paul discusses a serious moral issue, he almost always appeals to the cross and resurrection of Jesus, which epitomized for him the pattern of the good news. Subsequent generations of Christians have appealed to various aspects of the Gospel story, but also to the Ten Commandments, the cardinal virtues, natural law, judgments about consequences, and so on. As we shall see, the story of Jesus is a *paradigm*, a normative pattern or exemplar that can be creatively applied in different circumstances. Disciples do not clone their master's life; they follow the master through discerning imaginations, graced emotions, and faithful community.

Christians have often substituted a false norm for the story of Jesus by projecting their own values and biases onto it. These counterfeits are exposed by a deeper reading of the Gospels, which are the enduring standard against which all portraits of Jesus must be measured. The sentimental Jesus of middle-class piety hides the cross of poverty and oppression; the Jesus of Western imperialism is refuted by the nonviolence of the passion accounts; the Jesus of patriarchal tradition wilts under the evidence that the Nazarene chose the powerless and marginal to share his table. Liberation theologian Jon Sobrino reminds us that "whenever, in the course of history, Christians have sought to reinvest Christ with his totality, they have returned to Jesus of Nazareth."[3] In other words, they return to the one portrayed in the Gospels.

That return necessarily takes into account the best of historical scholarship because this story is about a particular human being at a definite time and place. If we are ignorant about the hopes and fears that drove his culture and the structures that shaped it, we will inevitably misunderstand the words and actions of Jesus, since they were directed, first of all, to his contemporaries. Misunderstanding their original meaning, we will be prone to misreading their import for today.

History, however, cannot convey the full import of the story. Every journey of Christian discipleship begins in an encounter with Jesus Christ, who is not an idea or a memory but the present risen Lord, who summons a wholehearted response from each generation. Those who hold aloof from this demanding and mysterious encounter cannot fully understand Jesus or the One whose reign he proclaimed. That intimate knowledge belongs to participants, not spectators.[4] Scripture tells us the astonishing news that we are invited to be the friends of God, who know and are known by God intimately. While history can describe a person's context and résumé, it cannot make us that person's friends. We have to make a living connection. Friendship necessarily involves encounter and personal engagement through mutual self-disclosure and commitment.

Christian faith asserts that an analogous, if far more mysterious, personal engagement is possible with God in Christ. That contact is not reducible to the language, symbols, and practices of various Christian traditions that are necessarily used to interpret it. In the final analysis, the Gospels are "good news" not because they convey a set of ideas about God but because they disclose Immanuel, God acting in our midst. Through this story the self-revelation of the central character occurs to the eyes of faith. Response to that revelation requires the action of the Spirit, personal decision, community, and struggle with the weakness and obscurity that faith never eradicates.

––––––––––––––––––––– I. A THREEFOLD APPROACH –––––––––––––––––––––

The canonical scriptures of Christian faith are held together by the story of Jesus of Nazareth, who came at the climactic moment in the history of Israel to proclaim and inaugurate God's reign or kingdom. Take away the story of that event and that person and almost nothing would remain of the collection of writings called the New Testament. In this human life Christians discover the path that leads to God, and they meet the One who invites and accompanies them on this way of service, witness, suffering, and reconciliation. Disciples follow Jesus as the Way, not as the terminus of the journey. The story that shapes the New Testament will also shape their lives and identities. Disciples are not above the master: they should expect the same treatment if they take the same path.[5]

I propose that a particular method of critical reflection can assist those who have already begun to walk on the way of discipleship. We can better discover that way by combining three avenues of reflection: (a) the New Testament story of Jesus, (b) the ethics of virtue and character, and (c) the practices of Christian spirituality. These complement each other, like a tripod or a three-legged stool. First, let us describe how these three approaches relate to each other before addressing them individually.

1. How are we to get at this story? Or better, how can we let this story get to us? Here is where character ethics and spirituality come into play. An *ethics of character and virtue* offers the most adequate approach to the *story of scripture* because that story aims to transform not only our individual actions but our "hearts," that is, the whole embodied person as related to others. That story becomes our story as we appropriate it progressively through imagination, emotions, convictions, and actions. The other, more common types of ethics are based respectively on obligation and on consequences. They grasp a more limited portion of what the canonical texts offer. If scripture were primarily a manual of behavioral rules, then the ethics of obligation would be the best way to approach it. If it were a program for social reconstruction, a utilitarian or pragmatic ethics would be the optimal way to read it. Although the Bible contains rules and undoubtedly has a political dimension, it cannot be limited to these aspects.

Taken as a whole, scripture is the story of a people called into existence and led by God to be a distinctive community. The Hebrew Scriptures disclose who

Yahweh is and who the chosen people should be in response to the covenant. The story that runs through the Old and New Testaments sets the pattern for Christian identity, for the "sorts of persons" Christians are called to become.[6] Since character refers to the "sort of person" someone is, character ethics would appear to be a better candidate for interpreting scripture than an ethics of oblig- ation or one of consequences (although both of these ways of doing ethics can play a useful, if limited, role in depicting the moral life and in understanding scripture[7]).

✳✳✳ Character attends to the whole person. It asks what sorts of people we are becoming through our actions and relations with others. We become what we do, for better or worse. Our actions and relations become habits that gradually shape the stable personal core we call "character." Virtues and vices are the dynamics of character, the habits of the heart that carry convictions into action and shape the way the person views the world and responds to it.[8] People can, of course, have fairly well defined characters that are corrupt.

Unfortunately, most contemporary character ethics remain at a relatively for- mal level. The moral philosophers who are willing to describe the structure of the good life usually shy away from describing its content.[9] In a pluralistic cul- ture such as ours, advocating one set of human values seems to imply intoler- ance of other ways of living. The first problem, therefore, is that contemporary character ethics is reluctant to specify moral content, that is, *what* this way of life should be. Second, even when moral philosophers are willing to provide definite content to the good life, they are often agnostic about *how* we can develop the prescribed virtues.

2. The other two legs of our methodological tripod balance off these deficits of virtue ethics. *The New Testament, taken as a whole,* provides quite definite content to the moral life. *Spirituality,* the third leg of our methodological stool, complements *exegesis and ethics* by spelling out practices that foster the habits of mind and heart that gradually transform the character. "Spirituality" refers here to classical traditions of Christian practice and community, not the undefined and idiosyncratic amalgam of activities that is currently referred to as "spiritu- ality." The purpose of traditional spiritual practices is not the fostering of spe- cific virtues but deepening the relationship to God.

3. A sound understanding of *virtue ethics* will check the common tendency to use *spirituality* as an instrument for self-enhancement. Authentic spirituality's commitment to values beyond the self can counter any perfectionist tendencies in virtue ethics. Virtues are acquired indirectly, when one is concerned with val- ues greater than the virtue itself. The virtuous life shifts attention from per- sonal perfection to more important concerns like beauty, justice, and

friendship. Analogously, spiritual practices affect the practitioner indirectly; in fact, they are distorted when used as tools for developing the self. For example, worshiping God in a community where the diverse body of Christ is fully represented may foster the virtues of gratitude and solidarity; however, using worship as an instrument to develop these qualities would be self-defeating. If the intent of worship is not God but personal growth, then God is being reduced to a means, which is a form of idolatry.[10]

4. The combination of *ethics of character and the content of the New Testament story* moves *spirituality* beyond the descriptive to the normative. Spirituality has often been a private pursuit of holiness without accountability to any community. Or, as an academic discipline, it has been a merely historical description of certain practices and communities. In a normative Christian spirituality, however, certain habits of the heart are mandated and others are proscribed; certain ways of relating are right and others are wrong. They are measured against the normative paradigm of the life and actions of Jesus. Some spiritualities can claim a bogus normativity, as when the author makes his own individual experience the measure for the spiritual journey of everyone else. Like mushrooms blooming in the damp shade of a log, this type of normativity tends to crop up when the practices are isolated from an expansive tradition and the light of critical reflection.[11]

Spiritual practices and the message of the New Testament have moral dimensions inherent in them. Christian ethics looks to bring out these implications so they can reshape character, community, and action in society.[12] Often enough, these dangerous implications remain latent, and any attempt to bring them to the fore will be resisted by those who want to keep their piety safe and comforting. For instance, the practice of Eucharist has inescapable moral dimensions to it. When understood against the stories of Jesus' table fellowship with sinners and outcasts, the ritual of sharing food blessed and broken in Jesus' name, is itself a socially significant action. Worship in this way means that we should treat distant neighbors as guests at our own family table. Christian ethics does not have its own agenda and then turn to spiritual practices and biblical symbols to dress it up in an attractive manner. The task of ethical reflection is to draw out the implications of the rituals and symbols of faith for life.

5. *Spirituality and character ethics* emphasizes personal engagement in a way that can be salutary for critical *biblical exegesis*. This engagement requires different skills from those honed in scholarship. Commitment to critical distance, probing questions, and attention to unspoken agendas help the scholar move beyond the original naivete of encountering the work of art.[13] After hermeneutics has helped someone climb the ladder of criticism, however, it can leave one

stranded at the top, somewhat remote from the original encounter with the text. Virtue ethics and spirituality will not eliminate critical distance. They should return the reader to a renewed encounter with the text, a fresh encounter enriched by criticism but not stranded in intellectual distance. If a Shakespearean scholar came to know so much about Hamlet that she couldn't stand to witness an actual production of the play, something would have gone wrong in her literary criticism.

"Beyond the desert of criticism, we wish to be called again," wrote Paul Ricouer, a master of hermeneutics.[14] The goal of criticism is not intellectual detachment but this "second naivete," which experiences the literary symbols not innocently and literally, as in the initial naivete, but "as if."[15] The scholar needs a different set of skills to close the circle, to appreciate the religious text from the inside, as a participant in a way of life rather than a spectator from outside. Closing the circle is less likely to occur in the academy, where the Bible is analyzed. It requires spiritual practices, disciplines of meditation, practice, and service. It requires a different social location, namely, a community of faith where the religious discourse is embodied in a way of life. Liberation theologians remind us that the actual praxis of the gospel is the precondition for understanding it: the Way looks different when you are on it.[16]

6. Finally, *scripture and spirituality* are not instrumentally related to *virtue ethics.* They are not motivational levers to get people to do what they ought to do but don't feel like doing. This persistent American heresy shapes many a Sunday sermon in which the Bible and liturgy are employed to foster a particular agenda, from social activism to family values. Worship and word are means to persuade the congregation to commit themselves to moral ends that are already clear. With a different audience one would simply use a different rhetoric.

This rhetorical strategy takes a more sophisticated shape in some recent forms of Catholic moral theology, where the content of morality is sharply distinguished from moral motivation. Moral obligations are claimed to possess intrinsic truth value which does not depend on extrinsic appeals. Support from scripture or the example of Jesus may assist those who cannot grasp the intrinsic value of ethical norms, but is unnecessary for the morally mature. They have no need of any such motivational "training wheels" to grasp the autonomous worth of moral norms.[17] Motivation, however, cannot be so readily separated from moral content, since why we do something often enters into the very meaning of what we are doing.[18] Often, different motivation changes the meaning of the action. Nonviolence understood as participating in the cross of Christ has a meaning different from Gandhian nonviolence. They are not the same moral practice outfitted in disposable rhetorical garments.

Let us now take a closer look at how we will read the New Testament and the
story of Jesus, the first of the three components in studying Jesus and ethics.
The next chapter will address the other two components, virtue ethics and spirituality.

─────────────────── II. SCRIPTURE: AN ENGAGED READING ───────────────────

What strategies of engaged reading are demanded by this connection of spiritual practices, virtue ethics, and scripture? Readers who are seeking meaning
rather than a detached, objective picture of Jesus cannot treat the New Testament text as a relic. They must enter into conversation with it, bring their questions and concerns into "the world of the text," and interrogate it from new
angles. They also must let the text interrogate them and allow its strangeness
to upset their familiar frameworks and assumptions. It must enter the world of
the reader to generate fresh meaning.

The canonical text of scripture provides the ultimate norm for Christian
spirituality and virtue ethics. There is no point in trying to clear the vast and
dense forest of biblical scholarship; perhaps it will be more realistic to indicate
briefly where the space for our discussion is located in the forest. First, I will
look at what an engaged reading of scripture means today; second, at the role
that historical scholarship plays; and finally, I will turn to a cameo of Christian
transformation in Paul's Letter to the Philippians.

A New Quest for Meaning

In the latter decades of the twentieth century, scripture is being read more
through ethics than through history. This change of perspective came from two
factors: the quest for meaning and diminished confidence in "objective" history.
Studying the historical context of the work and the intention of its author no
longer satisfies the contemporary quest for meaning, if it ever did before.[19]

Let us first examine the way in which the interests of the reader have moved
to the fore. Contemporary readers are increasingly seeking *meaning*, that is,
truth that one can live by. Skepticism about timeless, universal truths and the
pressure of personal and global needs is producing a more engaged reading of
texts, including scripture. What do the texts that formed our culture mean for
today? How are we to draw on scripture's normative vision to respond as faithful communities facing today's challenges? Classical texts are not museum
pieces, carefully preserved by scholarly curators, or relics valued for their testimony to the thoughts of long defunct authors. The new forms of biblical criti-

cism (contextual, narrative, rhetorical, reader response, etc.) address these new questions of meaning.

History provides a necessary perspective on the past, that of the observer who is as objective as possible; it needs to be complemented by another equally valid perspective, that of the participant. The writer Tobias Wolff distinguishes between "the facts" and the stories he has related in his memoirs. The latter are the actual events as lived through by himself as a boy and later interpreted as an adult in their retelling. Memory is anchored in the facts even while it colors them. Both perspectives are necessary. Wolff recommends that if you want to know about World War II, for example, you should read the most accurate descriptive account of the events you can find, always with the awareness that even they are recounted from the particular perspective of this historian. Then you should read at least one book written by someone who actually lived through the war to see what it looked like from the inside.[20] Memory and chronicle are complementary vehicles of truth, even when they do not exactly coincide. The Gospels are presented as "good news" for the readers, who are invited to enter the story as participants in its ongoing reality.

Virtue ethics and spirituality encourage engaged participation in the story of scripture because they put a primacy on meaning. They seek to answer the questions, How should we live? How are we to respond to the gracious call of God in Christ? These questions do not prize meaning at the expense of truth because meaning that is ungrounded is an illusion. Historical and contextual study can help determine as best we can how Jesus actually lived and what he called for. We cannot, however, appreciate the truth of that story unless we are willing to let it engage us. A reading of the Bible that aims at transformation cannot stop at historical information. Sandra M. Schneiders writes, "Here the objective is to go beyond simply discovering what the text says to asking if what it says is true, and if so in what sense, and what the personal consequences for the reader and others might be." Spirituality and virtue ethics can play a significant role in this existential quest.[21]

An engaged reading will also discover that not all of scripture's meaning has been positive; it contains prejudices and has perpetuated them. Some forms of engaged reading focus on these biases. A "hermeneutics of suspicion" seeks the social interests that shaped biblical materials that foster sexism, exclusive nationalism, and other forms of oppression. Texts that subordinate women or exclude other groups from Yahweh's supposed concern for justice are scandalous. What should be done with them? Should they be excised from the canon? Elisabeth Schüssler Fiorenza, the most prominent feminist hermeneutics scholar, proposes that the canon of scripture is hopelessly androcentric and should be replaced by a new canon or norm of faith. The liberatory experience of women should be considered as the source of God's revelation and the norm by which biblical materials should be judged.[22] Others suggest that the oppressive texts reveal the sinful limitations of biblical authors and contexts rather than the intentions of God.[23] While a necessary critical tool, the hermeneutics of suspicion can leave the reader at such critical distance from the story of Jesus that a "hermeneutics of appreciation" is impossible.

An engaged reading may require painful self-examination. It challenges supporters of the status quo as well as those who reject it. Beyond acknowledging their "social location" of class, race, gender, and educational status, readers must also question their level of religious maturity. Walter Wink writes, "No scholar can construct a picture of Jesus beyond the level of spiritual awareness that she or he has attained."[24] Immaturity blocks us from understanding what we have not yet experienced, and people at different levels of maturity may read the same biblical passage in different, even opposing, ways. The study of history has the same limitations because "historical reconstruction proceeds by analogy from our own experience."[25] If accurate knowledge depends upon wisdom and religious maturity, the task of biblical interpretation becomes all the more demanding.

Historical Analysis: Limits and Usefulness

Historical analysis of the story of Jesus has limits that need to be taken into account. In recent decades, the historical-critical method has lost its monopoly on interpreting scripture. We have moved from a culture that prized historical fact and objectivity to one that evaluates systems of ideas primarily by their capacity for transforming individuals and society.[26] Before describing the positive role for historical scholarship, we should acknowledge its limits:

1. Historical method promised an objectivity it has been unable to deliver. Nineteenth-century scholars aimed for a scientific history that could objectively determine the truth about the past. That project has been met with skepticism in a postmodern age that rejects Enlightenment pretensions to universal truth. Historical method cannot demonstrate the truth of assertions about what Jesus of Nazareth did and said. In part, this is due to the scarcity of evidence available about his life. More significantly, history as a method produces judgments of probability rather than certitude. It can establish with some probability that a saying of Jesus originated with him and whether there is any historical basis to a particular interpretation of Jesus.[27] It cannot prove beyond doubt that Jesus did or did not say something.

2. The limitations and bias of the historian inevitably influence the interpretation of historical data. Many contemporary scholars have abandoned the ideal of establishing who Jesus was with scientific objectivity because the historical project cannot be separated from the author's own convictions.[28] Those interests cannot be discounted. This does not mean that all history is merely ideological; rather, historians need to admit their biases and learn from other perspectives. Not all biblical scholars are convinced of these limitations. For instance, the "Jesus Seminar" reports its results as scientific determinations of what Jesus actually said. The seminar operates under the debatable assumption that the passion narratives and the eschatological sayings attributed to Jesus were fabricated by later communities and editors of the Gospels. Theological preferences, consequently, play a significant role in their supposedly objective historical judgments.[29]

3. The long-running "quests for the historical Jesus" have produced quite different accounts.[30] Recently, the historically sophisticated critics John P. Meier and John Dominic Crossan have spelled out elaborate methodologies to preserve their historical analyses from theological bias.[31] Nevertheless, the resulting portraits are strikingly different. Meier stresses the Jewishness of Jesus, emphasizes the imminent coming of the kingdom of God, acknowledges some miraculous works of power, and concludes that Jesus believed that, despite his impending execution, he would participate in the messianic banquet beyond death. Crossan downplays the Jewishness of Jesus, expectations of the kingdom, a messianic mission, and any transcendent dimension to the ministry of Jesus. He recasts him as a wandering Cynic sage who would be remembered for his pithy observations. The sayings of Jesus that Crossan accepts as authentic promote an egalitarian tolerance that looks remarkably like the ideals of a 1990s liberal.

4. The "historical Jesus" constructed by scholarly research cannot function as the norm of Christian faith. History can study the human face of Jesus but cannot draw any conclusions about what should be believed about him as the Christ of God. Raymond E. Brown, an accomplished historical critic, cautions that history cannot dictate conclusions about Christology. The "historical Jesus" is what historians can agree upon through applying critical methods to the limited evidence available. This construct cannot give a complete factual profile of the person who lived in Palestine in the first century C.E.[32] Brown argues that the Synoptic Gospels bear a closer resemblance to Jesus of Nazareth than the "historical Jesus" of scholars does. Their portraits do not edit out the story's religious and theological dimensions, as historicial criticism must do. Although the

portrait drawn in Luke or Matthew was tailored to a particular community, the Synoptics intended to write about Jesus rather than use him as a mouthpiece for their own ideas.[33] These portraits are the baseline for other ways of interpreting the text.

Does this editorial work mean that the Gospels are less true than a scholarly reconstruction of the historical Jesus? New Testament scholar Barnabas Ahern used to make an instructive analogy on this issue. Rembrandt painted a number of portraits of his mother. Are they more "true" or less "true" than a passport photo would have been, if photography had been possible in the seventeenth century? Rembrandt's personal knowledge and affection for his mother made the portraits less accurate but more true. Given the choice between the four Gospels and a documentary videotape of the same events, most of us would probably choose the Gospels. The perspective of the participants, interpreted through loving memory, has a distinct advantage for knowing the full truth about Jesus. Christian faith also holds that the Spirit of the risen Lord dwells in communities and believers to make present to them not just the meaning of the Gospels but, more importantly, the One who is the central character of the narratives. Faith seeks to encounter the living Christ, whose human face is revealed in the person of Jesus of Nazareth. The Gospels present good news about God's presence and power, not a nostalgic chronicle about a hero from the past. Historical methods remain descriptive at best, since they cannot address the transcendent and personal reality at the heart of the biblical story and the early Christian communities.

The Usefulness of History

The fact remains that Christianity is a historical religion. It asserts that God's self-disclosure occurs in human history and that certain revelatory events (exodus, exile, cross and resurrection, and so on) determine how subsequent generations are called to respond to God. The new forms of literary and rhetorical criticism do not advocate abandoning historical investigation of the life and times of Jesus. They do object to an exclusive reliance on historical method, which severely limits scripture's capacity to be the ethical and theological norm of a way of life.[34]

Since 1980, Jesus scholarship has moved in a direction that this volume will draw upon. New research into Second Temple Jerusalem has more clearly located Jesus in his Jewish context. Archaeological and social-scientific research has clarified Jesus' social context. Some common positions emerge from the many new studies of Jesus.[35] Healings and miracles are not dismissed out of hand but are seen as works of power that would have been expected from a religious leader in his time. Jesus' death is widely attributed to the threat he posed to the Sadducean authorities, which became critical after the Temple incident. With E. P. Sanders, some deny that Jesus was seen as a political revolutionary, yet many concur that his preaching and actions posed a political challenge to the established powers in Israel.[36]

A number of scholars acknowledge a specifically religious dimension to Jesus, in sharp contrast to others who picture him as a sage or a wandering philosopher.[37] There is greater agreement that Jesus was a person of Spirit, a holy man in touch with the numinous dimension of reality. Marcus J. Borg argues that a positivist worldview prevents many today from appreciating that life is more than two-dimensional. Jesus needs to be seen as one who had access to the divine and mediated numinous power into everyday life. Scholars like N. T. Wright, John P. Meier, and Ben F. Meyer see greater continuity between the actual life of Jesus and the subsequent traditions.[38] Serious scholars such as James D. G. Dunn, Marinus de Jonge, and Wright posit some confession of Jesus as Messiah in his lifetime which formed the basis for the unanimous designation of Jesus as the Christ after his death.[39]

Recent Jesus scholarship continues to debate eschatology. Following Albert Schweitzer, some hold that Jesus did speak of the end of the world and was wrong. Others argue that he was not mistaken because he did not in fact expect an imminent end to history. The early church put such language in his mouth. Still others believe that he did speak in eschatological terms; the world he saw ending, however, was not the space-time cosmos but the world of Second Temple Judaism and the political status quo of Israel.[40] This renewed interest in eschatology marks off this recent scholarship from its immediate predecessors, who either bracketed eschatology as myth (Rudolf Bultmann) or dismissed it as an alien imposition by the Gospel writers on the story of Jesus (the self-styled Jesus Seminar).

While Christian faith is not based on the conclusions of historians, it cannot be widely variant from counterevidence without producing intellectual schizophrenia in its adherents. If it could be proven conclusively that Josephus and other sources were wrong about the execution of a Galilean named Jesus around 30 C.E. and that this person never existed, then the act of faith would be mistaken since it would be directed to a myth or an ideology rather than to a living reality that is the risen Lord. The move by Bultmann and others to finesse the problems of historicity by divorcing the Christ of faith from Jesus of Nazareth led to an empty outline that was quickly fleshed out by the philosophy of the day, in Bultmann's case existentialism, rather than by the paradigmatic stories, encounters, sayings, and events of the Gospels.[41]

The new contextual criticism indicates how important knowledge of the world of the biblical text is for ethics. Contextual criticism considers the text as it stands in relation to its environment instead of seeking the earliest strata of the New Testament text on the assumption that the most primitive layer reflects the actual sayings or deeds of Jesus.[42] Social-scientific knowledge remains descriptive, but it provides a necessary background for normative debates of Christians today. The methods of social science can uncover, with a fair degree of probability, the political, economic, and cultural patterns of Israel and Palestine that shaped the biblical writings. The contextual approach also attends to the life of the early communities to provide leads to the person and message of Jesus.[43]

Communities are the primary locus of Christian moral discernment because the New Testament texts emerged from and were addressed to communities of faith. The texts are best interpreted by believing communities rather than by an isolated scholar bracketing any faith convictions. As Christian communities today wrestle with the contemporary world, they should look to the precedents of biblical communities engaging their own context, namely, the world of politics, economics, and so on, represented in the text.[44] This is why historical study is necessary in an engaged reading: without the right information about their context we will not understand how they addressed their world, and we will be less able to bring an analogous reading to bear on our own contexts.

This is how the Gospel story of Jesus gives content to the formal patterns of virtue ethics and is normative for the practices of spirituality. They become Christian to the extent that they are rooted in the historical person of Jesus of Nazareth, who is also acknowledged as the risen Lord. Discipleship connotes obedience, and obedience connotes accurate listening to the authoritative sources. The one whom believers relate to in faith is the same one who lived the life that the Gospels witness to. It is not helpful to presume that we already know who Jesus is or was. Historical studies can make scripture strange again, a voice from a time and place quite distant from our own, which can then open new and unexpected possibilities for us.[45]

New studies of the sociology of Palestine uncover cultural dynamics radically different from the contemporary first world. This research serves as a needed corrective to scholarship and piety that presume that the cultural values represented in the world of Jesus are largely the same as in our own. Ancient Palestinian society was structured by three cultural values that are quite different. First, religion was not a distinct aspect of culture but the horizon of everything else—politics, economics, social relations, and so on. Second, honor and shame were primary factors in society, since reputation counted more than property. Respect was gained through association, and disgrace could haunt a family for generations. Finally, it was a world of "limited good," where goods existed in limited and relatively fixed quantity. One person's gain came at the expense of others.[46] Contrast that with a world in which wealth is seen to be produced by inventive use of capital, where personal accomplishment and property are the key to reputation, and a secular world where religion is relegated to the private sphere. When the world of the text opens up to us, we find it to be quite different from our own. Then the words of Jesus that challenged the structures of his day can challenge the different structures that dominate us unwittingly.

Focusing on the Gospels

I will focus on the canonical Gospels as the basis of the story of Jesus. I accept on theological grounds the validity of the canon or "list" of works that were accepted by the Christian communities as uniquely authoritative for the life, worship, and beliefs of the churches.[47] These works were endorsed because they were of apostolic origin, whether actual or attributed; they were addressed to and accepted by important Christian communities; and they conformed with the rule of faith, the standard beliefs of the earliest Christian communities.[48] The New Testament will continue to be interpreted by believing communities, but it will always have authority over every interpretation and community practice.[49]

Every theology has to make some selection from the range of biblical material. I will concentrate on the Gospels and some material from Paul because they vividly present the story of Jesus as the norm for Christian life. The identity of Christians is shaped by the particular encounters, parables, and sayings of the Gospels as well as by the overall narrative shape of cross and resurrection. Paul, the earliest of the New Testament writers, witnesses to the same narrative structure as the Gospels, but without an actual narrative text.[50] I agree with Richard B. Hays that the pattern of cross and resurrection, which is the core of Pauline theology, is the "master paradigm" of the Christian moral life.[51] The Synoptic Gospels fill in that basic narrative structure in ways that are indispensable for Christian discipleship. Their parables, stories, and teachings shape Christian imagination and dispositions to act in ways that conform to Jesus. If the New Testament consisted of the Pauline writings alone, the profile of Jesus would be very sketchy indeed. We would know the end of his journey but precious little about how he got there. Paul's life had been radically transformed by encountering the crucified and risen Lord, but he had not known Jesus as a companion on the road that led to Jerusalem.

The Transformation of Identity: Paul in Philippians

What does it mean to say that the Gospel story of Jesus is the norm for Christian identity? Paul in his Letter to the Philippians gives us a glimpse of how radically the life of Jesus affects the Christian. The cross and resurrection changed the most fundamental orientation of his life. Jesus is the norm not just for Paul's behavior but for the core of his experience. Although the final chapter will treat identity at length, the topic is so central to the New Testament moral vision that it must be mentioned now as we conclude this methodological overview of scripture.

Identity refers to the conscious dimension of character, the deliberate core of personal experience that is shaped by our most basic commitments and convictions. Identity names that which stays the same in the stream of consciousness, the continuity to a personal history. Although never fully articulate, it is the basic "sense" of who we are. It is the horizon of our uniqueness, but, curiously, it is not individualistic. Identity is better captured by looking at our most important relationships than by introspection. I am a son of these parents, married to this person, member of this church, working in this profession, standing for these causes and against those menacing forces. The New Testament stresses this relational side of identity. The right question is not Who am I? but Whose am I?[52] To whom do I belong? To what am I committed? Personal continuity is determined by the persons and causes to which we have committed ourselves, and the persons who have promised themselves to us. Identity comes from identification with specific people and causes.

Paul's sense of identity was radically changed when Christ broke into his life on the road to Damascus. Years later, he recounted that turning point to the Philippians. He had left behind everything that he had identified with in the first part of his life: "circumcised on the eighth day, a member of the people of Israel, of the tribe of Benjamin, a Hebrew born of Hebrews; as to the law, a Pharisee; as to zeal, a persecutor of the church; as to righteousness under the law, blameless" (Phil. 3:5-6). What he had counted as gain now was loss "because of the surpassing value of knowing Christ Jesus my Lord" (3:7). Christ has grasped him, and Paul strives to grasp Christ by entering into the center of the experience of Christ, sharing his sufferings and knowing the power of his resurrection. That is why he forgets what lies behind and strives like a runner to cross the finish line (3:12-14).

Paul's life was literally trans-formed, reshaped from one pattern into another. As he died to his old self and came to life in Christ, his conversion replicated in him the core pattern of the life of Jesus. He no longer belongs to his old allegiances; he now belongs to Christ. His identification is intimate and charged with affection. Christ has embraced him, and in a response of gratitude and hope, Paul strives to live wholly for Christ, to belong to him fully. That response shapes his emotions and his actions, but it is rooted in a new identity.

He is not fully one with Christ yet, so he responds generously to the urgent call within him.

The logic of his argument in Philippians runs along a chain of identity: because Christ has identified with our human condition, Christians can identify with him. Their calling is the same as Paul's since all of them have been embraced by Christ. Therefore, Paul can move from their calling to the life of Christ to his calling and back again, because Christ's destiny is also theirs. In the first chapter, Paul commands the Philippians to be guided by the calling that he knew to be in them: "Only live your life in a manner worthy of the gospel of Christ . . ." (1:27). He immediately spells out in graphic terms what the gospel standard is. In response to their rivalries and self-assertion, Paul bluntly tells them to put the interests of others ahead of their own. He appeals not to an abstract moral standard but to the basic shape of the story of Jesus: "Let the same mind be in you that was in Christ Jesus" (2:5). Then he relates the famous hymn of how Christ emptied himself in becoming human and a servant, even to death on the cross, and how in response God raised him up so that the whole universe would acknowledge him as Lord. That is "the mind" that should be in them: the story of Jesus should be integral to them because they belong to Christ. His example should convert them from self-assertion to service, from contentiousness to humility and loving acceptance.

In the third chapter, Paul gives his own life as a corroborating example, as an embodied instance of the exemplary life of Christ. As he was called to die to the old ways and live only for Christ, so too are they. The argument thus runs from the calling of the Philippians to the normative story of Jesus to the analogous example of Paul. Paul is appealing to their basic identities: "Whose are you? You are Christ's—so act like it!" They have not undergone a personality transplant any more than Paul had lost his own fiery temperament.[53] Instead, they have all been brought into a radical new relationship with God in Christ, and that life had to be expressed in the way they lived.

Paul repeatedly makes this same appeal to the normative structure of Jesus' life in his letters. The "indicative" of the story of Jesus grounds the "imperative" of what Christians are called to do and become. He reminds the Romans that their lives turned around when they were baptized and plunged into the death of Christ. "Therefore we have been buried with him by baptism into death, so that, just as Christ was raised from the dead by the glory of the Father, so we too might walk in newness of life" (Rom. 6:4). "Walk" was a commonplace metaphor for living morally, journeying on the Way. At root, the imitation of Christ comes from participation in his life and death and rising. Christians so belong to Christ that his life, his Spirit, is in them, reshaping their very identities.[54] That life forms not only the pattern for their behavior but also the energy and impetus to "walk in the newness of life."

Even though the discussion of identity will come at the end of this book, it is appropriate that it stand also at the beginning. Becoming a Christian was a life-changing event for the New Testament writers, a transformation of the roots of personal identity. Christian moral perception and dispositions stem from the new identity that has been given them in Christ. Before moving into these three dimensions of moral psychology, however, we need to conclude our methodological prelude by discussing virtue ethics and spirituality and the operation of the analogical imagination.

CHAPTER 2

Virtues, Practices, and Discipleship

V IRTUE ETHICS AND SPIRITUALITY are the best ways to appropriate the moral vision of Jesus witnessed in the New Testament. In this chapter I will discuss them in turn, then address practices, which are the common ground that links the two.

I. ETHICS OF VIRTUE AND CHARACTER

Why choose virtue ethics to be the optic for examining the story of Jesus? First of all, it is necessary to select one form of ethics. It is impossible to give an account of Christian moral life without opting for some form of moral philosophy. Every theology contains a philosophy as an inner moment, because it must operate from some model of human experience. I believe that virtue ethics provides the most comprehensive account of moral experience and that it stands closer to the issues of moral life. As such, it is superior to the other common ethical approaches, an ethics that focuses on obligation and one that emphasizes consequences.

Second, these other approaches to ethics are not very promising avenues for engaging scripture. Certainly scripture specifies moral obligations and promises certain consequences for behavior; however, its primary way of guiding moral life is through narrative and images. An ethics of principles abstracts general norms from the particular images and narratives of religious discourse. These resources are raw material from which universally valid norms of action can be extracted. The other common approach looks to consequences. It looks to the pragmatic results and socially beneficial outcomes that biblical material

27

can produce. A utilitarian will be tempted to use religious symbols and stories rhetorically to motivate people to act rightly. Religious believers are apt to protest that using religious language to advertise other values utterly misses the point.

A brief description of the scope and emphases of virtue ethics will help to begin our discussion. The key term in virtue ethics can be defined generically: "a virtue is a disposition to act, desire and feel that involves the exercise of judgment and leads to a recognizable human excellence, an instance of human flourishing."[1] There are a variety of philosophical theories of virtue and no consensus on which virtues are central. Different traditions and cultures give different meaning to the same virtues. Courage, for example, may refer to steadfastness in combat in one culture, or to following one's conscience against social pressure in another culture. The various forms of virtue ethics have certain common features: (1) Moral evaluation focuses on the agent's character; actions are important because they display and reinforce the agent's values and commitments.[2] (2) Good character produces practical moral judgments that are based on beliefs, experience, and sensitivity more than on (or instead of) moral rules and principles. (3) Since virtues and vices develop over time, a moral psychology usually describes the process of maturation. (4) Since virtues lead to and are components of human flourishing, some account of human fulfillment is given, usually of a social rather than individualistic type.[3] (5) Increasingly, attention is paid to the cultural shaping of virtues and what relation, if any, exists between specific historical manifestations of virtues and more universal human traits.[4]

The first third of this chapter will argue that virtue ethics provides the most appropriate avenue to approach the scriptures and the life of Jesus for three reasons, which will be considered in turn: (a) It fits the narrative form of the New Testament and can explain how the particular story of Jesus shapes the moral character of individuals and communities. (b) It attends to the deeper levels of moral existence which the teaching of Jesus addressed: the heart, the personal center of convictions, emotions, and commitments. (c) It fits the dominant mode of moral discourse in the New Testament, namely, paradigms that establish certain patterns of disposition and action that guide action.

Character and Narrative

Virtue ethics, with its attention to character, is the appropriate way to approach scripture since it discloses the character of God. The framework for New Testament ethics is set by a narrative, the story of the life, death, and resurrection of Jesus of Nazareth, through whom God brings history to its turning point.

Narrative also sets the basic structure of the canonical literature of Israel as it relates the story of the chosen people moving from the patriarchs to exodus and Sinai to exile and return. As in any narrative, characters are central. The tensions and reversals of plot gradually define the central characters over the course of the story. The New Testament reveals who Jesus is and how he responds to God. The story exercises normative force because the character of God determines the appropriate ways to be faithful.[5]

Virtue ethics offers the most promising avenue to appreciate the role of Jesus in the New Testament. He does not come teaching timeless truths or moral principles but proclaiming a radically new initiative of God, the resurgent reign of God. The entire life of Jesus forms the basic norm of Christian ethics. His life gives content to what it means that Yahweh is returning to Israel in power: the blind see, the deaf hear, captives are released, the poor have the good news announced to them first. The character of Jesus emerges over the course of the story of his life. In order to grasp the ethical import of biblical texts that relate the life story of a human personality, it makes sense to use the comprehensive moral category of character.

Scripture does not simply exemplify the insights of virtue ethics, because it raises issues that are beyond the scope of philosophical ethics. Philosophical accounts of the moral life do not consider human sinfulness, which compromises moral agency and necessitates radical transformation. Philosophy likewise does not discuss the impact of God's grace on individuals and communities. In some canonical works, such as the Letters to the Galatians and the Romans, great emphasis is placed on the inability of human beings to move from who they are to who they should be. The gulf is attributed to sin, which generates self-absorption and moral impotence. It will take more than clearer information or more accurate reasoning to heal this moral paralysis, "for I do not do the good I want, but the evil I do not want is what I do" (Rom. 7:19). A more radical transformation of human capacities by divine grace and healing is called for than philosophers imagine. Although not every New Testament author emphasizes the debilitating effects of sin to this degree (Matthew, for instance) the need for radical change is a pervasive theme.

Virtue ethics is generally better at depicting formation than transformation. Aristotle's developmental model of character stresses continuities, not reversals; it does not expose moral perversity and evil in the human heart. Moral weakness is discussed but not human evil. Since philosophical virtue ethics does not usually address human evil, it does not adequately account for conversion, the dramatic or gradual reversal of a life that redefines the character.[6]

The story of the disciples, by contrast, begins in a transforming encounter with Jesus that repeatedly upsets the status quo. Some New Testament writings depict this transformation as a gradual approach. The Synoptics describe the disciples struggling through a long process of learning and unlearning, culminating in the scandal of the cross, which finally penetrates their resistance to the radical call of Jesus. Paul takes a more dramatic tack, in line with his own abrupt conversion. He combines stark images of radical conversion with a developmental framework of sanctification. The main source of moral growth is not the individual seeking perfection, but the patient grace of God that reconfigures interior dispositions to reflect the attitudes of Christ. Paul urges the Galatians to cooperate with "the fruit of the Spirit . . . love, joy, peace, patience, kindness, generosity, faithfulness, gentleness, and self-control" (Gal. 5:22). Nevertheless, Christians are expected to cooperate with the Spirit through the same dispositions, attitudes, and decisions that virtue ethics analyzes so effectively.

The Heart of the Matter

The second promising fit between virtue ethics and the New Testament is their common concern with the deeper level of moral living. Virtue ethics focuses on the personal sources of moral life: not only explicit intentions but emotions, needs, habits, and commitments. As such it is suited to the New Testament's emphasis on the "heart," the personal center that infuses acts with meaning. The psalms, prophets, evangelists, and authors of pastoral letters go beyond behavior to the heart. They probe the motivations and intentions behind action and the basic orientation of life. They ask about what sorts of persons believers are gradually turning into under the influence of the Spirit of God and life in community. Biblical ethics goes beyond rules and principles, though they are not ignored, to the level of transformation of character.[7]

As we saw in Philippians, Paul urges the congregation to have "that mind that was in Christ Jesus" (Phil. 2:5). They needed to change the roots of their behavior, to live no longer for themselves but for others, as Christ had done in becoming a servant, even to dying on the cross. The Gospels convey Jesus' concern with transforming the fundamental dispositions of the heart. In the most extended discussion of morality in the Gospels, Matthew's Sermon on the Mount, Jesus does not offer a detailed code of conduct. He seeks a more radical "righteousness" in the heart: nonviolence, forgiveness, purity of heart, simplicity, radical trust in God, and indiscriminate hospitality. The focus of virtue ethics on the inner dynamics of disposition and motivation fits well with this biblical emphasis.

The most persuasive testimony for the necessity of radical transformation of the heart comes not from Jesus but from his disciples. If they are paradigms of anything in the Synoptic Gospels, they are models of misunderstanding, false projection, moral obtuseness, and faithlessness. From beginning to the end of Mark's Gospel, the apostles are not so much evil as thick: they don't get the parables; they don't understand about the loaves; they don't grasp Jesus' repeated insistence that he is headed for the disgrace of the cross; they persist in thinking the rich have an advantage in salvation; they jockey for positions of honor in a movement whose teacher stresses humble service; they sleep through Jesus' agony and turn and run when he is arrested. They will not relinquish the dream of the apocalyptic Messiah who would finally bring down divine wrath on the enemies of Israel and appoint them to lead the victorious people.

The disciples are not just foils for the evangelists—they are figures with which every reader possessed of even minimal self-knowledge can readily identify. Instinctively, we balk at the radical message of Jesus; if it were less threatening, it would be easier to understand. He calls not for a change of behavior but for a change of heart and identity. If you would change the fruits, you have to go to the roots: no one expects to gather figs from a thornbush (Matt. 7:16-20).[8]

Like all the other prophets of Israel, Jesus insists that external obedience to commands was not enough. He commends specific dispositions of the heart that produce a more profound obedience: mercy, gratitude, radical trust in God, and nondiscriminating love. Behavioral commands cannot get to the heart of the matter. True gratitude, for instance, is a free and uncoerced response, a generosity that echoes the generosity of the giver. Jesus does not command the feeling of gratitude, but the practices that nurture gratitude and mercy. Spirituality collaborates with virtue ethics at this point, because dispositions are nurtured by certain practices.

The attention of virtue ethics to moral psychology supports the biblical practice of moral discernment. The interior movements of the heart are the medium through which God's invitation and direction are experienced. James M. Gustafson reminds us that the basic question for the believer is not What should I do? but What is God enabling and requiring me to do and to be?[9] God's "enabling" registers in the movements of hope, repentance, and gratitude which the Spirit stirs deep within. Christians need to sort out the various movements of their hearts in order to determine where they are being called by God. The ethics of virtue gets at this more fundamental level of human experience better than the alternative ethics of consequences or obligation.

Paradigms for Patterning a Way of Life

The third convergence between virtue ethics and the story of Jesus is the importance of moral paradigms for guiding a way of life. Virtues are internally shaped by cultural stories that indicate how to be fair, honest, or chaste. Virtues take on different forms from culture to culture because they are backed by different paradigmatic stories.

Paradigms are the most basic vehicle for New Testament moral teaching. Richard B. Hays distinguishes four main modes in which the biblical texts offer moral instruction: rules, principles, paradigms, and symbolic world.[10] Hays concludes that paradigms are the most basic vehicle for moral teaching in the New Testament. These paradigms are not simply examples of moral rules and principles; rather the moral norms are specified through the paradigmatic events and encounters of Jesus' life. For instance, the command to love the neighbor gets its uniquely Christian meaning through the paradoxical parable of the Good Samaritan (Luke 10:25-37) and the passion narratives, not through any general description of "love" or "neighbor." As we shall see in the next chapter, paradigms exercise a normative role through the analogical imagination, which seeks to act in novel circumstances in ways that are faithful to the original pattern.

The most fundamental paradigm for Christian life is found in the basic shape of the life of Jesus, which was spelled out in the christological hymn of Philippians 2. Christians are called to be conformed to the pattern of self-emptying obedience and service in radical trust of God. New Testament authors frequently invoke that paradigm, as when Paul exhorts the Corinthians to generosity in sharing their goods with the needy communities in Palestine, "For you know the generous act of our Lord Jesus Christ, that though he was rich, yet for your sakes he became poor, so that by his poverty you might become rich" (2 Cor. 8:9).

Each virtue of the Christian moral life is shaped by the story of Jesus and preeminently by its conclusion, the cross and resurrection. The sayings and encounters of the life of Jesus provide the particular incidents that shape justice toward generosity, direct compassion to surprising recipients, and contour mercy to the forgiveness received from God. The virtues that were prominent in the life of Jesus ought to be noticeable in his disciples. While different eras will emphasize different facets of this life, these interpretations should reflect a life which was loving, faithful to God, compassionate to the suffering and oppressed, dedicated to justice, self-forgetful and God-centered, wise, courageous—as well as all the qualities listed in Paul's encomium to love in 1 Corinthians 13. I think it better to avoid lengthy analysis of the meaning of *agapē* and turn to the stories, encounters, and parables where its meaning is fleshed out in terms that are both concrete and universal.

Virtue ethics appreciates the role that paradigmatic stories and exemplary figures play in defining particular virtues. Dictionary definitions of virtue are inadequate for two reasons. First, virtues take on a different meaning in various cultural contexts. Courage, for instance, was far more physical and martial in the Athens of Socrates than it is today, where the life of the *polis* does not depend on citizens holding the battle line against the enemy's charge.[11] The virtue of courage is recast in the Letter to the Ephesians as spiritual resistance to cosmic forces of evil.[12] Second, since virtues are skills, they need examples to show what they mean practically. They have to be displayed concretely to convey their tactical meaning. In order to grasp how courage and integrity operate, we need accounts of persons who have shown these virtues in the tangle of circumstances. We are more likely to learn these lessons from literature than philosophy. A dictionary definition of "honesty" is pallid compared to, say, John Henry Newman's *Apologia Pro Vita Sua*.[13]

When we look at the story of Jesus through the lens of virtue ethics, three main issue come into focus: perception, dispositions, and identity. Jesus challenges his hearers to be transformed in each of these dimensions, and they form the material for the second part of this book. Chapters 4 and 5 will focus on *what* Christians ought to see. Chapters 6 and 7 will expand on *how* Christians should desire and discern what to do. Finally, chapter 8 will discuss how Christian life together should flow from *who* we are.

―――――――――――――――II. SPIRITUALITY AND ITS PRACTICES―――――――――――

The term "spirituality" is currently used to refer to something quite different from what I will refer to. *Spirituality* here means the practical, affective, and transformative dimension of a religious tradition. It is accountable to the norms and convictions of a faith community. The practices that express spirituality are pedagogical and transformational. They are the basic repertory for an engaged reading of the story of Jesus.

The Contemporary Clamor for Spirituality

The topic of spirituality calls for extensive ground clearing because it is currently being used in a very curious fashion. Consider the celebratory description that appeared recently in the *New Republic*: "Spirituality ... is simply religion deinstitutionalized and shorn of any exclusionary doctrines. . . . You can claim to be a spiritual person without professing loyalty to a particular dogma or even understanding it."[14] The same connotation is expressed when people say, "I am not a religious person, but I am very spiritual." A number of the undergraduates I teach use the term in this sense. They appeal to personal spirituality as an alternative to being part of a tradition or worshiping any articulated deity with any specific community. "Religion" often connotes to them institution, doctrines that assert some truths and rule other ideas out, respect for the authority of some tradition, formal worship, and affiliation with a specific group of people. All these factors threaten to stifle personal engagement with the sources of deepest meaning. The *New York Times* reports that Americans are increasingly interested in the spiritual dimension of life, but not necessarily in mainstream churches, where attendance has remained roughly the same for the past fifty years.[15]

Even in this looser meaning, "spirituality" usually seeks another dimension to life, which is higher or deeper or more interior than the "two-dimensional" world of ordinary experience. It is important to seek contact with that dimension, usually out of a sense of inner urgency or need for integration, healing, or personal depth. This pursuit often takes the form of regular practices: walking in the woods or on the beach, meditating to music, or seeking solitude to repeat some cherished mantra. One student told me he finds God when he is rock-climbing without ropes, a way of worshiping that seems literally "nearer my God to Thee." New Age religious seekers blend a medley of spiritual practices while ignoring the traditions and convictions that originally grounded these devotions. These tourists in the spiritual realm practice Buddhist chanting, Native American vision quests and sweat lodges, tantric yoga, astrology, ersatz witchcraft rituals, and the like. Some practioners are searching to experience something deeper without having to interpret what it is or having to commit themselves to it. What else could we expect in a consumer culture that is dominated by an ethos of entertainment? Without the intellectual and ethical resources of a larger community that can critically assess spiritual experience and practices, however, these individual forays into the spiritual are susceptible to many problems.[16]

These pop understandings and exotic practices can give spirituality a bad name. They distract us from a more significant interest that is occurring in mainstream churches and synagogues. Members and fellow travelers are seeking ways to deepen their personal engagement and experiential knowledge of what they profess. Usually this hunger for the sacred does not replace communal worship but supplements it with practices of prayer, asceticism, and service. Often they are rediscovering practices that have long been part of their particular ecclesial traditions. Certainly this development is a mixed phenomenon, like every grass-roots religious movement. It can be a hunger for spiritual experience rather than for God. It can be self-absorbed or crassly pragmatic, techniques for personal enrichment rather than practices of holiness and service.[17] The critical resources of a larger tradition can offer a useful antidote.

Spirituality: Traditional and Lived

Authentic forms of spirituality have always been a vital part of major religious traditions. In the 1960s a number of young secular American Jews went off to Tibet and Nepal to learn meditation. Thirty years later, the next generation is finding spiritual depth in new versions of traditional Jewish mystical and cele-bratory spiritualities such as the Lubavitch movement. In Christianity every time of major renewal witnessed—or was caused by—the emergence of a distinc-tive way of living Christian faith. Some individual or group married the promise of the gospel to the deepest needs of the times. Witness the anchorites of the Egyptian desert, Benedictine monasticism in the Dark Ages, Franciscan and Dominican mendicant monks in the high Middle Ages, eighteenth-century Protestant pietism, American revivalism, and Mother Teresa's missionaries working with the abandoned poor in Calcutta and AIDS patients in New York.

These historical spiritualities typically originated in the intense experience of a founder who was able to articulate distinctive practices and communal forms so that others could share the founder's way of relating to God, other people, and nature. Subsequent generations often articulate that vision in more systematic and theological terms so "Benedictine" or "Jesuit" spirituality is elab-orated for the church as a whole. Here, "ecclesial spirituality" is not an oxy-moron.[18] Over time the community of faith needs a variety of spiritualities, just as the apostolic church needed four Gospels. There is no single, official Chris-tian spirituality. Different times, perspectives, and personalities encourage a variety of ways of being Christian, even though the appearance of a new spiri-tuality almost always threatens the keepers of the institutional church.

"Spirituality" in the traditional sense means almost the opposite of the cur-rent popular notion of spirituality. It signifies practical ways of praying, serving, and living that connect the faith convictions of a tradition to a particular time and place.[19] Like pop spirituality, it arises out of a hunger for the sacred and a need for personal transformation, but its practices are consciously located in a tradition with articulate beliefs, normative values, and communal worship. Its practices of prayer and service are accountable to larger traditions and commu-nities of faith, which they simultaneously renew by infusing new insights, per-ceptions, and practices. Some spiritualities, like Latin American liberation theology, are more politically radical; others, like the "Promise Keepers," are rel-atively conservative and less ecclesial. Problems arise when a lived spirituality is cut off from an adequate reflective framework, that is, from traditions and com-munities that could provide normative theological and ethical guidance. In their absence, spiritual practices are often justified by appeal to unexamined cultural commonplaces or narcissistic good feelings which are ripe for self-deception.

Most Protestant communions have historically been less receptive to new spiritualities than Judaism and Roman Catholicism. New movements of intense religion with well-defined identities (often called "sects") often left the Protestant churches in which they originated in order to form new denominations. Pietist movements from the Mennonites to the Methodists evoked the specter of antinomian enthusiasm in the established churches. Catholic sects were incorporated into the church as new religious orders.[20] Protestant theologians often used "mysticism" as a term of opprobrium, charging that pietists bypassed Word, sacrament, and institution to seek direct contact with the divine. Catholicism historically has not pitted mysticism against orthodoxy. In the late twentieth century, however, movements of spiritual renewal such as charismatic prayer groups, spiritual direction, lay retreat houses, meditation groups, and Bible-study fellowships are being accommodated in American Protestant communions. Theologians such as Marcus J. Borg employ the categories of spirituality to express the experience of Jesus Christ for contemporary readers. Borg started to understand Jesus when he "began to see Jesus as one whose spirituality—his experiential awareness of Spirit—was foundational for his life."[21]

Spirituality Defined

Spirituality, in the sense used here, refers to the practical, affective, and transformative side of authentic religion. It is grounded in two convictions: (a) that there are dimensions of reality that are not immediately obvious; and (b) that contact with those dimensions can heal personal alienation and fragmentation.[22] Historical theologian Bernard McGinn proposed this definition:

> Christian spirituality is the lived experience of Christian belief in both its general and more specialized forms. . . . It is possible to distinguish spirituality from doctrine in that it concentrates not on faith itself, but on the reaction that faith arouses in religious consciousness and practice.[23]

Spirituality is concerned not only with acts that are explicitly related to God but with the more pervasive awareness of God expressed by Ignatian spirituality as "finding God in all things."[24] Its practices are not only interior; rather, they integrate bodily actions and public commitments with convictions that are rooted in the person's affective and cognitive structure. Authentic spirituality is not confined to an individualistic "care of the soul," since its practices and frame of reference are communally based and oriented to action with and for others. In the framework of the story of Jesus, a spirituality that is purely inward and unrelated to moral transformation and action must be considered unauthentic.

Since spirituality can be studied as well as practiced, *lived spirituality* can be distinguished from *reflective spirituality*, that is, the study of this religious self-transcendence by a variety of academic disciplines, including theology, history, psychology, anthropology, sociology, and ethics.[25] Lived spirituality usually is expressed in "first order" language that is experiential and practical. Reflective spirituality, or spirituality as an academic study, uses "second order" language that is more general, abstract, and critical.

Ethics has an important role to play in any authentic spirituality. Because spirituality emphasizes disciplines that are practical, affective, and transformational, it shares common ground with forms of virtue ethics that are interested in the psychology of moral life.[26] Like virtue ethics, which stands consciously within a tradition, the type of spirituality discussed here is located within a normative tradition. Ethics encourages the study of spirituality to move beyond historical, psychological, and sociological description to normative reflection. Authentic spirituality is not antinomian, but it does differ from morality and ethics in some important respects.

Spirituality often addresses regions of experience that go beyond the usual range considered by morality and ethics. At one end of the spectrum, radically evil threats to meaning such as the scandal of the Holocaust and ecological devastation have generated contemporary spiritualities.[27] At the other end, the witness of heroic sanctity and mystical union with the Good have also sparked new spiritualities.[28] In addition, morality does not emphasize personal transformation and holistic integration to the degree that most forms of lived spirituality do. This omission could be explained by moral philosophers' usual reluctance to take disintegration (alienation, sinfulness) as seriously as spirituality does.

There are forms of lived spirituality that stand in tension with ethics. Some practitioners want spiritual practices to "do the work" of ethical reflection by immediately and intuitively grounding their actions or way of life. They wait for direct inspiration of God rather than engage in the critical practice of discernment. Conversely, some ethicists consider the practices of spirituality to be sectarian because they are not accountable to public criteria of truth and meaning.[29] Reflective spirituality can expand the scope of ethics beyond a strictly formal or impartialist account.[30]

Spiritual Practices: Pedagogical and Transformational

Spiritual *practices* are the core of authentic spirituality and provide the link between the New Testament and virtue ethics. Through the regular pedagogy of spiritual practices, God's Spirit works to transform Christians. Theology studies ultimate questions and doctrines; reflective spirituality primarily studies practices, their contexts and rationales. Ways of life are constituted by a set of practices. Some practices are indispensable for being a Christian community; without participating in practices of worship, service, witness, forgiveness, and so on, such communities would not be Christian.[31] Practices inculcate this way of life through regular, committed disciplines of study, meditation, and compassion which develop certain intellectual, moral, and religious capacities.[32] In the second part of this book I will discuss specific spiritual practices that develop the particular moral capacities that are the focus of this study.[33] The practice of intercessory prayer sharpens moral perception. The practice of meditating on scripture and discernment evoke and direct moral dispositions. Finally, the practice of the Lord's Supper, together with its constituent practices of forgiveness and solidarity with the poor, deepens Christians' sense of identity.

I will concentrate on practices that have always been central to the Christian way of life and draw their inspiration from the example and commands of Jesus. Unlike the exotic practices of today's pop spiritualities, the formative disciplines of Christian spirituality are not esoteric or idiosyncratic. They are not hobbies or occasional exercises that depend on sporadic bursts of good intention. Practices are committed exercises, activities that we deliberately set time aside to do regularly, like reading scripture twenty minutes a day in a particular setting or worshiping every Sunday with a particular community. Spiritual practices are usually cooperative enterprises, like showing up every Saturday afternoon to work at a soup kitchen, or becoming involved in the lobbying efforts of Bread for the World. These spiritual practices form the capacities of Christians by being both pedagogical and transformational. We will now look at these aspects in turn.

Pedagogical

Practices are the matrix for virtuous dispositions. When regular practice moves from mere repetition to settled habit, that habitual behavior can gradually evoke the right dispositions to make the behavior virtuous. We instruct our children not to lie and to tell the truth. They may initially follow our advice because they are docile or want to receive approval and avoid blame. However, the habit of telling the truth can deepen into the disposition to be honest. Certainly, there is nothing automatic about awakening moral dispositions. Some learn honesty through a dramatic experience, but for most of us the process is more organic. We see the worth of what we habitually do. It is far easier to learn the value of what we are accustomed to doing than to discover the value of behavior we have assiduously avoided. What children once did for extrinsic reasons, they eventually come to do for its own sake. The habit moves toward a virtue when it is done for the right intention. Maturing young people begin to act more from conscience and less from the super-ego. As they learn the satisfactions of honesty and integrity, they become disposed to be honest in speech and relationships. They are "disposed to"—that is, they "lean toward"—or have a readiness for open and candid speech. They are not inclined to deception because it goes against the grain of their character. It rarely occurs to them to ask, "Should I be honest here?" or "What good will it do me to tell the truth to her?"

Spiritual practices evoke and train the dispositions just as sound habits foster virtues. This is a central reason why spirituality and virtue ethics complement each other in analyzing Christian ethics. Both appreciate how practices form dispositions of character. For instance, because our parents said night prayers with us as children, we might learn to talk to God. In time, that habit of talking to God may catch on with us even when our parents are not around. Regular conversation with God can deepen into a sense that God cares for us, that we are inextricably related to God and God to us. Gradual confidence, possibly reinforced by biblical language and images, may grow into a deepening sense of dependence on God and trust in God's graciousness. The regular habit of conversation moves beyond perfunctory prayer or formal speech into the intimate conversation appropriate for friends. Inevitably, times of dryness and doubt will stretch us, and we may be forced beyond familiar ways of prayer. What may have been originally a duty becomes a welcome, if mysterious, part of daily experience.

Both moral and spiritual practices set us up for the right dispositions. They channel good intentions into habitual behavior, and those habits evoke and train the dispositions of the heart. Habits are often considered to be unreflective patterns of response to certain stimuli. "Does the name Pavlov ring a bell?" we joke. However, stimulus-response is not the whole story. Habits that are reflectively entered into shape character. Over time regular practices can strengthen commitments so we enact them with a certain ease and even delight. Attentively performed habits lead to the formation of moral dispositions.[34]

Of course, nothing is automatic in moral or spiritual pedagogy. One worshiper may be simply going through the motions while another may be entering into the same eucharistic ritual as an expression of her deepest commitments and identity. Like moral virtues, spiritual dispositions are not always affectively charged. I once heard a rather ascetical spiritual director counsel, "Spiritual joy is the kind of joy you do not feel." Though it was hardly persuasive at the time, his formulation now seems to me to have some wisdom. Done over time, spiritual practices become habits, and those routines can be the matrix of the deep work of the Spirit. They do not have to engender noticeable feelings in order to deepen dispositions; in fact, most writers predict that the enthusiasm of the beginner has to fade for deeper transformation to occur.

Religious practices do have a certain logic to them that can be instructive, just as the practice of telling the truth can gradually disclose the value of honesty and integrity. Spiritual practices have moral dimensions inherent in them. There is an agenda in the symbols and practices themselves. Ethical reflection draws out the implications of the rituals and symbols of faith for life.[35] Theologian Langdon Gilkey tells how the inner logic of praying the Lord's Prayer eventually had a telling effect on the white churches of the South. Gilkey taught at Vanderbilt's School of Divinity in Nashville during the struggles for civil rights. He said that civil disobedience and moral rhetoric of the movement were not the actual fulcrums of change for white churchgoers. Under the pressure of events and the media, they began to realize that when they prayed "Our Father" they were acknowledging that African-Americans were also part of the same family of God. Either they had to stop that practice, or they had to acknowledge that segregation did not fit with their most cherished prayer. Unfortunately, most American Christians have resisted this insight; otherwise Sunday morning would not still be the time when the nation is most segregated.

Transformational

The pedagogy of spiritual practices is aimed at transformation of individuals and communities. These practices help us break from unauthentic ways of existence in order to embrace a more authentic level through the power that comes from a more radical level of reality.[36] This radical reorientation "trans-forms," that is, moves us from one basic shape to another. The phenomenon of religious conversion may precipitate a movement of transformation, but regular spiritual practices will be needed to sustain the initial reorientation. They provide the structures for deepening and expanding a religious conversion.

In a Christian context this transformation is primarily attributed to the grace of God, but it also involves human cooperation. Although this synergy has eluded theologians' attempts to describe it precisely, the analogy of human friendship is instructive.[37] No human technique can bring about a relation of genuine friendship: it is always a gift and a commitment freely bestowed. Analogously, no technique can cause a personal relation with God, since that occurs through God's gracious self-disclosure and self-communication. Nevertheless, new friends need to develop regular patterns of contact and communication for their friendship to grow. One experience of grace does not make for a deep personal connection to God. Deepening that relation usually requires prayer, service, community, growth in understanding, and so on. This is where spiritual practices come in.

The Gospels testify to the transforming power of Jesus Christ. Those who encountered him were changed, either by opening to his invitation or rejecting it. Authentic Christian practices continuously confront the believer with this transforming demand and power of Christ. That distinctive power of the Spirit of Jesus is translated into ordinary activities by spiritual practices. By integrating ordinary activities into the following of Christ, spiritual practices help the disciple infuse ordinary life with the gratitude, care, justice, and forgiveness that Jesus demonstrated. Liturgical theologian Don E. Saliers writes, "The exercise of such affections requires a continual re-entry of the person into the narrative and teachings which depict the identity of Jesus Christ."[38]

Spiritual practices train the *affections*, the deeper emotions and dispositions. It is important to distinguish the affections from feelings.[39] *Feelings* are transitory occurrences that may be genuine or not. The affections behind the Christian moral life are not simply spontaneous, like feelings. They can be tutored and evoked, for example, by the language of prayer or the rhythm of ritual. They can also be deliberately shaped by specific practices like hospitality, caring for the sick, sharing possessions, and forgiveness. These actions may first be done out of a sense of obligation, but over time they should evoke the dispositions of generosity, compassion, and justice. They become "second nature" to the maturing disciple. If we think that all emotions are purely spontaneous, it will seem odd to read New Testament commands to have certain emotions. Yet this is precisely what Paul does: "Rejoice always, pray without ceasing, give thanks in all circumstances: for this is the will of God in Christ Jesus for you" (1 Thess. 5:16–18).

Paul is not simply commending the feelings of joy or gratitude to the readers. He is mandating certain practices that will deepen these dispositions of character. Since feelings are spontaneous, it is pointless to command them. Deeper emotional dispositions, however, can be commanded by calling for the practices that embody them. God's intention is to form a certain sort of people distinguished by definite qualities of the heart. The practice of giving thanks to God inculcates a disposition, a readiness, to be grateful to God. Parents remind young children to say "Thank you" in hopes that they will become the sort of people in whom a sense of gratitude is ingrained and for whom expressions of gratitude will "naturally" arise at the appropriate occasions.

Affections lead to corresponding actions, and that roots them more deeply in the character. The affections give shape and direction to character. Unlike transitory feelings, affections are enduring dispositions that incline us to ways of acting. The affection of gratitude, for instance, notices and appreciates the generosity of others. In this way, it engenders a character-based readiness to act generously toward others. It makes no sense to appreciate a quality without wanting to embody it ourselves. In the same way, spiritual practices evoke and form dispositions in the Christian life, which carry over into ways of action that are consonant with the disposition.

Having discussed how practices tutor our moral dispositions and help transform our characteristic emotions and actions, it is now time to discuss the meaning of practices themselves.

--------------- III. PRACTICES: LINKING SPIRITUALITY AND VIRTUE ---------------

Practices and Techniques

Virtue ethics and spirituality share common ground in appreciating the formative role of habitual behavior. Good habits, entered into with the right intention, form virtuous dispositions in the character. Spiritual practices are ways in which the body mentors the soul, shaping certain capacities in regular forms of attention, service, and common action. The notion of practices has moved to the center of recent literature in virtue ethics and spirituality.[40]

Some troubling questions, however, challenge this focus on practices in the moral and spiritual life. Does a focus on practices make these processes self-centered? If I act virtuously in order to acquire a virtue, does that detract from the moral value the virtue is meant to serve? Doing the right thing for the wrong reason can derail a practice into perfectionism. Practicing friendship for the sake of personal growth would drain benevolence out of the friendship. Instead of choosing the good of my friend, I would become the focus. This would soon undermine the relationship, because who wants to be used as a means to another's psychological growth? Likewise, if I serve the poor in order to get to heaven, I am not loving the poor but using them for my own benefit. Here is the paradox: both friendship and service of the poor are transformative only if the intent behind them is not personal transformation. I believe that problem of perfectionism can be addressed in two ways.

In the first place, virtues are both means to the good life and components of it. A life of human flourishing necessarily includes fairness, honesty, compassion, and the like. They are never purely instrumental. We do not fight oppression and do the works of justice in order to get to a society where there will be no need for justice. Fairness and respect for others will be constituents of the good society. The relationship between virtuous activity and human flourishing does not neatly fit into the category of means and ends. Human flourishing is not an end state because all relationships remain in process and human flourishing refers primarily to how we live as we pursue worthwhile ends. The values we seek should characterize the way that we pursue them.

The point is even clearer in Christian spirituality, where "the good life" is loving communion with God and others. Paul makes it abundantly clear that even the most heroic behavior means nothing apart from love (1 Cor 13:1–3). Every spiritual practice is done in service of these relationships, not to make the agent a moral virtuoso. As Christian love deepens, it increasingly shifts attention away from the subject's needs and accomplishiments. Because love takes the other more seriously than it takes itself, it is self-forgetful and self-transcending. Jesus does not command his disciples to become moral paragons but to make every effort to serve God's cause in the world. That reign of justice and mercy breaks into lives that are burdened by oppression and fragmentation. The compassion that drives Jesus takes its cues from the needs of people. That same compassion ought to characterize the self-emptying service of his disciples.

Second, practices must be distinguished from techniques. Practices are activities that are worthwhile in themselves; the enhancement and satisfaction they bring come from doing them well. Techniques are instrumental activities that produce benefits that are tangential to the activity. A technique requires certain skills and is judged by the quality of the good produced; a practice may involve certain skills but it is a good in itself and is judged by standards internal to it. Since different techniques can often produce the same benefit, the technique is not necessarily related to the good produced.

The boundary between technique and practice is not absolute. An activity that started out as a technique may evolve into a practice. Often we do not appreciate the full value of a practice when we first become involved in it. Practices are usually complex social activities that are intrinsically interesting and rewarding. They are rich human activities that draw us into themselves, thereby reorienting our initial intentions and motivations. The philosopher Alasdair MacIntyre relates how he got his young nephew interested in chess. He promised the boy that he would get a piece of candy any time he defeated his uncle in a chess match. This peaked the boy's interest so that he learned to play well, and he collected his share of candy. After a while, however, he became fascinated with the strategy and competition of the game itself and forgot about the candy. He began playing chess as a technique, but eventually was drawn into it as a practice.[41] Chess, like friendship or portrait painting or basketball, has its own rewards. The expansion of our capacities and the delight they bring are wrapped up in doing them well.

Some techniques are not complex enough to challenge our capacities sufficiently to become a practice. Shooting free throws is a skill that can never engage an athlete like the actual sport of basketball. In other cases, however, the same behavior can be a practice or a technique, depending on the intention we bring to it. For instance, painting landscapes in order to pay the rent is a technique. Painting as artistic expression is another matter. I may find better ways to pay the rent, but painting as a practice can bring a joy and an integrity that are wrapped up in the process itself. As the painter becomes immersed in the practice of painting, commitment to the integrity of the work grows. Although the landscapes produced may have some commercial success, paying the rent is not the primary intent behind the practice. Practices may have some indirect instrumental value, but they are primarily done for the values inherent in them.

The difference between technique and practice is perhaps more evident in friendship. The moral practice of friendship centers on the deepening relation of the friends. The friends will be enhanced by the loyalty, intimacy, and mutual support that are components of the practice of friendship. They will become richer human beings, more virtuous, precisely by taking the friend more seriously than they do any personal benefit. While the relationship may have begun as useful or entertaining to the parties involved, as it ripens into friendship those initial motivations become subordinate. The good of the friend and the quality of the bond become paramount as the parties give themselves to the practice.[42] Gradually they are changed by the deepening friendship as it develops their capacities for commitment, benevolence, reciprocity, and generosity.

A different intention can use a show of friendliness for self-interested purposes. It employs some of the behaviors that support friendship as techniques. For example, a sales representative may cultivate customers and show a personal concern for them, not primarily to make them friends but to increase sales. To complicate matters somewhat, two persons may have a relationship that seems to be a practice to one person while it is only a technique to the other. The customer may think that the sales representative is a close friend, but if he changes suppliers, he will discover the awkward truth.

Practices usually have evolved over time and have a structure that supports the values involved in them. The expectations of those entering into marriage are shaped by the authority the practice has gained over time. Newlyweds may have relatively self-centered, romantic intentions, but the discipline of married life should reorient their intentions over time so that it becomes a practice rather than merely a technique to meet their needs. The rules that govern the practice usually play an important role in shaping the intentions of those who participate in them. Like sports, many social practices have explicitly formulated rules that help define the practice and ensure its values.[43] The prohibition of adultery in the practice of marriage, for example, preserves the fidelity that makes marital intimacy possible. The uniqueness of the relation between spouses is embodied in their sexual exclusivity. This exclusivity helps create the conditions for trust and self-disclosure that are central to marital intimacy.[44]

Practices are the activities that make up a way of life, including the Christian way. The ritual of baptism, sharing life in community, solidarity with the poor, meditating on scripture, and mutual forgiveness are some of the concrete practices that make up a Christian way of life. They are rich human activities that are done together and have a history. They are worthwhile and meaningful activities that we engage in because they are good to do, not primarily because they produce something else. They can be done well or poorly, and we can get better at doing them. They have a formative effect on our characters when they are done well because through them our relationship with God in Christ develops.

The Practice of Christian Prayer

Reflection on the practice of friendship leads into reflection on Christian prayer, because prayer is the language of friendship with God. The various practices of prayer are the regular forms of attentiveness to and conversation with God that sustain a life of friendship with God. They are central components of the Christian way of life.[45] Understanding the Christian life as friendship with God illumines the pedagogical and transformative aspect of all spiritual practices. They help situate daily life in the horizon of God's friendship. Understanding these practices as expressions of friendship with God will also preserve them from degenerating into techniques. Friends enjoy regularly conversing with each other because that is the lifeblood of the friendship. The practices of Christian prayer have their own integrity; they are not means to personal growth or strategies to trigger peak experiences.[46]

The imagery of friendship with Jesus complements the more frequent term of discipleship in the Synoptic Gospels. Disciples may be expected to admire and revere their masters, but they are unlikely to become their friends because the difference of status is so great. In the final discourse of John's Gospel, however, Jesus assures his disciples, "I do not call you servants any longer, because the servant does not know what the master is doing; but I have called you friends, because I have made known to you everything that I have heard from my Father" (John 15:15). Jesus does not treat his disciples as slaves, simply giving them orders. The servant–master relationship has little room for the intimacy of friends. Jesus treats them like friends by disclosing who he is and where he is going. Jesus tells them that he is laying down his life for his friends; that is not what a master would do for his slaves. Typically, the disciples are bewildered and protest that they do not understand what is going on. Nevertheless, the candor of their objections hints at John's intent. Knowing Jesus is mysterious, but that knowledge grows through intimate conversation that is the basic medium of friendship.

The Pedagogy of Prayer

The practices of Christian prayer help us enter into the conversation that God has already begun. We start to pray not in a vacuum but in community through forms and rituals that have been shaped over time. The quintessential Christian prayer begins "Our Father," an expression that locates us with Jesus and countless others in intimate relationship to God. We are ushered into the conversation that Jesus has with God because we share the life of God's family. Christians can say the Lord's Prayer because they have entered into a new relationship with God, which reconstitutes them as children of God. They share God's life in such a way that they can honestly say "Our Father."[47] Whether groaning or exulting, Christians are not praying alone. God's shared life in the daughters and sons of God finds voice in the Spirit, who prays through them in ways that are intelligible to God (Rom. 8:26–27). They are not only on the Way, the Way is in them.

Praying the Lord's Prayer is a pedagogical practice, since it contains the basic modes of all private and communal prayer: praise, thanksgiving, intercession, and repentance. Christian prayer has its origins in this unique prayer, but it also learns from the psalms, prophets, and stories of Israel. They teach Christians how to express themselves freely to God and what sort of responses to expect from God.

Prayer and Transformation

The transformative effect of Christian prayer comes as it works to rectify our intentions and basic self-understanding. As with the initial stages of friendships, people begin to pray for a variety of reasons, some of which are probably self-interested. If they become committed to regular prayer, however, the practice should gradually discipline and correct these original intentions. Typically we begin to pray for what we want. After not getting what we want, we are gradually led to seek what we need, namely, a deeper and unconditional relation with God where we let God be the judge of what we should receive. Prayer may begin as a technique, but under the impetus of the Spirit it becomes a practice. Over time, a regular discipline of prayer has its own dynamic and rhythm that should shift attention from self-concern to the Other.[48] It moves toward wholehearted attention to the God who is revealed through Christ. Prayer becomes an activity that is done for its own sake, just as friends want to be in each others' company simply because it is good.

At the same time, friends are bound by common interests beyond themselves. Their common cause, whether sports or justice or the environment, enriches the bond of friendship and draws the best from them. Christian prayer, the discourse of friendship with God, pulls Christians beyond themselves to active devotion to God's cause in the world. It longs for God to reign in the whole of creation, for a deeper impact of God's liberating and healing Spirit. Intercession for the world naturally leads to service in the world. It inclines the Christian to enter into the way of the cross that is the path to life for all. Christian prayer pulls us into a way of life and is itself a component of that life:

> To pray constantly is to be disposed in this world before the face of God. Prayer is thus not an *aid*, psychological or otherwise, to the living of a spiritually healthy or ethically sensitive life. It is not a motivating set of techniques. Rather, prayer is part of having a life formed in joy, gratitude, awe and compassion. These capacities, which one learns to call 'gifts' when they are rightly understood, are directed toward God and all God's creation.[49]

Even prayers of intercession are not pragmatic strategies but exercises in locating our concerns in the concern of God and opening ourselves to finding God's way of responding, which quite often does not match our requests.

Christian practices of prayer can be done well or poorly. The norm for them is set by the story of Jesus. Christian prayer has certain qualities that ought to be ingredient to it, qualities that are "appropriate to" Christian prayer and define it.[50] Prayer should lead to deeper communion with God and greater docility to the indwelling Spirit's transformation of the heart and mind. Since Christian prayer is a form of communion, it should engender the qualities appropriate to the One it communes with. The narrative of scripture presents a set of qualities that ought to emerge in the prayerful relationship with God. As Saliers puts it, this connection is especially apparent in liturgical prayer: "To pray is to give oneself to the Christian story in such a way that there is an internal link between the emotions and virtues exercised in that life and the meaning of the texts, prayer and symbols enacted in the rites."[51] Although we do not pray in order to become reverent, humble, grateful, caring, and hopeful, these virtues are formed in paying wholehearted attention to God and seeing the world through the perspective defined by God's word. Christian prayer should engender the dispositions and actions of discipleship.

The practice of friendship is also instructive about the ebb and flow of emotion in prayer. True friends remain committed even when the other is not particularly entertaining or useful. Likewise, the relationship with God is more important than the felt experience of that relationship. The insights and feelings produced in times of prayer cannot measure their worth because most often prayer does not produce notable experiences or results. If contemplation leads to a radical acceptance of God even when it is not consoling, if it decenters the self so that others are appreciated and treated with respect, then it is genuinely Christian contemplation. Conversely, if prayer of intercession does not lead to greater gratitude and caring for others but to quietism and fatalism, it is not Christian intercession.

The most profound transformation that prayer brings about occurs in the core of our identity. Through participation in the practice we come to recognize what it means to be Christian. There are insights that come only from participating in the practices of a way of life. When young people tell Rembert Weakland, the archbishop of Milwaukee, that they are having a difficult time understanding what it means to be a Catholic, he tells them to participate in the eucharistic celebration with the same parish community every Sunday for six months and at the same time work in a soup kitchen for the poor. If they do these two practices, they will come to understand what it means to be a Catholic.[52] Perhaps they begin out of curiosity, but eventually the rhythm of the practices will redirect their hearts. They will understand the Catholic way of life from the inside and appreciate that God finds them in these regular actions. They will come to see grace in the ordinary, to perceive that their "*daily lives are all tangled up with the things God is doing in the world.*"[53]

Relatively simple and common practices of prayer can also embody and deepen the qualities of Christian life. They bring the ultimate relationship closer to the surface of daily experience, including the ordinary in that ultimate friendship. "Asking a blessing" or "saying grace," for example, sets the ordinary action of sharing a meal in the context of God. It encourages those who pray to recognize that this is the "daily bread" they asked God for and to look for God's gracious and challenging presence elsewhere in ordinary life. None of this is automatic; it requires doing the practice from the right disposition and intention and doing it regularly over time. The embodied rhythm of practices like asking a blessing or keeping the Sabbath can help us see the world in a different way, as a place where God's abundance can be found in food and leisure.

Since relationships are defined by the persons who are related, Christian prayer should lead individuals and communities into closer conformity with the character of Jesus, the Way that leads to God.[54] Scripture provides the profile of Jesus that becomes normative for the practices of spirituality. These practices are regular, concrete activities that tutor Christians in the ways of Christ. Embodied spirituality, therefore, links the content of the story of Jesus to lives that express the gospel. The practices of Christian spirituality provide peda-gogical avenues by which, under the power of God's spirit, the transformation called for by the Gospels is able to occur.

I will propose in the next chapter that the analogical imagination is the main bridge between the biblical text and contemporary ethical practice. Jesus did not come teaching timeless moral truths or a uniform way of life to be replicated in every generation. Rather his words, encounters, and life story set patterns that can be flexibly but faithfully extended to new circumstances. These pat-terns lead us to envision analogous ways of acting that are partly the same and partly different. As disciples become more conformed to Christ, their imagina-tion spots these patterns and carries them creatively into new realizations.

CHAPTER 3

The Analogical Imagination

I. THE BRIDGE OF IMAGINATION

T HE ANALOGICAL IMAGINATION bridges the moral reflection of Christians and the words and deeds of Jesus. It provides the cognitive content for obeying the command "Go and do likewise." That command of Jesus directs Christians to use their imaginations creatively to discover new ways of acting that are faithful to the story of the Good Samaritan and the complete story of Jesus. The adverb "likewise" sets the task for this chapter: How can we live creatively and faithfully? At one extreme, copying the action of the Samaritan is impossible. At the other, Jesus does not invite us to go and do whatever we want to do. Analogical reflection does not simply split the difference between the extremes, since that would be impossible. Instead, it plunges into the concrete details of the life of Jesus in order to become universal. It discovers in the details of parable, encounters, and sayings patterns that normatively guide us in new situations. That discovery and creative extension occur when the imagination enters deeply into the particular images and stories of scripture and envisions possibilities in our own context.

In the second part of the book we will discuss how other links to the narrative of Jesus are forged through transformed perception, dispositions, and identity. The analogical imagination grasps the patterns that guide these dimensions of the moral agent; they in turn sharpen the sensibilities to discover appropriate ways to act and live. It takes more than intelligence and cleverness to spot the relations between our situation and Jesus. The insights of the analogical imagination come to those who want to embody the way of Jesus in their lives and communities.

The path of imaginative reflection begins from the story of Jesus, not from abstract considerations of doctrine or moral principles. Theological concepts like grace, sin, and salvation help set the context for moral reflection. Yet they are "cooled metaphors" that originated in the religious imagination. General moral principles such as the Decalogue set the outer limits for moral reflection but rarely indicate the particular path to take. The analogical imagination integrates these background resources with an informed reading of the situation to discover a way of acting that is harmonious with the story of Jesus and faithful to the present call of the Spirit.

The analogies of scripture guide moral reflection but do not monopolize it. The interpretation of biblical images and stories needs to be defended on theological grounds, since most stories and images can be read in different ways. In addition, other sources of moral wisdom and accurate knowledge of the facts at hand have to be taken into account, a synthetic procedure as old as the prophets of Israel. For instance, the story of the exodus from Egypt inspired liberation theologians, but they did not move directly from the biblical text to action. They also had to engage in social and historical analysis of particular societies, discussion of consequences, and appeals to principles of justice. In the history of the West, the liberation from Egypt has inspired a wide variety of movements and has been used to support pacifist strategies as well as violent revolutions.[1]

In order to explore religious analogies we will take a test case of Jesus washing the disciples' feet. The creative and faithful work of the imagination to craft liturgical expressions parallels its use in moral reflection on scripture. Then we will discuss the meaning of analogy and the role the imagination plays in using biblical paradigms to make the story of Jesus concrete. Finally we will look at the role that the kingdom of God, the central image of Jesus' proclamation, plays in moral reflection.

Test Case: Footwashing and Discipleship

On Holy Thursday evening many Christian communities commemorate the Lord's Supper and the washing of the disciples' feet. John's account has inspired a number of rituals to remember and reenact the washing of the feet. I will describe three Holy Thursday rituals to chart how analogies guide action. Which of these is the most faithful and powerful reexpression of what Jesus did in John's Gospel?

First, we must look at the setting in John, since that is the foundation for these rituals. The footwashing stands at the pivotal point in the plot of John's Gospel. It opens the thirteenth chapter, which marks the transition from the messianic signs of the public life to the ultimate revelatory sign, the lifting up of Jesus on the cross and into God's glory. At the turning point of his life, Jesus is portrayed as a majestic figure who is fully aware of his origins in God and his imminent return to the Father (John 13:1–3). Loving his own to the end, he gets up from the table, takes off his outer robe, takes up the towel and bowl of a servant, and washes the feet of his disciples. They are dumbfounded and appalled. This act of hospitality belonged to a Gentile slave, someone who would not be contaminated by the impurity that clung to bare feet. The master is turning their world upside down.

When Peter quite sensibly objects, Jesus insists, "Unless I wash you, you will have no share with me" (13:8). No share or lot (Greek *meros*) means that they will have no future, no common destiny. Peter needs to be baptized, initiated, into the death of Jesus through accepting this gesture of radical service. If he is uncomfortable at the humiliation of Jesus, how will he understand the crucifixion? Faced with losing his tie to Jesus, Peter caves in, but as Jesus prophetically remarks, "You do not know now what I am doing, but later you will understand" (13:7).

When he is done, Jesus spells out for them the meaning of his scandalous behavior. If he, their Lord and Teacher, has washed their feet, they have to do the same for each other. Since they share his table and his destiny, they must share his way of loving and serving. After the meal, Jesus articulates his "new commandment," which pulls together all his signs, the washing of feet, and the future of the disciples: "Just as I have loved you, you also should love one another. By this everyone will know you for my disciples, if you have love for one another" (13:34–35) The dynamism of his radical love and humble service must pass into their lives and on to all people. As the community formed by the distinctive love of Jesus, from now on they must become the sign of God's liberation and salvation in the world.

What does this mean? If the disciples had taken Jesus literally, Christians would be washing feet every Sunday. They knew better than to copy him. He had given them an example, a demonstration, that graphically pointed to a distinctive way of loving service. They had to figure out from this sign how they could become a corresponding sign to the world. In the new commandment Jesus tells Christians to use their imaginations, to think analogically in moving from "as I have loved you" to "so you ought to love one another." John's expression in 13:34 echoes Luke's "Go and do likewise."

Here are three Holy Thursday rituals that try to capture the import of John 13:

1. In St. Peter's basilica in Rome, Pope John Paul II washes the feet of twelve men. Under the magnificent baldacchino of Bernini and surrounded by Michelangelo's opulent marble interior, the most prominent religious figure in

the contemporary world performs this service to the twelve, who are students from Roman seminaries and laymen.

2. At Holy Spirit Parish in Berkeley, California, the parish pastor takes off his chasuble, lays it on the altar, and washes the feet of one of the women from the parish. Then they reverse the process as she then washes his feet. Then both of them wash the feet of a dozen other men and women. They take bowls and towels to various parts of the packed church where chairs are waiting. All the adults and children who wish to participate get up from their pews and line up at the various stations. When they get to the chair, they remove their footwear, and the person who had been in line ahead of them bends down, washes, and dries their feet. Then they do the same for the person in line behind them. While the congregation is singing quietly, the process goes on until all have been washed. Then the eucharistic liturgy resumes at the altar.

3. In an inner city parish in Baltimore, the pastor, who is Irish-American, takes off his chasuble. Then he shines the shoes of twelve elderly African-American men.

Which one of these rituals best conveys the example that Jesus gave in John 13? Each of them highlights different aspects of the original. The poignant sight of the aging pontiff bending down at the high altar in St. Peter's is the closest reenactment of the three, yet it may be the least faithful to the message. For many women, the fact that all twelve of the "disciples" are male is a pointed reminder of who can be ordained to the priesthood in the Catholic Church. A Protestant friend told me, "I imagine that when you Catholics watch that on television, you probably are thinking, 'This is just what the Pope does on Holy Thursday.' But to someone from the free church tradition, it just looks weird." The opulent setting and trappings of ancient power make the gesture of humble service seem a token at best. The papal title of "servant of the servants of God" sounds like an oxymoron to an outsider.

The second ritual of congregational footwashing highlights not the person of the pastor but the responsibility of all to follow the example of Jesus. They literally wash the feet of one another. The prominence of women and children highlights the radical equality of the Christian vocation. The extension of the service ritual from altar out to congregation images the calling to move the ministry of the gospel out to the world. Everyone gets their hands wet and makes contact with the dirty feet of people who are probably strangers. The Catholic sacramental spirituality is evident in the ordinariness and concreteness of the action. It is a sign that effects what it signifies, and it points to a way of living beyond the liturgy.

The third ritual deeply moved the congregation in that inner city parish.

Shining other people's shoes resonated with the original example of Jesus. It is the work of the poor, traditionally of poor black men who still bear the effects of centuries of chattel slavery. It was a shocking reversal to see the well-educated white pastor shine their shoes. The message was not democratic equality but the last becoming first and the first becoming last, the kingdom of God's reparation of justice long delayed.

These rituals are all exercises of analogical imagination, since the planners tried to reenact the action of Jesus without merely repeating it. Although the third ritual uses different surface details, in my judgment it conveys the values and impact of Jesus' act better than the others. It harmonizes with the original on many levels that elude precise articulation. The one that came close to repeating John 13, the papal liturgy, may be farthest removed from its meaning. How do I make this judgment of relative similarity and dissimilarity? Spotting the appropriate analogy is to some extent a perception, an insight that comes from perceiving a complex resemblance. To justify my judgment, I would have to discuss the dynamics of John 13 and appeal to their analogical imagination in hopes that they would spot what I saw. Analogy illuminates what was hidden before and pulls the past into the present. As Mark Twain said, history doesn't repeat itself, but it does rhyme. The work of analogical imagination is to catch that rhyme. Let us now analyze this process more closely.

Analogy: Spotting the Rhyme

Christian moral reflection tries to imagine actions that will be appropriate to the problem at hand and faithful to the story of Jesus. The new actions will be analogical because they will be partly the same, partly different, but basically similar to the relevant portion of the story of Jesus.[2] Discerning what to do will engage the imagination, which is the capacity to bring together the concrete and general features of human experience.[3] Something is found in the story of Jesus that can be exemplary and paradigmatic for how to act today.

Broadly taken, analogy can be understood as the most fundamental way in which we learn. We begin to grasp what is unfamiliar by moving from what is familiar. If new experiences bore no resemblance whatsoever to familiar ones, they would be unintelligible. There would be no bridges from the actually known to what is not yet clear. Even to recognize how the new experience is different (unlike), we have to have some sense of how it is similar to familiar experiences (like). Narrowly taken, *analogy* means the product of analogical reflection, that is, an explicit statement of how one thing may be understood in reference to another. More broadly, "analogy is the repetition of the same fundamental pattern in two different contexts."[4] The "rhyme" between the two contexts is usually complex rather than simple. The classic analogical proportion involves four terms: not *a* to *a'* but *a* is to *b* as *c* is to *d*. The relation of the first two terms guides the pursuit for the fourth term, as in 2:4 :: 8:X. Knowing *a*, *b*, and *c*, we try to figure out what *d* should be. The answer for *d* fits the proportion; it is the appropriate number because it relates to *c* as *a* does to *b*. There are four terms in the basic analogy that guides Christian moral reflection on scripture:

(a) the biblical text in relation to
(b) its world and
(c) today's Christian community in relation to
(d) its world.[5]

The original relation is normative for the second pair, since the *prime analogate* sets the paradigm for the *analogue*. The primacy of the biblical material for contemporary reflection can be expressed thus: as *a* is to *b* so *c* should be to *d*. Put schematically:

$$\frac{\text{NT text is to}}{\text{its world}} \quad :: \quad \frac{\text{Christian community is to}}{\text{its world}}$$

Analogies exercise a normative function by implying actions and ways of living that are congruent with the prototype. The liturgical planners of the shoe shining needed to know the details and import of John's foot-washing, but they also needed to know something about contemporary America. The tension between the familiar background of John 13 and the unfamiliar sight of a white pastor shining the shoes of old African Americans triggered a shock of recognition. By hearing the rhyme, the congregation discovered simultaneously something about their world and the world of Jesus. The moral implications are drawn less by strict logic than by a sense of what is appropriate and fitting. If this is how Christians ought to love, what should we do about overcoming barriers of race and class, locating the Church in solidarity with the poor, and facing divisions within the parish itself? The ritual is the analogue, and the scene in John 13 is the prime analogate. The tension between features in the analogue that are similar to the prime analogate and those that are different sparks the graced imagination to see what should be done in response.[6]

"Analogical" stands in contrast to *univocal* and *equivocal*. Univocal terms are mere repetitions; there is no need for imagination where the terms are completely similar. Equivocal terms are utterly unrelated, leaving no room for imagination since they are completely dissimilar. Analogical thinking discovers similarity within difference by recognizing a common pattern within diversity. Analogical reflection does not abstract from the diversity, but relishes the uniqueness and variety of particular details, like washing feet and shining shoes.

The story of Jesus is the prime analogate for the Christian way of life. It cannot be copied univocally, like a timeless blueprint. There are many ways to be Christian, just as there are four Gospels. Nevertheless, the story of Jesus witnessed in all the Gospels continues to have authority over every attempt to be Christian. The varieties of Christian community and spirituality are accountable to this normative story. Without that accountability, the various expressions of spirituality and community would be simply equivocal. Discipleship would be vacuous, since there would be nothing and no one to follow. The challenge of Christian ethics is to think analogically, that is, to be faithful and creative at the same time.

Meaning in the Concrete:
William F. Lynch and David Tracy

William F. Lynch and David Tracy have fruitfully analyzed the analogical imagination. Lynch, a literary critic, and Tracy, a fundamental theologian, appreciated that Christian insight is to be found by plunging into the particulars of the gospel and human experience.

Lynch suggested that the analogical imagination engages the whole person. We use all the resources of our psyche and history "to form images of the world, and thus to find it, cope with it, shape it, even make it." [7] The task of the imagination is to imagine reality and to remake it. Imagination is the opposite of *fantasy*, which fabricates an image to evade reality. Imagination engages particular realities and places them in a context, an intelligible landscape.[8] Fragments of experience that are divorced from any context lack meaning and defy hope. When placed in context by the imagination, however, they make room for possibility. Threats do not monopolize our attention once they are construed as parts of a meaningful whole. They become amenable to change and transformation. Imagination fuels the virtues of hope and patience by making it possible to envision a future.[9]

Literature teaches us that the path to meaning goes directly through the definite and concrete. This path leads "straight through our human realities, through our labor, our disappointments, our friends, our game legs, our harvests, our subjection to time. There are no shortcuts to beauty or insight."[10] To discover meaning we need to plunge into the depths of the very particulars that stand in tension with universal truth or beauty. Unlike the analogical imagination, romanticism and Manicheanism fail to take particular realities seriously.

Analogies are grounded in particular objects, events, and stories. The analogical imagination plunges down into concrete particulars, "in such a way that the plunge down *causally generates* the plunge up" into insight. There is a causal connection, not a rupture, between the human love for the concrete stuff of experience and the quest for meaning in its fullness. "The mind that has descended into the real has shot up into insights that would have been inaccessible to pure concepts."[11] Lynch parallels the path of the hymn in Philippians 2 when he interprets Christ's descent as the cause of his subsequent ascent: "Christ moved down into all the realities of man to get to His father."[12] This is the appropriate path to discover meaning and freedom. The stuff of ordinary life is not to be dismissed or transcended, but engaged. The Word is made flesh and cannot be found dissolved from the flesh.

This path of descent-into-the-part leading to ascent-into-the-whole stands out in the works of Dostoevski, Shakespeare, and other classics. "Our hope must be to discover such symbols as can make the imagination *rise* indeed, and yet keep all the tang and density of that actuality into which the imagination *descends*."[13] Since the pursuit of meaning and beauty passes through the narrow gate of particularity, we should not read the stories of Jesus as a code to transcendent meaning. We have to find ways of plunging into their particular characters, shape, and detail so that the larger meaning is disclosed. The practices of Jesuit spirituality helped Lynch to "plunge down" into the stories of the Gospels. At the same time, he insisted that no single image can define reality. It takes a variety of analogies and metaphors to bring out the richness of experience. In the language of contemporary cognitive science, we need "multiple metaphorical mappings" to grasp experiences.[14]

Without adequate images to grasp experience, we find ourselves overwhelmed and unable to cope with hard reality. Lynch argued that the great American fear of death stems from the absence of images for passivity. We cannot cope with death because we lack a set of images that tell us that

> it is all right to lie down in good time and die, dependently leaving it to God to raise [us] up again. . . . As a mother would tell a child that it is all right to be human, so the high images of a culture should be able to tell us that it can be all right to be passive and to die. Then we could cope (because the imagination had coped) and would have hope.[15]

We cannot define death or the terror it induces. We try to bring various images to bear on it, as Lynch does: the mother encouraging her child, the natural process of "lying down" in death as in sleep, God raising us up as with Christ. These figures do not encompass the reality of death, but they illumine it from different angles and evoke appropriate moral dispositions of patient courage and trusting resignation into the hands of another.

David Tracy explores two other aspects of this process. The first is the "focal meaning" necessary for the subject to reflect analogically. This awareness of what we stand for makes it possible to converse seriously with others in our pluralist culture. Insight into the experience of others comes from making analogies to our own. This presumes that we have some focus of our own to appeal to. Second, Tracy contrasts analogical and dialectical imagination and claims that both have an important role to play in theological reflection.

Focal Meaning

We understand others by analogy with our own experience. They are not copies of ourselves, nor is their experience completely alien. Instead humans share similarities-in-difference. We come to know what others stand for, the "focal meaning" that organizes their lives, through comparison to the central meanings of our own lives. One particular life, if it is grasped with some honest awareness, bears some resemblance to another particular life. "We understand one another, if at all, only through analogy. Who you are I know only by knowing what event, what focal meaning, you actually live by. And that I know only if I too have sensed some analogous guide in my own life."[16]

In a pluralistic age we fear that different viewpoints are incommensurable. Ideologies divide groups, and the scandal of sectarian warfare in places like Bosnia and Kashmir make us wonder whether religious language is inherently private and divisive. Even interpersonal conversations originate in quite different points of view and struggle to find points of contact and resonance. Nevertheless, conversation partners do not have to possess the same focal meaning at the center of their lives in order to converse. They do have to respect the central meaning of the other and not reduce it to a reflection of their own or despair of finding common ground in their differences. Religious pluralism does not destroy the possibility of dialogue so long as all parties know where their own identity is grounded and respect the others. That is, religious language is not equivocal in relation to the language of other traditions.

Christians find their focal meaning in the event of Jesus Christ as witnessed in the Gospels and tradition.[17] By probing the particularity of this event, Christians can give a coherent account of their belief, which should have some intelligibility to thinkers who do not share that focal meaning. This particular event will be the source of insight for understanding the rest of the experience of Christians.[18] Presumably, if their interlocutors were skeptics who dismissed any possibility of focal self-understanding, they would find Christian focal meaning unintelligible.

Focal points of meaning can be appreciated by others who have a different perspective and different focal meaning as their "prime analogate." It is a mistake to settle for the lowest common denominator in conversing across viewpoints, or to abstract from particular traditions in order to move to a level of high generality in order to offend no one. Like literary classics, some central religious events and symbols have such depth that they can be grasped by people from different traditions. There may well be analogous events and symbols in another's tradition or experience that interact fruitfully with a focal event like the exodus or the cross.

When the Dalai Lama attended a Passover seder with reformed Jews, he was very moved by the power of the liturgy. The story of Israel's passage from slavery to freedom had special resonance for this religious leader, who was driven into exile when the Chinese army destroyed hundreds of Buddhist monasteries and killed many monks and scholars. He said, "In our dialogue with rabbis and Jewish scholars, the Tibetan people have learned about the secrets of Jewish spiritual survival in exile: one secret is in the Passover seder." The Dalai Lama urged Tibetans "to copy some of the Jewish determination and the techniques they have used to keep their identity, their religious faith, their traditions under difficult circumstances."[19] The concrete details of the story of the exodus evoke the universal appeal of courage under persecution and the hope of being freed from oppression.

The importance of focal meaning implies that analogical reflection requires more than attention and intelligence. We "hear the rhyme" of religious analogy because it harmonizes with something central to our identity. Unless my life has the event of Jesus Christ as its focus, it is unlikely that I would be able to grasp what was happening in those Holy Thursday rituals. If I do participate in the way of life that is Christian, I will more likely appreciate the ways in which contemporary events and experiences bear some similarity to the events of the Gospels. Some degree of transformation by grace and committed involvement in a faith community enables the religious imagination to recognize and appreciate analogies.

Dialectical Imagination

According to Tracy, Christian theology has two "classic" languages, one based on the analogical imagination and the other on the dialectical imagination. While analogical reflection emphasizes the similarities in the relations ordered to the prime analogate, the dialectical stresses the differences. Analogical discourse begins with experiences of the manifestation of God's graciousness in ordinary life and moves from that to try to understand God. Dialectical discourse starts with "the empowering experience of God's decisive word of address in Jesus Christ."[20] The dialectical imagination hears the word of God exposing the profound alienation of humanity from God. This word stands over against natural and human quests for meaning and ultimacy.

The analogical and dialectical approaches can both be found in the biblical canon. The negations of cross and apocalyptic insist that the fullness of Christ is "not yet," while the resurrection and incarnation maintain that the prophetic promise is "even now" being realized. Thomas Aquinas and Karl Rahner exemplify the analogical imagination in their search for harmonious relations between God, self, and world. The early Karl Barth, Rudolf Bultmann, Paul Tillich, and Søren Kierkegaard articulate the dialectical approach. Although contemporary theology does not stress individual sinfulness so much, liberation and feminist theologians express the social aspects of dialectical negation. They first denounce the pervasive oppression of social structures before announcing good news. Otherwise, the good news will merely buttress the sinful status quo.

Which of these two uses of the imagination is more basic to Christian theology? I agree with Tracy that analogy enables the biblical text to mediate between the original generations of Christians and subsequent ones. Dialectical negations are important for unmasking our illusions and deflating our presumptions, but they are secondary to analogical affirmations. There would be no possibility of dialectical qualifications unless there were some analogy between the experience of believers and that of the communities that gave us the New Testament. The Lord who gathers the assembly of the faithful today is the same Jesus who announced the reign of God, healed the sick, reconciled the outcasts, and brought good news to the poor. Unless subsequent Christians had some experience of comparable activity in their era, the scriptures would be a dead letter. The command of Jesus to "go and do likewise" makes sense when Christians approach scripture through the analogical imagination. Then they can discover the same power of the Spirit working in them that inspired the apostolic communities.

───────────── II. IMAGINATION IN CHRISTIAN ETHICS ─────────────

The analogical imagination plays a central role in Christian ethics because Christian discipleship is grounded in a particular person conveyed to us through the particular shape of the Gospel story. The universal claim of Jesus is bound up with the concrete details of his story. We do not discard the story after wringing certain concepts and dogmas from it. These theological products attempt to encapsulate aspects of the story, putting it in conceptual shorthand so it can be translated to other contexts. Nevertheless, as Jon Sobrino writes, "whenever, in the course of history, Christians have sought to reinvest Christ with his totality, they have returned to Jesus of Nazareth."[21] The meaning of the reign of God, the cross and resurrection, and the reconciling grace of God is inextricably bound up with the Gospel accounts. The Gospels were written not to give lessons but to witness to a person and an event. That is, the particulars of the Gospels point out to contemporary Christian communities where the same Lord is present in the particulars of their experience.

"As": The Copula of the Imagination

As Immanuel Kant wrote, if "is" is the copula of understanding, joining subject and predicate, then "as" can be called the copula of the imagination.[22] The verb "is" can be called the copula of understanding since it links one term to another. The little word "as" is the copula of the imagination because it connects something not well known to something better known. In the moral imagination, "as" links our questions of how to live with a normative pattern. In the new commandment of Jesus, the disciples ought to love "just as" Jesus has loved them (John 13:34). Jesus ends the parable of the Good Samaritan by asking the lawyer, "Which of these three, do you think, was a neighbor to the man who fell into the hands of robbers?" The lawyer responds, "The one who showed him mercy." Jesus then says to him, "Go and do likewise" (Luke 10:37). The Greek word *homoios* does not simply refer to "showing mercy." It points back to the compassionate deed of the Samaritan as the paradigm for Christian neighborly love.

In both John and Luke, the standard for action-inspired-by-love is a narrative pattern. The conjunctions "just as" and "likewise" refer moral reflection back to the prime analogate for guidance. Since that prime analogate displays a moral pattern, it functions in a morally normative way: you ought to act likewise. This type of guidance differs from the usual case of moral normativity, namely, a general principle shaping action in concrete circumstances. The biblical scenarios guide action in a more concrete manner. They call for action that is appropriate or "fitting" to a pattern of relations that is embedded in an image or story. Moral inquiry thereby becomes analogical because it asks what the paradigm suggests. The way to love or be merciful will embody analogy's similarity-in-difference, some basic resemblance to the original paradigm.

Jesus' disciples are to use the image of footwashing as a springboard and guide for appropriate dispositions and actions. They have to figure what would be appropriate to their own situations and also faithful to the scenario displayed in the footwashing. That account is too rich to be univocally reproduced. It embodies a rich constellation of aspects: reversal of roles, humble service, equality, concrete compassion, voluntary relinquishment, foreshadowing of the cross, and eucharistic overtones of sharing of life. Different aspects of that scenario will be more appropriate than others to the new situations faced by Christians. For instance, shining shoes might evoke many of these themes in an American urban setting but might be unintelligible in St. Peter's basilica on Holy Thursday. On the other hand, the footwashing image is a guide as well as a springboard. It is not completely open-ended, because it is incompatible with enviously clinging to privilege, dominating others, rank ambition, impersonal treatment, and harsh justice.

Although there are no rules for the precise application of analogies, there are boundaries beyond which the original pattern, or "prime analogate," is no longer recognizable. The normative role of the image, therefore, depends on the capacity to perceive the point where "difference" has eroded any similarity. Although recognizing an apt analogy necessarily includes a well-tutored intuition, providing reasons can help another to see the appropriateness of the analogy. This method was the mainstay of Roman Catholic moral theology for centuries. The tradition of casuistry thrived on arguing the subtle differences that new circumstances could introduce to standard moral paradigms. When contemporary casuists employ the same analogical moves, they often frustrate moral philosophers who want stricter procedures for determining what to do or avoid.[23] The most important ability in arguing from paradigm cases is the capacity to recognize when the new case no longer resembles the paradigm—in other words, when there are no longer parallels between them.

The imagination's capacity to spot analogies usually comes from education and grounding in a way of life. As Tracy wrote, Christians whose focal meaning is the event of Jesus Christ will be better able to discern God's presence than those who are only casual believers. The practices of spirituality sharpen the Christian's capacities to discern what is appropriate. They ground the person in a way of life by shaping perception and moral dispositions. At the same time, the doctrines of the faith and its moral principles also set parameters for analogical imagination.

The medical profession depends on the same combination of perception and education in a way of life. The practice of medicine begins with the art of diagnosis. Medical students are educated to think analogically. They learn the central repository of typical medical conditions and use them as paradigms to diagnose and treat particular patients. As they make their "rounds" in hospital training, they are shown cases that display certain patterns of symptoms that are typical of pneumonia, peptic ulcers, and the like. They learn to recognize similar sets of symptoms when they occur again in other patients. The categories they learn help sharpen their perception so that they notice what is salient in the information presented. A good diagnostician also possesses certain skills of communication and knows how to elicit the appropriate information from patients and to listen carefully when they are hesitant to respond. Over time, medical students develop the knowledge and sensitivity to recognize diseases and conditions that they have seen before.[24]

Christians learn the art of discerning what is appropriate to their way of life in a similar fashion. Spiritual practices of meditation, discernment, and life in community train the Christian's perception by appreciating biblical paradigms. They begin to "spot the rhyme" between present experience and the sayings and stories of Jesus. As they deepen the focal meaning of their lives by study and practice, they become more skilled at discerning how to live in accordance with the gospel. Jesus Christ is the "Rosetta stone" that helps them decode experience to recognize whom God is calling them to become.[25] Beyond discerning that call, of course, Christians also need to make prudent determinations of what practical steps to take. There are other norms besides scripture that guide Christian moral imagination: tradition, common human moral standards, relevant empirical data, and prophetic voices in society. Whatever these other sources have to offer must be tested against the basic norm of Christian identity, the canonical scriptures. This process of testing is synthetic, involving a good deal of cross-checking among the various sources. The precise weight given to each source varies with the problem at hand: no formula can be specified in the abstract.

The Vocabulary of the Imagination

Since the vocabulary of the imagination has considerable fluidity these days, it will be necessary to clarify the terms of this discussion.[26] Imagination has two principal functions, the reproductive and the productive. In its reproductive function, imagination recognizes images and patterns. As productive, it fashions metaphors, symbols, and paradigms—the last being the most important term for analogical reflection.

An *image* is a visual reality like a picture, but it is more selective. It highlights certain essential features of the object considered and ignores nonessential ones. An image is not an abstraction but a streamlined way of looking at something.

A *pattern* is more abstract than an image and is not necessarily visual. A pattern is "an arrangement of elements in any medium."[27] A pattern often connotes more determinate meaning than an image. It is closer to "gestalt," that is, a distinctive way in which various parts are organized into a whole. Gestalt psychologists have shown that we do not build up our perceptions bit by bit; instead we grasp the whole of which they are parts.[28] For instance, once we get beyond the rudiments of phonics, we learn to read by seeing words as units, not accumulations of individual letters.

Production, the second function of the imagination, moves beyond simple recognition to create patterns. It goes beyond the actual to the possible. Here one image is played off against another by comparison, contrast, or synthesis. One set of data is "seen as" something else. "As" is the copula of the imagination because seeing one thing *as* another joins two terms by pointing out some similarity.

A *metaphor* joins two terms from normally discrete domains of experience. When one term is seen through the lens of the other, similarities and new aspects appear. A metaphor often works both ways when we can see each one from the perspective of the other. When juxtaposed, their chemistry interacts. "My love" is seen as "a red, red rose," a conjunction that baffles only the most literal-minded.

A *symbol* is a compressed metaphor that shares metaphor's "double-edged" structure and figurative language.[29] "A symbol is a complex of gestures, sounds, images, and/or words that evoke, invite, and persuade participation in that to which they refer."[30] Symbols work by simultaneously concealing and revealing larger dimensions of meaning. Unlike a sign, symbol keeps layers of meaning in tension. Like a metaphor, a symbol's meaning cannot be spelled out abstractly.[31]

Paradigm is the most important term for understanding analogy. It comes from the Greek *paradeigma*, which means an architect's model, a precedent or example, or an argument by example. A pattern becomes a paradigm when it becomes an exemplar for other objects or actions. A paradigm is a privileged pattern; it is not just an interesting comparison but a model for action. Biblical paradigms are used as analogies, not as strict examples to be copied. Copying the footwashing scene in the twentieth century, for instance, can actually fail to capture its meaning. In an analogy, the prime analogate is paradigmatic for the analogue, but not as a blueprint. The prime analogate is a flexible prototype that suggests interesting variations.

Paradigms and Theory

Paradigm is crucial for our discussion because the story of Jesus norms the lives of Christians *as a paradigm*. Jesus is the "concrete universal" for Christian life because his story has universal import for Christians. Wherever they are, they ought to live in ways that conform to the life of Jesus. They ought to form the sorts of communities that embody Christ in the world. They are to use their imaginations to recognize certain patterns and to extend them to their own families, businesses, and societies. This movement from text to life usually occurs by analogical extension, not by abstraction. The sayings of the Gospel are not inductively abstracted into general principles, which are then deductively applied to life. For instance, Dorothy Day did not first construct a theory of hospitality to the poor based on the Gospels before she could apply it in the soup kitchens of the Catholic Worker. She read the Sermon on the Mount's commands against the background of Jesus reaching out to the marginal, and she saw what she had to do. Intellectually, the transfer from text to life took the more intuitive route of the analogical imagination rather than the high road of abstraction. Psychologically, Day's astute discernment of what to do arose from a converted and generous heart. She heard the rhyme because her values and habits were already attuned to it.

Theory plays a role in moral reflection, though perhaps it is less central than philosophers and theologians assume. Theology derives general concepts and moral principles from the stories and paradigmatic images of religious tradition. Abstraction and generalization enable them to travel more readily to new contexts. The concept of justification, for example, compresses the story of the sinner's acquittal before the divine justice on account of the free grace of Christ. Many stories stand behind it: the welcome of Zacchaeus, the gracious father of the Prodigal Son, Jesus' treatment of the woman about to be stoned for adultery. However, "justification" can become a merely technical term if it loses touch with its narrative roots. Moral principles do not depend to the same extent on a canonical narrative, but they often depend upon paradigmatic cases or maxims. When John Rawls wanted to reconstruct the theory of justice for modern liberal democracies, he translated the myth of the social contract into the thought experiment of "the original position," where the agreeing parties were blind to the status they would have in the society that their agreement would produce. [32] In spelling out the requirements of liberal justice he repeatedly appeals to this philosophical "myth of origin."

Theory played a background role in Dorothy Day's case. Frequent conversation with Peter Maurin integrated her gospel convictions into the larger framework of his homespun socialism and the spirituality of the Little Brothers of Charles de Foucauld, a religious community to which that he had once belonged. If Day had written more theologically, the Catholic Worker vision might be more widely understood. Certainly the Latin American liberation theologians have had a greater impact in other cultures than the Catholic Worker movement has had. This may be due to their ability to root their convictions about the poor in theoretical frameworks of critical sociology, exegesis, and theology. Nevertheless, they insist that transforming insight comes not from study-ing theory but from immersion in the struggle of actual poor and oppressed people. Engagement with the poor Christ reshapes one's frame of reference to see and respond to the world in a transformed way.

——————— III. THE KINGDOM OF GOD: METAPHOR AND ANALOGY ———————

How does the image of "the kingdom of God" work in Christian moral reflec-tion? The *basileia tou theou*, God's reign or realm, is the image most frequently used by Jesus in the Gospels. Every attempt to define it as a precise theological concept fails. As a moral image it seems equally elusive since it does not directly determine what should be done. I believe that God's reign is a metaphor that functions in two ways: it frames the disciples' view of the world, and it becomes a fruitful analogy in the parables of the kingdom.

A Framing Metaphor

The reign of God is a compressed metaphor because it joins terms from two domains of experience in a surprising way. Since the term has become a cliché, it probably has lost any element of tension or surprise for most Christians. Reli-gious language is often metaphorical because it takes a collision of normally unrelated experiences to convey the strangeness and power of God's action. It is a surprising assertion to claim that "God now reigns," because whatever nor-mally runs the world certainly does not seem to be a gracious and merciful deity. Its meaning, like that of other metaphors, is suggestive, not literal; it can-not be pinned down in definitions. Is the *basileia* a place, a "kingdom," or is it a region of authority, a "reign"? Is it a state of mind and heart or a social real-ity? Is it an event that is breaking into history or the goal of history?[33] The very elusiveness of the *basileia tou theou* is an advantage if it keeps us from taking lit-erally what should be taken metaphorically.

Most fundamentally, the reign of God is a "metaphorical frame" that struc-tures Christian experience.[34] It is a basic horizon or framework within which everything else is apprehended. It works like the presuppositions of the "New-tonian universe" did for scientists before the advent of relativity theory. Isaac Newton's laws of matter and motion set the basic coordinates for understand-ing physics and the other sciences. Einstein replaced the metaphorical frame of Newton's mechanics with a more comprehensive theory of space and time, mat-ter and energy, that now frames the discussion of most science.[35] This shift had profound cultural repercussions. A closely ordered universe became less certain

and more relative, even for people who had never heard of W. Heisenberg's
uncertainty principle.

Jesus' proclamation that God had finally begun to reign called for a comparable change of metaphorical frame for his disciples. "God's reign" means God
acting in power—or the world according to God. It is the horizon within which
everything else is apprehended. At long last, the history of Israel was coming to
its promised fullness. God is acting graciously to set this world right, to return
humans from their long exile, and to constitute a new community of reconciliation and peace. Or, as Jon Sobrino translates this reality in broader terms:
God is the God of life and acts to liberate the world from the forces of death,
the anti-kingdom.[36] From the preaching of Jesus on, time and individual experience must be understood in terms of images from another domain, the rule
of a just sovereign. The metaphor of the sovereign God returning the people
from exile is the fundamental presupposition that lies behind the entire ministry of Jesus and the experience of his disciples. In the next chapter we will consider what that meant for them.

Religious conversion inevitably involves a change in our basic metaphorical
frameworks. We suspend many of the familiar ways of looking at the world and
our own lives; they have broken down and need to be replaced. Dispositions
and actions that used to be appropriate no longer fit this new way of looking at
the world. The New Testament writers attempt to convert the imaginations of
Christians by parables, metaphors, and stories. They want their readers to see
life in a new way and to act in radically different ways. They claim that they have
found a new identity in Christ that is more fundamental than the basic categories that have defined who we are.

Parables of the Kingdom: Fruitful Analogies

The kingdom is not only a frame for reflection; it is also spelled out more clearly
in the parables and sayings of Jesus. Jesus never told the disciples what the kingdom is, but he prefaced many parables and sayings with "The kingdom of God
is like . . . ." These parables invite us to see God and our world in fresh terms.
God acts like a shepherd seeking out lost sheep, a woman searching for a coin,
and an anxious father worried over his son who has gone off to a distant country with his inheritance (Luke 15). The parables become analogies that disclose
aspects of who God is and how we should respond to God's reign. They function metaphorically more than paradigmatically. Since they usually refer to
God's ways of acting, they are paradigmatic for us by implication. If God is this
merciful, then we should be this merciful too. Jesus' parables do not give a blueprint for action; instead, they tend to subvert the world of the status quo. So

Matthew's parable of the workers in the vineyard does not tell us how to combine generosity and fairness; rather, it demolishes any notion that God operates according to the logic of *quid pro quo*. God's reign will not be business as usual.[37]

All of the parables of Jesus are geared to evoke insight in metaphorical fashion. Every metaphor associates two terms that do not belong together. The tension between the two provokes an insight that reveals new depths in familiar material. In the parables, ordinary life is set against an extraordinary background. Fields are bought, merchants make deals, sons refuse to work in the vineyard, women lose coins, fathers welcome back wastrel sons but with unexpected consequences and extraordinary joy. Jesus lets these metaphorical puzzles stand on their own; he does not distill out a moral as if they were Aesop's fables. We have to get the insight by catching similarities where we least expect them to be. The surprise that parables evoke is the disclosure that ordinary life is cracking open to reveal One we never thought was there:

> The logic of the parabolic method contains the implication that the "mystery" of the Kingdom—the riddle of God's presence, power, and purpose, and of human duty, value and goal, will unfold itself not in the systematic exploration of the myth or symbol of "the Kingdom of God" but through reflection on and response to features of real life delineated and imaged in parable.[38]

The parables turn moral reflection back to what God is doing. They open us to One whose ways are decidedly not our ways. Even when they are more paradigmatic, they call for actions that go off the scale of ordinary behavior. A merchant sells everything he owns in order to buy a single pearl. A patch of ground receives the seed and brings forth an enormous harvest of grain. Sleepy members of a bridal party let their lamps go out and are excluded from the wedding party; they get no second chance. These stories hint that God's reign is more abundant and more consequential than we would like to think.

For those who have ears to hear, the analogical imagination highlights relevant aspects of the parables and infers distinctive behavioral consequences. If we imagine that the reign of God is like reading the sky for signs of impending weather, it encourages us to pay attention to the extraordinary action of God in the daily routine. When we imagine that the kingdom is like a wedding banquet, we recognize how necessary it is to respond to the invitation. These moral consequences flow integrally from the respective metaphors and the dispositions they engender. Appropriate actions are not tacked on to the parable as an afterthought; the parables entail the actions analogically to the extent that we let them challenge us. Although the parables of the kingdom are more analogical and metaphorical, the Gospels do offer material that is more directly paradigmatic for human response. The actions and sayings of Jesus give more definite content to the nature of God's reign. He calls people to enter into the reign of God by doing the sorts of things that he did with the same motives.

Deceptive Analogies

When do metaphorical frames and paradigms go astray? Actions may be judged to fit the world as it is seen through a particular set of lenses, but what if the lenses distort reality? Then the action might be appropriate in a narrow sense but could be disastrous in other ways. Metaphorical frameworks exercise a normative role because they rule in certain dispositions and rule out others. They make some actions seem appropriate and others inappropriate. At times, metaphors can be worse than inadequate; they can be positively misleading when they distort reality and lead to immoral consequences. They become "evil imaginations of the heart."[39] During the Cold War, American and Russian strategic planners located their thinking about nuclear deterrence in radically different metaphorical frameworks. The American planners thought about nuclear strategy in the highly technical terms of computer-modeled war games. They played out various scenarios of thermonuclear conflict on large video screens. Their Russian counterparts thought of nuclear war in terms of Tolstoy's *War and Peace*. Mother Russia could once again absorb enormous suffering and still endure longer than its adversary; its triumph would mystically emerge from defeat and devastation.[40] Were these evil imaginations of the heart? Certainly they propped up a regime that relied on a balance of terror and they might have justified all-out nuclear war. It is difficult to fathom why Christians tolerated such a threat to God's creation for decades.

Biblical stories and images have been used to justify actions and ways of living that are incompatible with the authentic values of Jesus. Misogynist interpretations of the Genesis account have underwritten traditional discrimination against women. Attitudes in the Pauline literature about the subordination of wives to husbands and the place of women in the liturgical assembly have been extrapolated into divine principles for all times and places. The image of the kingdom of God has undergone similar distortion. It has underwritten a number of patently un-Christian social arrangements and policies. The crusaders combined the language of the kingdom with their martial ethos to justify the slaughter of the inhabitants of the Holy Land. Oliver Cromwell had few scruples about brutally crushing the Irish in the name of the kingdom of God.[41] Nineteenth-century American Protestants transposed the Puritans' "city on a hill" into the ideology of "manifest destiny" by aligning the kingdom of God with a jingoistic and racist nationalism. Revivalists of the same period transposed the reign of God into a purely inward and sentimental reality.[42]

Clearly, invoking biblical images does not guarantee fidelity to the way of Christ. When cultures are dominated by vindictive chivalry or nationalism, the language of the kingdom can be a rhetorical cloak. God is enlisted to fight on their side, and they become convinced that their slaughter is doing the Lord's work. The analogical imagination judges certain action to be appropriate based on the compatibility between the proposed course of action, the facts of the situation, and certain paradigmatic frameworks. The entire process also depends on the level of moral sensitivity and virtue of those who are discerning what to do. The images of the Gospel will easily become evil imaginations of the heart to those whose hearts are unwittingly dominated by self-serving and evil dispositions. They will still think analogically, but they will draw the wrong implications. The course of action that will seem fitting will be appropriate to their own purposes rather than to the mind of Christ.

There are resources within scripture and Christian tradition to unmask the evil imaginations of the heart, but often they have not prevailed. Movements in the larger culture can shame Christian communities back to living the gospel vision with integrity. The churches become sectarian when they presume that they have a monopoly on wisdom. The biblical authors showed no such defensiveness about borrowing moral insight from other cultures, on the assumption that the God of all the earth works in many ways. When churches become sectarian, they have confused their little institution with the kingdom of God. In nineteenth-century Europe, it was not the churches who championed the rights of workers against predatory capitalism but socialists and other radical reformers. In this century, secular feminists drove the protest against entrenched sexism in social institutions, including the churches. Criticism of anti-Judaic polemics in the New Testament has arisen from the scandal of the Holocaust. Eventually these prophetic movements awakened Christians and their institutions. Other movements such as abolitionism and civil rights were deeply rooted in biblical religion from the outset.

Literal readings of biblical imagery can be unfaithful to their trajectory of meaning. Norms and paradigms that push the boundaries of cultural arrangements in their original biblical setting should not be used to canonize our present institutions. For example, Ephesians 5 challenged the male-dominated structure of marriage when it mandated both husbands and wives to "be subject to one another out of reverence for Christ" (Eph. 5:21). Marriage relations should be analogous to the love of Christ for the church. True, the passage counsels wives to be subject to their husbands and husbands to love their wives as they do their very bodies. However, that position represents a genuine advance toward mutuality from prevailing Jewish and Greco-Roman patterns. The ideal of mutual submission after the example of Christ stated in v. 21 should continue to push beyond patriarchal definitions of marriage relations.

The Southern Baptist Convention amended its Faith and Mission Statement in 1998 to state, "As the wife submits to her husband's leadership, the husband humbles himself to meet his wife's needs for love and nurture. Wives, on the other hand, are created to be 'helpers' to their husbands."[43] The Southern Baptists defended traditional family roles by combining a literal reading of Ephesians 5 with the reference in Genesis 2:18 to "the woman's" creation, thereby flattening out the trajectory of the original passages.[44] More careful attention to the context of Ephesians and Genesis would have revealed not a fixed formula for family relations but a leaven that should keep challenging families in every culture. The tension between the Letter to the Ephesians and its cultural context should be maintained when using it analogically to guide Christians today in respect to our culture's suppositions about gender roles. That analogy would not support one-sided subordination of either party; it would also challenge a contractual marriage based on individual self-interest, often carefully calibrated in a "score card" of credits and debits. Combined with Jesus' own unconventional acceptance of women in his ministry, Ephesians' imagery should press Christians to move contemporary gender roles toward greater mutuality of respect and service. Otherwise, the creative dynamic of the analogical imagination is blocked by a literalism that is actually unfaithful to the biblical text.

The journey of discipleship began with Jesus' call to see that something radically new was breaking into history. Jesus' healings, exorcisms, and prophetic preaching were signs that God was acting in a definitive way. They were evidence that had to be noticed so that people could begin to respond to God's initiative. The Christian way of life begins in how we perceive what is going on. The Gospels give us a new set of metaphors and paradigms, new lenses, to look at the world. Our experience looks different when seen through the lens of the kingdom of God that Jesus announced and the cross and resurrection, which cracked open history so that God could reign. In the next chapter we will look at Jesus' announcement of the reign of God and how that called for a new vision for those who believed they were seeing the inauguration of the world according to God.

PART 2

Christian Transformation

W E NOW MOVE FROM DISCUSSING the three sources of this approach —New Testament studies, virtue ethics, and spirituality—to consider the transformation of persons and communities. The ability to see pertinent analogies between scripture and life depends on the character and faith commitment of the person who is exercising the analogical imagination. The way looks different when you are on it. Christian discipleship affects the entire person, particularly the capacities of moral perception, dispositions, and identity. The gospel challenges each of these dimensions of moral psychology; spiritual practices tutor these capacities to produce lives faithful to the way of Jesus Christ.

Chapters 4 and 5 describe how the call to recognize the dawn of the kingdom of God summons us to the compassionate vision expressed in the Good Samaritan. The practice of intercessory prayer locates all of life within the framework of the reign of God. Chapters 6 and 7 discuss how the healings and encounters of Jesus evoke particular moral dispositions that enable Christians to "go and do likewise." Practices of biblical meditation and discernment guide disciples in the way of the cross and resurrection. Finally, chapter 8 considers how the practice of the Lord's Supper, or Eucharist, shapes the identity of Christians in community. The practices of forgiveness and solidarity with the poor are necessary components of this central act of Christian worship.

Distinguishing various aspects of moral psychology and spiritual practices may give the impression that experience can be divided into closed compartments. In fact, change in any aspect of moral psychology will alter every other aspect. When someone gets married or has a religious conversion, that change in personal identity can be expected to produce a different moral vision and reorient the person's basic moral dispositions. Similarly, the same spiritual practice influences more than one aspect of moral psychology The practice of forgiveness shapes Christian identity, but it also shapes perception, since a forgiving person sees enemies and strangers in a radically different light. They look different when we see them as those for whom Christ died. The same practice should deepen specific Christian dispositions of gratitude, repentance, compassion, and nonviolence. What is distinguished here for analytical purposes is integrated in walking the way of discipleship.

Finally, Christian transformation is not an end in itself. The disciples of Jesus are earnest about furthering the reign of God in the world and deepening friendship with God, not about becoming moral paragons. If they were, they would not be his disciples.

CHAPTER 4

Perception

The Pharisees and Sadducees came, and to test Jesus they asked him to show them a sign from heaven. He answered them, "When it is evening, you say, 'It will be fair weather, for the sky is red.' And in the morning, 'It will be stormy today, for the sky is red and threatening.' You know how to interpret the appearance of the sky, but you cannot interpret the signs of the times." (Matt. 16:1–3)

JESUS COMES TO PROCLAIM that Yahweh is finally bringing the history of Israel to its climax. God is beginning to fulfill the promises that had sustained the chosen people through exile and centuries of foreign domination. God's final gracious initiative is breaking out in their midst but, strangely, many of the people cannot perceive it. Some of the leaders insist on manifest proof that would remove their doubts. Usually the Sadducees and Pharisees were opponents, but they come together here to demand more evidence for Jesus' claims. He warns them that the signs of God's approach are as easy to read as the weather: just look at what is going on. If they cannot discern the obvious, whose fault is it?

The Christian life begins with the gracious approach of God, not human initiative. In order to respond to God's approach we have to recognize it for what it is. We have to perceive what is going on before we can interpret it and decide what to do. *Perception* is the ability to notice the morally relevant features of a situation and the readiness to respond appropriately. However, perception is not a matter of simply "taking a look" at objective reality. What we perceive depends on the sort of character we have, because that defines our point of view. As the saying goes, "To a pickpocket, all the world's a pocket." Perception is integrally related to dispositions as well as identity because our habitual dispositions determine what we perceive. Moral perception relies on specific character traits, especially the virtues of empathy and compassion.

75

Perception is, therefore, the first aspect of moral psychology to consider in relation to Jesus. Jesus insisted that people pay attention to what was happening in their midst because God was doing something new. The opening of Mark's Gospel opens announces this breakthrough and demands a response:

> Now after John was arrested, Jesus came to Galilee, proclaiming the good news of God and saying, "The time is fulfilled, and the kingdom of God has come near; repent, and believe in the good news." (Mark 1:14–15)

The history of Israel has reached its climactic moment; God is making a definitive move that requires repentance, a radical reversal of mind and heart. History is coming to its climax, not to its end, and the people of Israel are being summoned to judgment and grace. A sense of urgency runs through Mark's fast-paced narrative: God's time has begun; each person must decide to seize this opportunity of grace or it will pass by.[1]

Jesus was convinced that the reign of God was dawning, and that conviction lay behind everything he said and did. It should also be the basic horizon within which his followers also apprehend experience. Whenever God's gracious initiative breaks into human experience, inviting and commanding a response, the reign of God is being extended. Where God reigns, a different way of life becomes possible—for those who are willing to notice what is going on. Attending in faith to the "signs of the times" can help us discern how God is enabling and requiring us to respond.[2] Since God's reign is characterized by mercy and justice, compassion for the suffering and oppressed is a central dimension of it.

In order to understand how Jesus transforms moral perception we will consider: (1) what he said was happening, namely, the breaking into history of God's reign, God's action to set things right; (2) compassion as the virtue that sees others in the way that God does; (3) how contemporary virtue ethics helps unpack what this compassionate vision involves.

I. GOD HAS BEGUN TO REIGN

The good news of Jesus announces an event, not a set of doctrines, sage advice on how to live a better life, or a roadmap to get to the world to come. Coming on the heels of John the Baptizer's prophetic denunciation of Israel's status quo, this announcement caught people's attention. Each of the Synoptics begins the account of Jesus' public life with this announcement (Mark 1:14–15; Matt. 4:17, 23; Luke 4:42–43). Fifty of Jesus' parables and sayings spell out the phrase "reign of God" and its paraphrase "kingdom of heaven." While there is scholarly consensus on the centrality of the *basileia tou theou* in the preaching of

Jesus, there is little agreement on what precisely Jesus meant by the term. Each of the evangelists interprets it according to a distinctive theological agenda, and in John it fades into the term "eternal life." Jesus took the conventional story of Israel and retold it in surprising and subversive ways. Therefore, the first order of business will be sketching the expectations that Jesus' contemporaries had for Yahweh's deliverance.[3]

Jewish Expectations of the Kingdom of God

Israel was still in exile in the first century C.E. More than four centuries had elapsed since the return from Babylon, but the Lord's pledge of restoration was yet to be fulfilled. The people still waited for the rich promises of Isaiah 40–55 and Zechariah to come true. As long as foreigners occupied the land, the Messiah had not come and Torah was not observed in Israel, and Yahweh had not definitively returned to the chosen people. These promises had not been fulfilled in the Maccabean revolt against the Hellenists in 164 B.C.E. and the brief time of independence that followed. One revolutionary leader after another had risen up to claim the mantle of the Maccabeans and to usher in the Lord's reign. They counted on divine intervention to make their revolutions succeed, but all failed. N. T. Wright assures us that

> anyone who was heard talking about the reign of Israel's god would be assumed to be referring to the fulfillment of Israel's long-held hope. The covenant god would act to reconstitute his people, to end their exile, to forgive their sins. When that happened, Israel would no longer be dominated by the pagans. She would be free.[4]

The complete return from exile would be a new exodus in which Yahweh would definitively deliver the people and would finally be manifested as king of the whole world. The Lord would return in glory to the spiritual center of the nation, the Temple that Herod had reconstructed, and would restore the Davidic monarchy.

Israel was hoping that God would come and straighten out this world; it was not longing for life in some transcendent realm. This event would usher in the final stage of history, and only in that sense would it be the end of the world. All the prophetic images of restoration are set within space and time: captives will be set free, the lame will walk again, the poor will receive just treatment, crops will flourish, people will grow old in peace on their own land and see their great grandchildren, and all nations will stream to the Temple for instruction in the Torah. This vision has political implications precisely because it is this-worldly. Ezekiel and Jeremiah had warned that when the Lord comes to reign, others will be cast off the throne. There will be a great battle with the entrenched forces of evil, and the Lord will emerge victorious. A purely spiritual or dualistic hope would not have inspired the Maccabean revolt or the insurgent movements against Roman rule. Curiously, the early church and subsequent eras transmuted this eschatological vision into the expectation of the destruction of the space-time cosmos.

Although the exile taught Israel that Yahweh was God of all the earth rather than the foremost among many deities, the struggle against Syrian, Hellenistic, and Roman conquerors in the intervening centuries made their hope more nationalistic. If God is just and has chosen Israel, God would have to deliver them from their present humiliation and vindicate God's name before the nations. This urgent hope was "eschatological," since it longed for the end of the present age and the definitive revelation of God, which would inaugurate a new era of history. In the book of Daniel, composed in the second century B.C.E., this hope finds "apocalyptic" expression as well. Colorful symbolism codes the story of the final overthrow of tyranny, and the text plots out a timetable for God's judgment and vindication.[5]

In the time of Jesus this expectation of national deliverance took different forms and advocated different religious strategies.[6] The Essenes forsook the Temple and sought this kingdom in the heavenly court that worshiped God. They withdrew to monastic seclusion at Qumran. The Pharisees and their rabbinic successors emphasized fidelity to Torah as the condition for God's vindication. Taking on the yoke of the kingdom meant accepting the yoke of Torah. Hellenistic Jewish thought took a more philosophical turn by identifying God's reign with a cosmic providence. Local insurgents attempted to seize the mantle of deliverance in sporadic movements that were closer to banditry than to revolution.

Jesus envisioned the reign of God in ways quite different from these contemporary alternatives. God's reign permeated nature and ordinary life and was not confined to the celestial court, as the Essenes held. He did not identify God's sphere of influence with obedience to Torah, but extended it to those whom the Pharisees considered sinners for their disregard of the Law. God's reign had an immediacy and a personal quality of relationship that were absent from Hellenistic philosophical conceptions. Finally, Jesus repudiated violence as a strategy to provoke God's political vindication of Israel.

It is impossible for us to recreate the rich expectations of Second Temple Judaism for the coming the God's reign. It is important to probe that symbolic world so that our metaphorical frame lines up with theirs. Otherwise our analogical imagination will operate without the assumptions Jesus had. God's return to Israel, the defeat of evil, and the exile-ending forgiveness of sins are more than a myth. We do not have to accept the whole worldview as fact in order to use it paradigmatically.

Jesus and the Kingdom of God

The people of Palestine would have understood the image of God reigning, since it was familiar from patterns of prayer and worship. How did the people of Israel expect the Lord to reign? Their history testified to One who delivered them from slavery, forged a covenant bond that demanded a committed response, established them in the land, and guided their destiny through leaders and prophets. The Lord who is sovereign over all nations acts on Israel's behalf:

> Clap your hands, all you peoples;
>   shout to God with loud songs of joy.
> For the LORD, the Most High, is awesome,
>   a great King over all the earth.
> He subdues peoples under us, and nations under our feet.
> He chose our heritage for us,
>   the pride of Jacob whom he loves. (Ps. 43:1-4)

This reign of God will extend to all creation as well as to the people of the covenant, as the Psalms' images of regal enthronement celebrated:

> The LORD is king, he is robed in majesty;
>   the LORD is robed, he is girded in strength.
> He has established the world; it shall never be moved;
>   your throne is established from of old;
>   you are everlasting. (Ps. 93:1-2)

Jesus appealed to the same texts, but subverted his contemporaries' assumptions about how the deliverance would occur. If they stayed on their course to armed insurrection, the nation would undergo a terrible catastrophe. Although subsequent generations would make Jesus' prophetic warnings into predictions about events after death, Jesus' contemporaries heard them as judgments about themselves. Like the people of Jeremiah's time, many preferred violent military solutions to relying on God to act in God's own ways. Within thirty years they would revolt against the Romans, and instead of bringing down Yahweh's delivering power, they would bring about the destruction of the Second Temple, the devastation of Jerusalem, and a more radical exile.

Jesus proclaimed that God was beginning to reign and performed specific actions that ushered in, inaugurated, that new reality. His healings and exorcisms brought the power of God into direct confrontation with the real source of evil, which was not the Romans but the satanic forces of evil. His parables were the seed that he sowed, which led to judgment about the ones who heard it. The way in which his audience received the announcement revealed their character: some were impervious, others superficial, others stifled by worldly cares, and still others were receptive and proved abundantly fruitful (Mark 4:1–20). None of his symbolic actions, however, had consequences as momentous as the consequences of his assault on the Temple system. All four Gospels testify to this event as pivotal in his ministry; they cite it as the principal accusation that led to his death. Preaching parables was one thing, but condemning the central religious institution of Israel as corrupt was a capital offense.

This incident has been traditionally called the "cleansing of the Temple," as though it were a reformer's attempt to bring the sacrificial system back into line with the Temple's original mission. A closer reading of the text of Mark 11 and its parallels (Matt. 21:12–27; Luke 19:45–48; John 2:13–22), however, yields a more radical meaning. Jesus was actually condemning the Temple system and its guardians in the name of God and prophesying its destruction. The Temple was the center of the life of Israel, and it had become corrupted. Unless the nation repented, it would be destroyed by the pagans. This prediction is not a post-factum reflection of the 70 C.E. destruction of the Temple by the early Christians, because the prophetic action and prophecy exactly fit the historical mission and teaching of Jesus.[7]

The biblical texts that Jesus cites to justify his outburst reveal a sweeping condemnation. "My house shall be called a house of prayer for all nations" comes from Isaiah 56, which states the Lord's intention that Gentiles will be welcomed to sacrifice there, in contrast to the people of Israel and its leaders, who are strongly criticized in the rest of the passage (Isa. 56:9–12; 57:1–21). Even more damning is the line from Jeremiah: "but you have made it a den of robbers" (Mark 11:17). It comes from Jeremiah's harrowing prophecy (7:3–15), which condemns Israel for thinking that they could find safety in the Lord's house while committing theft, murder, adultery, and idolatry. They have not listened to the divine call to repent, and so Jeremiah prophesied that the Lord would destroy this sanctuary of Solomon as utterly as he had destroyed the sanctuary of their ancestors at Shiloh. In a few years the Babylonians did just that.

Just as in the time of Jeremiah, the Second Temple had become the focus of expectations of national deliverance; Yahweh's presence protected Jerusalem against the nations.[8] If it came to a violent struggle for national survival, would not Yahweh have to defend Jerusalem against the enemies of Israel? The Temple incident is bracketed in Mark by the story of the fig tree (11:12–14 and 20–22), another enacted parable that echoes a destructive prophecy of Jeremiah. When the Lord comes to gather the fruits of his planting, Israel is barren

(Jer. 8:13). Jesus is hungry but finds no fruit on the fig tree so he curses it as a sign of the judgment that awaits Israel and the Temple. Jesus banishes the money changers from the Temple because without them people could not change their money in order to purchase animals for sacrifice. The regular sacrifice of animals was Israel's vital contact with its Lord; take that away and the whole Temple system becomes useless.[9]

This prophetic action brings the emerging reign of God into direct conflict with the Sadducean Temple establishment. Jesus so identifies himself with the message that he sees his actions as bringing in the day of the Lord. He is not just proclaiming the kingdom; he is enacting and "performing" it.[10] He dramatizes that the path of violent nationalist revolution is incompatible with the way in which God reigns. He advocates "turning the other cheek" and follows this nonviolent path to his death, forswearing defense or retaliation when he is surrounded by his enemies. Ironically, the Temple incident has often been cited to justify Christian resort to physical violence and warfare. If Jesus could use force to accomplish his aims, may not his followers engage in justifiable wars? This convenient reading misses the point of the enacted parable and the consistent way of peace that Jesus walked at the cost of his life.[11] Again, these actions lose their messianic import when read from a modern or postmodern secular mind-set rather than from the mind-set of Second Temple Judaism. That rich symbolic framework gives Jesus' actions a significance that eludes those who portray Jesus as a wandering Cynic philosopher who preached equality and inclusiveness.

Jesus' welcome of sinners and outcasts added insult to the serious injury inflicted by his attack on the Temple system. By offering forgiveness of sins and reconciliation with the family of God, Jesus was doing what had been reserved to the Temple system. Eating with sinners and outcasts and inviting them into his company posed a direct threat not only to the Pharisees' insistence on observing purity laws but also to the Sadducees' monopoly on the system of sacrifice. Consider the story of Zacchaeus in Luke 19. This tax collector had made a fortune by collaborating with Romans and squeezing revenues out of his fellow Israelites. The Romans put tax collecting out for bids. Above the fixed amount that had to be turned over to the local authorities, the collectors could keep the additional money they extracted by hiding behind the threat of Rome's soldiers. In all, it seems unlikely that Zacchaeus would have won any popularity contest in Jericho. Jesus singles out this outsider from the crowd and invites himself into Zacchaeus's house for dinner. The crowd, which must have included victims of his extortion, grumbled in anger. Zacchaeus is moved by Jesus' unusual treatment to repent and restore fourfold whatever he had taken by fraud. At this Jesus welcomes him back into the people of Israel. "This day salvation has come to this house, because he too is a son of Abraham. The Son of Man came to seek out and to save the lost" (Luke 19:9–10).

If Jesus is able to forgive sinners and reconcile them with the Lord, then the Temple is being reconstituted in his own ministry. It is no longer necessary to go to the Temple and perform the prescribed rituals under the guidance of the priests to ensure grace and mercy. Since sin had caused Israel's exile, this proclamation of forgiveness signifies that Israel has finally returned home and the Lord has returned to Israel. This could only mean one thing: in Jesus' ministry the climax of Israel's story is already occurring and the exile is over at last. Forgiveness of sin was not an isolated rapprochement between an individual and Yahweh; it was a profoundly communal event. Individuals were reconciled and forgiven as part of the whole community of Israel that is being restored to God's favor. These repeated demonstrations of reconciliation in Jesus' healings, exorcisms, and table fellowship with sinners and outcasts meant that he was offering a replacement to the central institutions of Israel. The reign of God was breaking out in Israel but not in the Temple or in the discussions of Torah. "Jesus offered membership in the renewed people of the covenant god *on his own authority* and *by his own process*. This was the real scandal."[12]

What did Jesus have to say about his own connection to the emerging reign of God? Typically, he invited the curious to pay attention to the works he was doing and to draw their own conclusions. They had to perceive what was going on in front of them. His encounters, healings, exorcisms, preaching, and association with outcasts were prophetic "performances." They indicated that Jesus thought himself to be intimately involved with the reign of God. When he was doing these things, the God of Israel was doing them. Jesus' opponents did not miss the point. After Jesus has told the paralyzed man in Mark 2 that his sins were forgiven, "some of the scribes were sitting there, questioning in their hearts. 'Why does this fellow speak this way? It is blasphemy! Who can forgive sins but God alone?'" (Mark 2:6, 7). Jesus called them on their opposition and cured the paralytic "so that you may know that the Son of Man has power on earth to forgive sins" (2:10). Many in the crowd were astonished at what he did and glorified God for it. Others, like the grumbling scribes, saw the same event and failed to perceive what was going on.

This same invitation holds in analogous fashion for the curious in subsequent generations: pay attention and draw the inference for yourselves. When John's disciples came to Jesus asking, "Are you the one who is to come, or are we to wait for another?" he told them simply to notice what he was doing. "Go and tell John what you hear and see: the blind receive their sight, the lame walk, the lepers are cleansed, the deaf hear, the dead are raised, and the poor have the good news brought to them" (Matt. 10:2-5). The plain facts become evidence to those who are willing to pay attention with an open heart. Those who are not ready to respond will not be able to perceive. Those who do perceive what is occurring are the ones who "enter into" the reign of God. Those who do not are not judged by Jesus; they exclude themselves. John's Gospel reiterates this theme: Jesus has come not to judge the world but to save it. Judgment takes place as people decide to turn to the light that he brings or to shun it (John 3).

The announcement of the reign of God generates resistance. This is a central feature of this Gospel paradigm. Why could some people see God's presence in Jesus' words and actions while others saw the power of the evil one? Perceiving God's action requires a willingness to be affected by what one sees, an initial disposition to respond favorably to what is good and true. The good news is inviting to those who have "ears to hear" (Matt. 19:12). It sounds threatening to those who are closed. "Having ears to hear," that is, a readiness to perceive, is a precondition for correct interpretation. Without that openness many of the most knowledgeable guardians of Israel's traditions missed the message that was the culmination of their history. Their intellectual preparation did not make them open to healing and transformation.

The Kingdom of God and Early Christianity

The early Christian communities told a new version of this same story. In the Synoptic Gospels, the words and actions of Jesus give content to God's reign. The final battle is joined with the true forces of evil, which turn out to be not the Romans but the satanic powers of darkness.[13] In his exorcisms and miracles and climactically in his crucifixion, Jesus confronts the powers of darkness. These works of power demonstrated that God was doing battle with the powers of death. "But if it is by the Spirit of God that I cast out demons, then the kingdom of God has come to you" (Matt. 12:28). Literally, the reign of God "has come upon" those who see Jesus casting out demons by the Spirit of God. The rule of God is literally breaking into the midst of the human community—it is not "within you" as a spiritual possession but "among you" as an irruption into the ordinary fabric of human relations. Mark's account crackles with the energy of this cosmic conflict. When Jesus approaches, the powers that hold people in bondage and sickness cry out and beg not to be expelled by his superior force. They try to get a handle on this power by naming Jesus, but he silences them (1:21-28; 3:7-12; 5:1-20).

Matthew puts more emphasis than Mark on the fulfillment of the expectations of God's coming in the person of Jesus. Growth and steady expansion of the kingdom complement Mark's picture of God's power confronting the forces of death. Those who hear the message and obey the commandments of Jesus become sons and daughters of the kingdom (Matt. 13:37-38). The risen Christ already reigns over the world, even though his kingship will not be fully realized until the end of the world and the judging of the nations (13:30, 40-43). Matthew also emphasizes divine judgment and the consequences of rejecting the invitation to the messianic banquet (21:33-45; 22:1-14). The community of believers gathers at the feet of the New Moses, who teaches them how to respond to God in obedient faith and earnest service, foreshadowing the gathering of all peoples into the kingdom.[14]

Luke emphasizes that God's reign will be socially transforming. He presents a cameo of the public career of Jesus at its outset. Jesus claims that the promise of God in Isaiah is now being fulfilled in him:

> The Spirit of the Lord is upon me,
>   because he has anointed me
>   to bring good news to the poor.
> He has sent me to proclaim release to the captives
>   and recovery of sight to the blind,
>   to let the oppressed go free,
>   to proclaim the year of the Lord's favor. (Luke 4:18-19)

This good news soon provokes murderous opposition not from demons but from the darkness in the people themselves. Why did this good news scandalize the people of Nazareth? Perhaps they were threatened by the hints of the "jubilee year," which would release all debts and restore confiscated lands.[15] Perhaps they were offended at the audacity of this local youth claiming to be the fulfillment of the prophetic promise. Anticipating the climax of the narrative, they try to push him off a cliff, but he passes through their midst and goes on his way. In the Acts of the Apostles, the second half of Luke's work, the good news goes out from Jerusalem to the whole world, always marked with the mixture of joy and suffering that characterized Jesus' life.

The Synoptics make clear that God's reign comes into history through human response; it is not a theophany that reorders the world by sovereign power. The parables about the wedding banquet communicate the indispensable necessity of responding to the invitation: if the invited guests fail to respond, there will be no banquet. The king who wants the celebration will be frustrated if no one shows up (see Matt. 22:1-10). God's mercy and justice are extended into the world through human response and witness to this radical invitation. Unless it is responded to, there is no gracious relation initiated: God does not reign over us unless we agree to let it happen. Mark relates how unbelief can frustrate the power of God. When Jesus returns to Nazareth, "he could do no deed of power there except that he laid his hands on few sick people and cured them. He was amazed at their unbelief" (6:5–6). He wanted the world according to God; they preferred it the way it was, and they got their wish.

Outside the Synoptic Gospels, the language of the kingdom or reign of God is not so prevalent, but the central message that God is irrupting into human history is consistent. Paul and John move analogically from the symbolism of the kingdom to the concerns of their own contexts, although John has revised Paul's expectation of an imminent parousia. The message about Jesus seems to supplant the announcement of the reign of God; or rather attention shifts to the event of his death and rising, which marks the definitive break from the old order. Those who want to respond to the reign of God have to undergo the same passage from death to life that Jesus went through. By the time that the Gospel of John was composed, it had become clear that the first generation of Christians had made a mistake in assuming that the Lord Jesus would return soon to judge the world and bring history to its close.

Paul captures the tension of the kingdom imagery in his teaching that there are two competing ways of living. This tensive state functions in Paul much as the kingdom of God in the Synoptics: it is "already/but not yet." This formulation combines the "already" affirmation of the analogical imagination with the "not yet" negation of the dialectical imagination. The saving event has occurred but it is not complete; it has not been extended universally.[16] This "already/but not yet" situation is not peaceful coexistence. When it comes to the lives of individuals, it is more a collision than a mere tension. Paul uses the central paradigm of the dying and rising of Jesus to articulate this tension between two eras of time that have collided. The point where the two eras meet is the cross. Yet they have converged in a curious way; the collision is not over and done with. The dying and rising of the Lord continue in the daily life of the churches. Citing his credentials as an apostle to the recalcitrant Corinthians, Paul writes that the pattern of Christ's death and rising is there to be seen in his sufferings and ministry: "For while we live, we are always being given up to death for Jesus' sake, so that the life of Jesus may be made visible in our mortal flesh. So death is at work in us, but life in you" (2 Cor. 4:11–12). The future resurrection overlaps with present sufferings.

Put in other Pauline imagery, the life of the flesh, of self-enclosed existence, still remains an option for those who live "in the Spirit." Paul sees the tension between the two eras of time internalized in the struggle between flesh (living an existence oriented to the self) and spirit (living a life oriented toward God). The past has not been canceled by baptism; otherwise there would be no point in exhorting Christians to act according to the new way of life. The self-absorbed life of "flesh," which has been made obsolete by the cross of Christ, has not completely disappeared in the victory of the resurrection because Christians are not yet risen in Christ. Paul has to exhort his readers, "You have died to sin and now live for Christ: so act like it!"

The tension between dying to death and living to life is not confined to the individual sphere alone—nor even to the human sphere. This new life of resurrection and Spirit must become a way of life in communion with those who are also "in Christ." The communal body of Christ extends the event of salvation, the beginnings of God's reign.

In the Gospel of John the reign of God has already arrived and its "not yet" character is played down, at least for those who are part of the fellowship of believers. John has been described as the Gospel of "realized eschatology," since it asserts that many of the features of the last times are already occurring: judgment, resurrection, eternal life, intimate friendship with God.[17] Perhaps this realized eschatology addresses the early communities' belief that Jesus would soon return in glory. John responds that he already has returned: the last times are present right now. Even though John is removed from the era of Second Temple Judaism by decades, the "here and now" portrayal of the last times is more in accord with Jewish eschatology of Jesus' day than the imminent expectations of the Lord's return found in the earlier letters of Paul.

The "already/but not yet" quality of the kingdom is found in John in the conflict between those who welcome the light and those who reject it. The light is rejected by those to whom it was sent because those who live a lie have deep reluctance about being confronted by the truth. Those who live in truth have an affinity for the light:

> And this is the judgment, that the light has come into the world, and people loved darkness rather than light because their deeds were evil. For all who do evil hate the light and do not come to the light, so that their deeds may be exposed. But those who do what is true come to the light, so that it may be clearly seen that their deeds have been done in God. (John 3:19–21)

Perception is a function of character; it is not a morally neutral faculty but one that sees only that which the person already values. Transformation of the person down to her most important values, therefore, is necessary to correct the vision of the heart.

Since the reign of God was welcomed by all the wrong sorts of people, the sinners and prostitutes and outcasts, we may ask what made them able to perceive God's approach. Was it because they had no need to defend a status quo that despised them? Were they aware that they were not self-sufficient? The New

Testament hints at these attitudes but points more to another key moral disposition that opens our eyes to where God is acting: the virtue of compassion is
the key to perceiving where God is to be found.

<hr />

II. JESUS AND COMPASSIONATE VISION

How does faith in the reign of God transform our perception today? First, it
places all experience in the framework of God's gracious action, since it trusts
that God continues to approach the world in power. Second, it tunes our sight
to become compassionate vision, to notice those that Jesus paid attention to.
Luke's parable of the Good Samaritan shows that compassion is the optic nerve
of Christian vision.

The Reign of God in Our Midst

If God's reign continues to break into our world, it must be noticeable. Perceiving the kingdom of God does not mean knowing the time or place of its
arrival.[18] The knowledge that counts here is not informational (Where? When?)
or theoretical (What exactly is the kingdom? How does it fit systematically with
other theological and philosophical concepts?). Concerns about when God's
reign will be manifest shift our attention away from practical response to the
urgent summons to enter it. Repentance, conversion, joining with others who
are welcoming God's reign must take priority so we actually enter this new
regime.

The dialectical imagination uses the metaphorical frame of the kingdom to
highlight the "not yet" character of our experience. God's future has broken into
the present so sharply that the present has become *passé*. Everything should
look different if we believe that it is not ultimate but transitory. The approach
of the reign of God ought to relativize the values and allegiances that usually
rule over our lives. Paul derived great moral freedom from his conviction that
nothing less than God should define Christians. As Paul reminded the Corinthians, whether you are wrapped up in business, marriage, sorrow, or grief,
don't let them define you, "for the present form of this world is passing away"
(1 Cor. 7:31). Even though he was mistaken about the imminent end of the
space-time cosmos, Paul's insight is still valid. Perceiving the nearness of God's
ultimate vindication should prevent us from taking anything but God as the
final meaning of our lives.

The analogical side of Christian imagination looks for places where God's
saving initiative is "already" occurring in nature and society. Life in the world

is permeable to the presence and power of God, particularly where life and freedom are "not yet" realized. The metaphorical frame of the kingdom "funds" our vision with these analogical and dialectical expectations; it enriches and tutors our receptivity. As William James put it, "*My experience is what I agree to attend to. Only those items which I notice shape my mind*—without selective interest, experience is an utter chaos."[19] The horizon of the kingdom alerts us to pay attention to ordinary experience in a new way. This "selective interest" makes us ready to see the ordinary as something more. Certainly, adequate interpretation is necessary, but first something has to be occurring in experience to interpret.

Perception funded by this hope opens us to those extraordinary times when God makes particular initiatives in the lives of individuals and communities. Gustavo Gutierrez writes of the journey of Christian discipleship: "This walking has its point of departure in an encounter with the Lord."[20] For some, like Gutierrez, that encounter comes in sharing the lot of the poor. Others may encounter the Lord in the awesome majesty of nature or in the strength to endure during times of depression and rejection. For still others it may occur in the healing support of community and in the ordinary rhythms of family and friendship that unfold a surprising constancy and vitality. In some moments a more direct awareness of God's presence breaks into peoples' lives that seems qualitatively different from any other experience. When hope for God's reign perceives these moments, we can see them as God inviting, calling to repentance, and healing. At those times of breakthrough, especially, the reign of God comes near to us and calls for response.

According to the parables of Jesus, however, we ought to be looking for God's reign to break into the fabric of ordinary life. That is the world that God intends to reorder. God approaches us through our daily interactions with others. The invitation may come from quite unexpected and unwelcome sources, not from the sort of people or events that we are comfortable with. Encounters and confrontations can call us to compassion, forgiveness, and love. The discerning believer glimpses another dimension, which is the presence of the One "in whom we live and move and have our being" (Acts 17:28). A call to repentance emerges from conflict and misunderstandings. The suffering of others claims us for a practical solidarity with them that mirrors God's solidarity with us all. As Karl Barth put it, the command of God always comes cloaked in another command.[21] So do the invitation and healing grace of God: they accompany and underwrite particular human interactions. A morally perceptive religious person, therefore, discerns not only the morally relevant features of the situation but also how they are related to God. The paradigms provided in the story of Jesus sharpen perception to notice that ordinary life resonates with the extraordinary, at least for "those who have ears to hear."

The Good Samaritan: Compassionate Vision

The parable of the Good Samaritan is a classic paradigm of perception and blindness. The parable was told in response to the lawyer who asked, "And who is my neighbor?" He wanted to know who was covered by the love command. Jesus replied:

> A man was going down from Jerusalem to Jericho, and fell into the hands of robbers, who stripped him, beat him, and left him half dead. Now by chance a priest was going down that road; and when he saw him he passed by on the other side. So likewise a Levite, when he came to the place and saw him, passed by on the other side. But a Samaritan while traveling came near him; and when he saw him, he was moved with pity. (Luke 10:31–33)

All three see the beaten, stripped man by the roadside, but in a deeper sense only one sees him. The priest and the Levite notice him but keep their distance in order to avoid any contact that might defile them. He might be a Gentile or even a corpse. He enters their field of vision but not their field of compassion. They cannot afford to perceive his full reality because his condition is threatening. They screen him out before his desperate situation can complicate their journey.

The parable invites us to imagine what their motivation might have been by summoning up our own history of avoiding needy strangers. If we use our imaginations honestly, the parable becomes a window on the world of Jesus and a mirror to our own existence. Anyone who has walked past the homeless and brushed off beggars in the street is no stranger to this parable.

Why does the Samaritan come to the wounded man's aid? He sees the victim and is moved with compassion. "Pity" is a pallid translation of *esplangchnisthē*, which means being shaken in the depths of the womb or bowels, a wrenching gut reaction. The Samaritan has a visceral compassion for the man that goes beyond pity. Compassion was the ingredient missing from the sight of the priest and the Levite. The Samaritan sees the man as a fellow human being in terrible trouble. The others' perception was funded by categories of corpse, Gentile, and defilement so that avoidance seemed natural. The priest and the Levite did not let themselves be affected by his plight. Any inchoate feelings of pity or shock were neutralized by wariness, disgust, or fear—or perhaps they felt nothing at all.

The Samaritan has no such emotional immunity. He is not only touched by the sight; his compassion impels him to do something to help the victim. His subjective capacity of being receptive to suffering goes beyond pity to empathy: he "feels with" and "feels into" the situation by apprehending the situation as the man in the ditch experiences it. *Empathy* refers to the affective, imaginative, and cognitive capacity that enables us to enter and identify with the experience of others. *Compassion* refers to the most active and engaged form of empathy, namely, that disposition directed particularly to those in great need or suffering.[22] Compassion bridges the gap between perception and effective action. He knows immediately what action to take:

> He went to him and bandaged his wounds, having poured oil and wine on them. Then he put him on his own animal, brought him to an inn, and took care of him. The next day he took out two denarii, gave them to the innkeeper, and said, "Take care of him; and when I came back, I will repay you whatever more you spend." (10:34–35)[23]

His compassion is no fleeting sentiment; it looks ahead to the victim's continuing needs. Knowing that the man has no resources and might take a while to recover, the Samaritan generously provides two days' wages for his care and gives his assurance for any further expenses he might incur. He knows that if the man could not reimburse the innkeeper for additional care, he might land in debtors' prison. The surprising alacrity and intensity of the Samaritan's response is typical of Jesus' parables, where the extraordinary keeps breaking out of the ordinary. The Samaritan surpasses the care that would be appropriate for a fellow countryman to aid this stranger, who might belong to his ethnic group's worst enemies.

At the end of the parable, Jesus turns the lawyer's original question back on him. He asks, "Which of these three, do you think, was a neighbor to the man who fell into the hands of the robbers?" The lawyer replies, "The one who showed him mercy." Jesus tells him, "Go and do likewise" (10:36–37). The parable does not answer the original inquiry because it was the wrong question. "Who is my neighbor?" poses the question in insider/outsider terms. "Neighbor" shifts from the object of love to the subject who shows love: "Which of these three, do you think, was a neighbor to the man . . . ?" Jesus tells a parable about perception in order to let the lawyer see that his moral categories are too constricted. The only question that is relevant is "Are *you* a neighbor?" The parable is not a didactic exercise but a device to help the lawyer get this insight for himself.

The Samaritan does not pause to ask whether the man in the ditch is his neighbor. That question hedges empathy by drawing a clear line between neighbors and outsiders. It steps back from the scene and inquires whether loving this person falls within the range of duty. Instead, the Samaritan brings himself near to the victim, identifies with him, becomes neighborly to him. The original question tried to establish the boundaries of love: "Whom do I have to love?" It gets turned around in a way that cancels boundaries: "To whom can I show love?" Compassionate sight leads to merciful action when "neighbor" becomes adverbial, "neighborly," a characteristic of generous response, rather than a clearly bounded nominal category that encompasses some people and excludes others. "Neighbor" no longer demarcates the "non-neighbor" whom I do not have to love. Non-neighbors are not the ones under scrutiny; I am.

Jesus does not tell the lawyer what to do as an active, outgoing neighbor. Rather, that is left up to the analogical imagination. The "likewise" is up to each person to figure out in different situations. Anyone who can use her analogical imagination to stand in the place of the lawyer has a new model for looking at others. It instructs the imagination, goads our sympathy beyond its usual parochial limits, and calls us to acknowledge that we too have received undeserved mercy from others and from God.

Making a Samaritan the hero brings a dialectical edge to the command to "go and do likewise." A Jewish audience would have been shocked by holding up a Samaritan as an exemplar, while discrediting the respected priest and Levite. Jesus stretches the limits of vision and compassion precisely where fear, enmity, and inconvenience want to constrict them. Samaritans were religious heretics and national enemies of Israel. "Good Samaritan" has become a natural coupling in cultures shaped by the New Testament, but for Jesus' contemporaries it would have been as palatable as speaking about "the good terrorist" or making a crack dealer the hero of an urban drama. In recent times Samaritan radicals had dumped a corpse in the Temple during Passover, defiling it so that the feast could not be celebrated. The shock of reversal in this parable is similar to the footwashing in John 13, which displays the meaning of Jesus' new commandment of love. These are the two places in the Gospels where "love" is spelled out directly. Instead of defining love conceptually, they portray it in dramatic and disturbing action. When a national enemy gets the hero role and the host at table puts himself in the role of a slave, our usual way of perceiving the world is turned upside down.

This parable has become an effective paradigm for compassionate responsibility in Western culture at large. "In Christianity, building on Judaism, the practice of medicine was profoundly influenced by the story of the Good Samaritan."[24] The sick were given a preferential position they had lacked before. In studying people who were active volunteers in their communities, Robert Wuthnow discovered that half of the nonbelievers and two-thirds of churchgoers cited the parable as part of their motivation for serving the needy.[25]

———————————— III. VIRTUE ETHICS ON MORAL PERCEPTION ————————————

Virtue ethics shares the Gospels' concern for moral sight and blindness. From Aristotle on, character ethics has considered the problem of moral perception as a central issue in the moral life. Both traditions realize that the quality of moral perception is determined by the moral quality of the agent and community. What we see is a function of the sorts of persons we are. An ethics of virtue reflects on the habits of mind and heart that we bring to situations in ways which can inform our understanding of perception in the ethics of the Gospels.

Moral perception is the active ability to grasp the human significance of a situation, to be receptive to its significance for benefiting or harming people. Moral perception depends on the affective skills that we bring to the interaction of human beings in particular encounters where moral values and problems arise. Virtues of empathy, honesty, and fairness, for example, enable the moral agent to appreciate others on their own terms. Moral perception is an accomplishment that depends on moral maturity. It will be determined by character, that is, by the explicit commitments and the cognitive, emotional, and imaginative development we bring to the situation. Martha Nussbaum writes that moral knowledge "is not simply intellectual grasp of propositions; it is not even simply intellectual grasp of particular facts; it is perception. It is seeing a complex, concrete reality in a highly lucid and richly responsive way; it is taking in what is there, with imagination and feeling."[26]

Virtue ethics tries to consider the full range of psychological dynamics that undergird the moral life. Since character is an evolving process of integration and deepening of habits and commitments, ethics necessarily attends to the patterns of human maturing. We expect people to have the level of moral perceptiveness that is appropriate to their age. We blame them for not showing an appropriate level of moral maturity. The insouciance and carefree spontaneity that may be charming in an adolescent are not charming in a forty-year-old. By then they look more like the marks of an immature, irresponsible character.

Kantian and utilitarian ethics usually ignore issues of perception because they concentrate on a later stage in moral reflection. They begin ethical thought with intentions already shaped and ready for moral scrutiny rather than with moral perception and the formation of intentions. Virtue ethics pushes the inquiry one stage back to ask how we came to describe this situation as a problem of justice or respect in the first place.

The first stage of moral perception, therefore, is *attention*, which Iris Murdoch describes as "a just and loving gaze directed upon an individual reality."[27] Attention means seeing what is there without projection or fantasy. This is not a morally neutral stance but an attitude made possible by the virtues of fairness, respect, and love. Paying attention to the full truth of the situation is itself a moral accomplishment because it requires the discipline of getting egotistical concerns out of the way, seeing the situation as it is rather than how I want it to be.

Character Ethics and Moral Perception

Philosophers who study character have distinguished several features of moral perception, which will be considered in turn. It is necessary because action is always particular. It occurs prior to conscious deliberation and judgment. It is rooted in the values, dispositions, and habits of the perceiver, not in a separate faculty. Finally, it does not automatically accompany knowledge of moral principles.

Virtue ethics acknowledges that thought and action are always anchored in the world of contingencies and particular persons, even though they are informed by more general concepts and principles. We act in specific situations constituted by the interaction of specific persons within an environment that has definite capacities and limitations. Anyone over the age of four realizes that life is not just the raw material for our plans and will power. Intentions emerge through interactive reflection and experimentation that discover the environment's potentials and anticipate the likely reactions of people and institutions.

Although these general moral features are easier to express conceptually, they cannot determine action in specific situations. Aristotle wrote that "in a discussion of moral actions, although general statements have a wider range of application, statements on particular points have more truth in them: actions are concerned with particulars and our statements must harmonize with them."[28] Consequently, accurate discernment of particular conditions becomes central to the moral life.

According to Plato, if you knew the meaning of a virtue you would know how to practice it. Aristotle, like subsequent realist philosophers and pragmatists, insisted that we do not move from abstract definitions of virtue to moral action with the same ease that we move from axiom to corollary in geometry. Moral reflection is more complex and ambiguous than geometry because morality operates in the practical realm of contingent circumstances, multiple perspectives, partial insight gained from engagement, ambiguous consequences, and so on. For Aristotle, excellence in morality means to respond "at the right time, toward the right objects, toward the right people, for the right reason, and in the right manner—that is the median and best course, the course that is the mark of virtue."[29] The virtuous action is always the most appropriate one insofar as it *fits* all the particular features involved in a unique situation. As a result, ethics resembles an art more than a theoretical science.

The moral agent has to be able to improvise, to be alert to surprising and recalcitrant facts. Because the terrain of action has such complex contours, moral rules and principles need to be flexible in order to guide action. Aristotle claims that moral rules should be outlines for conduct rather than completely determined directives. They have to be more like tape measures than rigid yardsticks: the tape measure is more useful for three-dimensional objects because it is flexible.[30] Like the principles of navigation, moral rules need to be applied by an experienced agent. The pilot does not navigate by charts and instruments alone. His experience has given him a fine eye to read the subtle shifts of wind and water, light and shadow. The morally astute person needs similar perceptiveness and experience to chart her course in life's tides and shoals.

Consider how moral perception operates in a specific case. A plant manager wonders how to determine a fair wage for employees who perform a variety of functions in a manufacturing business. Let us imagine that the manager is a person of some moral maturity who is sensitive to this problem. He notices that there are moral issues embedded within the particular facts of the workplace. He knows that his industry has not faced attitudes of discrimination that are supported by institutional arrangements.

He might begin with a general principle and then try to apply it. He could try to spell out the principle that "equals should be treated equally" to determine what is a fair wage for different sorts of work. The principle could be translated into a more specific norm: "equal pay for equal work." He would need further reflection because the term "equal" remains ambiguous in this maxim. It would forbid different wages for men and women working on the assembly line. But is it discriminatory to pay the line workers more than clerical workers but less than truck drivers? If the physical toll taken on teamsters qualifies them for greater compensation, what about the danger of repetitive stress injuries to the hands and wrists of computer workers? In order to determine what is a fair wage, the manager would have to wrestle with the concrete conditions of work, the levels of skill and exertion involved, the relative value added to the product by the work function, historic prejudice against adequate pay to work done by women, and so on.

Perception as Precondition for Judgment

Moral perception occurs before we consider what steps to take (deliberation) and actually decide on what to do (judgment). As we deliberate over what to do, our original perception is often sharpened by closer examination of the unique contours in which we will act. In turn, this deliberation focuses our initial vague awareness that something must be done into a judgment to pursue a specific course of action.[31]

It takes finely tuned affectivity to perceive what is morally relevant in a situation. For the morally perceptive person certain aspects of the situation are "salient" facts, "jumping out" from the complex situation. Emotion cooperates with cognition here. Emotions are not passive, "gut reactions" to stimuli. They are more like antennae seeking relevant clues in the situation. Emotions direct our attention to grounds for fear or hope or gratitude. They are active and informative insofar as they point out the "import" of factors in the environment, that is, their relevance to our needs and purposes.[32] Although rationalist philosophers tirelessly remind us that emotional reactions can be erroneous, they are often accurate initial estimates of practical import. A purely unemotional state, if such a condition could ever exist, would miss the humanly significant features in our interactions with others. To see someone in pain and be unaffected by it is possible only for a morally stunted character.

Emotions and cognition do not operate on separate tracks. Emotions are evaluative perceptions, and many intellectual attitudes are rich with affect. Our initial affective impressions can draw us into engagement or repel us. This initial apprehension occurs more directly and intuitively than through articulate ideas. That is why we often use analogies from sense perception, such as sight or touch, to describe this immediate recognition. Perception, however, can be "funded" by experience and reflection. We do not perceive raw bits of sense data, since past experience fuses with perception, funding it with significance and direction. Two people walking past a refinery can catch the same scent. One of them thinks it smells like rotten eggs, while the other may recognize it as a sulphur compound and realize instantly that something dangerous is happening in the refinery.[33] The second one does not deliberately interpret the data; he grasps the data as colored with significance.

In the case of the factory manager, his sensitivity may well be heightened by understanding the persistent discrepancy between wages paid to women and men and by being familiar with current discussions of justice in the workplace. If he knows that his clerical workers face the possibility of repetitive stress injuries, he might be more sympathetic to their claims for equal pay than if he believed that the line workers and teamsters were the only ones whose work put them at risk.

Let us develop our case study further. The plant manager notices that one programmer is more productive than her peers; she anticipates problems in software applications, knows how to tailor programs to the plant's limitations, and can coordinate innovations with other programs in the plant. The manager realizes that her contribution exceeds her standard compensation. He knows she is not being treated fairly. If he pays her more, will her coworkers be offended? If he writes a glowing evaluation of her, will she be promoted to company headquarters? If he raises her salary, will the union that represents the line workers object on the grounds of their historic wage superiority to officeworkers? The manager must weigh the moral valence of all these factors, even though some may be quite murky.

We hope that our office manager would be sensitive to possible inequity, even if he does not immediately know how to redress it. Noticing these salient facts does not necessarily indicate what to do. He has to examine the situation more carefully and imagine some possible courses of action. Perhaps recalling some principle of justice will help focus his intuitive awareness into a moral judgment about what to do. Perhaps his judgment may be guided by a troubled conscience which cannot tolerate letting the situation persist because it disturbs his own sense of fair treatment. In any case, emotional awareness will work together with rational reflection as he moves toward decision.

No Single Faculty of Perception

Like conscience, moral perception is not a separate psychological function.[34] Although we sometimes speak of conscience as a distinct faculty in a person, more accurately, conscience is the whole person engaged in moral judgment. *Conscience* is "a personal, self-conscious activity, integrating reason, emotions, and will in self-committed decisions about right and wrong, good and evil."[35] Analogously, moral perception is a function of the whole person which engages reflective, emotional, and imaginative capacities. It includes honest assessment, sympathetic appreciation, attentiveness to relevant detail, memory refined into useful experience, social skills, virtuous dispositions, and practical "know-how."

Imagination evokes empathy and calls on relevant memories. The common-sense maxim of the golden rule teaches us the basic strategy of empathy: How would you feel if you were on the receiving end of this action? Empathy imagines the situation from the other parties' viewpoints. Imagination also culls certain patterns from past experience that might be relevant in the present dilemma. It creatively weds these regularities with the distinctive and unrepeatable features of the present. The analogical imagination, which can be tutored by the symbols and stories of scripture, detects repeated patterns and improvises creative solutions in new settings.

Empathy and compassion usually do not function consistently across the whole gamut of experience. It is physically and psychologically impossible to have universal empathy for every person we encounter or hear about in the media. Most of us are more receptive to certain types of experience than others and more alert to certain types of people than we are to others.[36] Race, class, gender, age, and ideology can make some people highly sensitive to particular problems within their group while permitting them to gloss over the same suffering when it happens to other types of people.

In our ongoing case study, the whole character of the manager will influence how he perceives and responds to this situation. The manager brings a personal history that has been shaped by his family and society. If he has internalized certain prejudices, he will probably not consider this talented officeworker's performance as especially meritorious. Suppose she is Asian-American, and he has always believed that Asians are "naturally" gifted at organizing data and working with computers. He may unconsciously harbor resentments against Asian-American women for outperforming him in school. He may resent the fact that his own children do not do as well in mathematics and science as some of their Asian-American classmates. Alternatively, he may be uneasy about competent women or presume that males generally deserve higher pay because they are their families' "breadwinners." He may fear that rewarding her efforts could make her ambitious to take over his job. If he is aware of these biases, he might counter them, but if they are unconscious, they could easily warp his perception about what fair treatment would be for her. Each of these prejudices blocks the sort of empathetic transfer upon which the golden rule relies. They reinforce the belief that she is sufficiently different from him so that he cannot easily imagine how he would feel if he were in her situation.

If the manager is fortunate enough to have an experienced peer or superior whose judgment he trusts, he could discuss the case with that person. If she can recall similar cases from her own experience, she might be able to help him see differently. She might relate how difficult it was for her to be one of the few women hired at her level and describe the problems she encountered in the corporate culture. If she is a friend, the manager may be more likely to understand the office-worker's situation empathetically, thereby gaining a particular reference that could counteract some of his prejudices about Asian women. We expand our own vision by learning from those we admire because we trust their insights and can identify with the choices they have made.[37]

Moral Principles and Perception

Knowing moral principles can support astute moral vision. Moral maxims and principles can help us focus on certain features of the situation that we might have otherwise missed. Knowing that "equal opportunity" is a component of social justice may help us recognize that some policies which claim to be racially blind, for example, are in fact cementing current inequities into permanent barriers. A physician well trained in the "principle of double effect" may be more astute at spotting when an outcome occurs as the direct result of an intention and when it occurs indirectly. The "hard sayings" of the Gospel may come to a Christian's mind when faced with a threatening confrontation. The facts that would prod someone else to retaliation might suggest nonviolent endurance instead. There is of course no necessary connection between knowledge of principles and moral perceptiveness. It is possible for a moral philosopher to be obtuse about other people. The knowledge of principles becomes practically insightful only when the principles are embedded in habits formed by reflective experience and deepened by committed practice.

Some people who have rich experience and good character may have an intuitive but inarticulate appreciation of what is morally important in a situation. Aristotle urges us to pay attention to the judgments of people of practical wisdom, even though they may not be able to justify them by appealing to moral principles. "For experience has given such [people] an eye with which they can see correctly."[38] It usually takes time and a wealth of reflection to acquire this eye for what is salient. Although young people may be geniuses in mathematics or science, we do not expect them to be wise because they lack experience navigating life's complexities.

Moral principles become practical by interacting with the particular situation. In our case, the maxim "equals should be treated equally" can help the manager inspect the situation for what counts as equal. To treat as equals persons who are unequal in some relevant aspects is a recipe for unfairness. He will need to move from general principles to the concrete case and back again, letting one clarify the other. Nussbaum writes, "Perception . . . is a process of loving conversation between rules and concrete responses, general conceptions and unique cases, in which the general articulates the particular and is in turn further articulated by it."[39] Rules are certainly useful to follow when it is impossible to scrutinize the situation exhaustively.[40] Habits of empathy and respect will anchor the general principles of justice in the lives of particular persons.

The main components of moral perception are habits of considerateness and attentiveness to the data, virtues of respect and empathy, imagination capable of understanding the other's hopes and fears, experience that has taught us how to place this situation in a larger perspective, honest self-knowledge about our preferences and prejudices, and humility to seek the advice of others to expand our own vision. The story of Jesus calls his disciples to develop the capacity to see justly and lovingly. Conversion requires confronting our blindness and reluctance to be engaged with people who are threatening or repulsive. The transformation of moral perception begins with admitting that we are blind, or at least quite selective in our compassion. People with even a little self-knowledge can identify with the priest and Levite in the parable of the Good Samaritan. They did not see because they could not afford to. The story of Jesus addresses the roots of our reluctance and calls us to conversion. The next chapter considers moral blindness and spiritual practices that can help stony hearts to become hearts that respond.

CHAPTER 5

Correcting Perception

I F MORAL PERCEPTION IS FAULTY, how can it be corrected? In this chapter we will look to religious prescriptions for moral near-sightedness and
blindness. The most dramatic prescription comes from theologians inspired by
Paul, Augustine, and the Reformers. They give classic expression to the dialectical imagination, which begins with the alienation of humanity from God and
its impotence to bridge the gap. Moral blindness is the ordinary condition in
humanity's fallen state. No one can cure blindness; that takes the miracle of
grace, which enters through the life-changing transformation called conversion.

The second approach makes a less severe diagnosis of the human condition.
It sees moral obtuseness as a case of myopia, and prescribes corrective lenses. It
aims to sharpen moral perception by discarding the old lenses of selfish existence and replacing them with the central images and metaphors of scripture.
Correction of sight works together with rectification of the heart's dispositions,
since hope, compassion, love, and obedient service are necessary to see aright.
This is the analogical imagination at work, highlighting the similarities and har-
monies rather than the dialectical differences between our ways and God's
ways. This approach usually presumes that a basic conversion to God has
occurred. It seeks to find God in the daily events of life as well as in peak
moments and major decisions.

While Paul's stark images of transformation presume the diagnosis of blindness, the portrait of the disciples in the Gospels supports the diagnosis of near-
sightedness that can gradually be corrected. Jesus' closest disciples take on his
perspective with considerable reluctance. Each of the Gospel writers portrays the
disciples' confusion and lack of faith, even at the end of Jesus' time with them.
They do not understand the parables. They jostle for preference even though

100

Jesus acts like a servant (Mark 10:35–45). They panic when he is arrested and scatter like sheep without a shepherd (Matt. 26:31). Completely misunderstanding the scriptural testimony about the Messiah, they are scandalized by the crucifixion and desert the cause (Luke 24:13–32). In John's account, they forget all that Jesus has said about being one with the Father and admit they have no idea where he is going (John 14:1–11). It is not so much that the disciples are blinded by evil; they just seem rather thick. These accounts are mirrors held up for future generations because we can recognize ourselves in the disciples' attitudes and questions. Clearly, we are all "successors to the apostles."

Although virtue ethics has not had much to say about moral transformation and the disciplines that help inculcate the skills of moral perception, Christian theology and spirituality have made these concerns central. They can provide resources for the moral life that are lacking in philosophical discussions of virtue ethics. At the same time, spirituality shares with virtue ethics the insight that moral perception is sharpened indirectly. It is a side effect of more important concerns and commitments. We will examine conversion and intercessory prayer, two common spiritual practices that can shape a compassionate moral vision that is centered on God.

I. CORRECTING PERCEPTION: FRAMES AND METAPHORS

Jesus spoke in images and parables in order to convert the imaginations of his listeners. They did not perceive what was going on because their normal way of viewing things blurred and distorted their vision. How did he get them to notice that something remarkable was happening, that God was drawing near to set things right? He dusted off traditional categories, such as God is king, the God of justice comes to reign, God tends the people like a shepherd. He also used homey examples with an extraordinary twist: a man buys a field but finds a treasure; you cannot put your hand to the plow and look back without ruining the furrow; seeds fall all over the field—some get lost but some yield an enormous harvest. The message is clear: pay attention, because in the fabric of ordinary life something extraordinary is happening.

Jesus was equipping his audiences with fresh images so they could use their imaginations. Moral perception gets sharpened when we start using our imaginations in new ways. New analogies and metaphors open up experience so that it is "seen as" something fresh and mysterious. Like new lenses they disclose details and depth that we had missed before. Just taking a look does not disclose the full significance of an experience. We need to try to see it from different angles of vision, to place it in different contexts that will progressively illumine more and more of the meaning of the event. Isaiah and Jeremiah paid close attention to the poor because they saw them in light of the exodus, when Yahweh rescued Israel and set a standard for Israel to follow. By contrast, Plato and Aristotle make almost no mention of the poor, even though Athenian society depended on slaves. Their foundational stories did not equip them to notice the poor; since they were not "seen as" important in a larger framework, the poor were not seen at all.

Experiences are "had" within different metaphorical frames that highlight some aspects and obscure others. At this level, analogies and metaphors are not mere decorations; now they become "frames" within which meaning gradually becomes clear. When life is taken to be a journey that leads to a destination, events and people are taken in a different light than when life and death succeed each other in an endless natural cycle of seasons.

What we can see is shaped by the basic analogies that frame our experience and the metaphors that we habitually employ. Although these frameworks are typically so familiar that we take them for granted, they are culturally produced, not naturally given. Action flows from these frames, because they make certain ways of acting seem appropriate. The actions are not logically entailed by the operative image, perhaps, but they seem to follow naturally from these seminal "root metaphors."[1] It seems that many of our assumptions that determine what is appropriate action are not based on articulated concepts or propositions. They are more likely contained in the analogies and metaphors that are operative in a culture rather than in explicitly formulated assumptions. Revolutionary proposals are rejected as "unimaginable." Customary frameworks are "pre-understandings" in the sense that they condition all our concepts and theories while usually operating below conscious awareness.[2]

If the basic analogies that we bring to scripture are incompatible with its content, we have a serious problem. We will distort the biblical content by transposing it into our familiar frameworks, or more likely, we will dismiss it as meaningless or irrelevant. Thomas W. Ogletree argues that most Americans assume that ethics is consequential: what is right is what produces good. Pragmatist Americans seek satisfactory solutions to specific problems. Or, since most of us are "anonymous utilitarians," we look for the policies that will produce the greatest goods for the greatest number of people. Finally, in the weakest ethical version, followers of expressive individualism seek personal growth and fulfillment. In any case this focus on consequences runs aground when it comes to the New Testament, which is not at all consequentialist.[3] Often we do not recognize our own frameworks until they collide with the strange perspectives of scripture.

Jesus used parables to shock his audience into recognizing that their ways were not God's ways. I will examine one of the most challenging parables, the Workers in the Vineyard (Matt. 20:1–16). Paul and other New Testament writers developed other central analogies to reframe the imaginations of the early communities. Here we will look briefly at how he uses the practice of Eucharist to open the eyes of the Corinthians to how they were mistreating one another.

Fairness and Grace: The Workers in the Vineyard

This parable generates a classic New Testament collision between two metaphorical frames of experience, namely, life as fairness versus life as grace. The drama that unfolds in the parable evokes the audience's basic assumptions about fairness only to confound them with a generosity that is troubling, even offensive. The parable does not critique our usual assumptions about what is fair and unfair; it subverts them. If life cannot be analyzed along the lines of fairness, our moral compass has lost magnetic north.

Matthew frames the parable with two verses that announce a radical reversal of expectations. The previous section had Peter questioning, "Look, we have left everything and followed you. What then will we have?" (19:27). Jesus assures them that this unimpressive band will judge the tribes of Israel and receive a hundredfold for whatever they lost—and inherit eternal life as well. "But many who are first will be last, and the last will be first" (19:30). At the end of the vineyard parable, Jesus reverses the reversal, "So the last will be first, and the first last" (20:16). The important will become unimportant and the unimportant will be important. In a word, all bets are off. Life under God's reign is not a ladder that rewards the ambitious climber; it is more like a ferris wheel where top and bottom are constantly being switched. This can be quite maddening if you have spent much of your life climbing the ladder. In the "world according to God" ambition is as pointless as any attempt at ranking ourselves or others on any scale at all, whether the scale of intelligence, achievement, social position, or wealth.

Reversal brings the element of surprise into the parables of Jesus. The parable sets us up for a shock just as a joke does. Jokes, puns, and "shaggy dog" stories set up a pattern and then shatter it. Certain regularities of language, imagery, or manners make us anticipate what will come next, and then we get jarred by the punch line. The surprise makes us laugh. It reveals that we were expecting something else. If you don't know the underlying conventions or fail to detect the pattern in the story, you miss the ironic twist. A joke that has to be explained always falls flat because there is no surprise. Humor rests on spotting the reversal, as when the Woody Allen says "I am two with nature." If you enjoyed that line it is because you know that Allen is the archetypal New Yorker and you are also familiar with the romantic exclamation "I am one with nature." I used that line during a talk in Hawaii and nobody got it.

Parables work the same way, breaking open the ordinary way of doing things, but in a mysterious rather than humorous way. Humor plays off a settled world in an ironic way; it may mock the world's pretensions, but it usually does so by drawing on some more subtle aspect of the way of life. Irony is amused, not revolutionary. Parables, however, crack open the settled world to disclose a background fraught with uncanny, even transcendent, meaning. Irony actually reinforces a world, while parables subvert it by showing that things really are not at all what they seem to be.

The familiar scene in Matthew's story is harvest time, when workers are urgently needed to bring in the grapes while they are at their peak. The landowner goes to the marketplace early in the morning to hire day laborers and agrees to pay them the usual daily wage. Three hours later, he goes back and hires some more, promising to pay them "whatever is right" (v. 4). He comes back at noon and again at three o'clock and does the same. Somewhat surprisingly, he returns at five and hires the day laborers who are left, but he does not mention how much they will receive.

As evening falls, the landowner instructs his manager, "Call the laborers and give them their pay, beginning with the last and then going to the first" (v. 8). There is usually a point when a parable gets odd, and this is it. Why not start by paying the ones who had worked all day? They would get their day's wage and leave. Instead, the landowner raises their expectations by giving a full day's pay to the ones who had worked only an hour. Jesus does not mention how much the landowner pays those who worked nine, six, and three hours. At any rate, we can imagine the growing anticipation of the ones who had been in the fields all day. Their turn finally comes, and what do they get? The usual daily wage and nothing more.

They are irritated. Most likely any congregation that is listening to the Gospel reading is also irritated. They too have been set up by the unfolding drama to expect that more would be given to the ones who had worked all day. Why do we expect this to happen? It just seems fair: equal pay for equal work. When the workers receive equal pay for unequal work, that is obviously unfair. This is the point where grumbling and complaints break out. The people in the pews hear the worn-out workers put their feelings into words: this just isn't fair. They worked twelve times longer than the latecomers and got the same pay?

The landowner gives three different reasons why his action is not unfair. First, they received exactly what they had agreed to at the crack of dawn. Second, if he chooses to be generous with the latecomers, why is that unfair? He can do what he wants with "what belongs to" him. (By contrast, the first group has received "what belongs to" them [v. 14].) Finally, he questions their motives, "Are you envious because I am generous?" (v. 15). To sum up, fairness has been observed, generosity leaps beyond fairness, and it looks like unfairness only to those whose sense of entitlement has made them envious of their fellows.

If this response does not offend our sensibilities, it is hard to imagine what would. That, however, is precisely what the parable is intended to do: raise our expectations about fairness and unfairness to the surface only to confound them. Our protests might occasion new insight into our own way of looking at the world. We do not believe that the last should be first, certainly not when the first deserve to be first. Hard work should mean better pay; good people deserve good treatment; those at the back of the line do not get to "cut in" to the front. The logic of fairness is clear: people should get what they deserve. The parable teases us with the ambiguity of what is "deserved." Strictly speaking, the first hired got what they agreed to, the expected daily wage. However, when they saw how the others were treated, their expectations naturally went up. What is fair has now changed. Or has it?

The landowner has acted fairly because he honored their agreement. They got what belonged to them. He is fair to them but generous to the others. What is to stop him from doing that? He is simply being generous. Perhaps he realizes that the workers who did not get hired all day would not eat that day. If the others do not appreciate his generosity, there must be something wrong with their point of view. Envy is organizing their perspective, not anger over injustice. The vice of envy is always comparative: others have gotten what I should have gotten; someone else's good fortune has come at my expense. The final words of the landowner are literally, "Is your eye evil because I am good?"[4] Elsewhere in Matthew, "the eye is the lamp of the body" (6:22), since it sheds its light on the facts. An envious eye sheds a harsh light on this situation. It produces no rejoicing at the good fortune of their fellow day laborers, only resentment.

Jesus seems to be drawing out our spontaneous reaction to show how inadequate it is in the new world of God's emerging reign. In the context of his ministry, this parable may have been a defense of his practice of sharing table fellowship with society's despised castes. Later in the context of Matthew's community, it probably gets reinterpreted as vindication of the "come lately" Gentiles over against the claims of the people of the covenant who have "borne the heat of the day" for so many centuries. Doesn't giving them the same reward as the Gentiles cheapen their accomplishment? It is puzzling that most of us identify with the ones who worked all day rather than the latecomers: perhaps that says something about our own sense of entitlement. We cannot identify the landowner with God, since that treats the parable like an allegory. Jesus seems to be clear that reward is not the issue but generosity. The logic of grace simply goes beyond the logic of fairness, but it does not violate it. Generosity does not calculate the relative worth of its recipients but comes out of the abundance of the giver. Grace has everything to do with God and very little with those who receive it. When God's grace irrupts into history, moral rules and the structure of justice are not abolished but surpassed.

In the metaphorical frame of fairness, the scales of justice must balance. Compensation evens everything out in the long run as the good are rewarded and the wicked punished. The frame of fairness presumes that we know what are the true standards and who measures up against them. But if the logic of the landowner is put in the place of justice, we do not know what the standards are. Our imaginations have to be retooled drastically to make sense out of a world of such cosmic generosity. Jesus uses natural abundance as a sign of God's refusal to be selective in loving humanity and as a paradigm for the duty to love indiscriminately: "Love your enemies and pray for those who persecute you, so that you may be children of your Father in heaven; he makes his sun rise on the evil and on the good, and sends rain on the righteous and the unrighteous" (Matt. 6:44–45).

Different conduct is appropriate in a world framed by fairness than would fit a world framed by generosity. The frame of fairness indicates that we should love the good and shun the evil. Fairness takes its measure from the recipients. Some deserve love and forgiveness; others do not. By contrast, the frame of God's generosity calls for loving indiscriminately. Indiscriminate generosity takes its measure from the One who loves. It does not calibrate levels of entitlement. That measure is not impossible for Christians because they are in fact members of God's family and empowered by the Spirit to love in God's way. God rules by mercy and measures us by God's own willingness to create and save. In a word, the world according to God is not fair; it is gracious. Those who want to enter it have to read the world and themselves in a new way and act accordingly.

Defective Perception: Myopia or Glaucoma?

The language of metaphorical frames may be misleadingly intellectual, as though moral perception can be corrected by simply replacing one set of root metaphors with another. Comparing moral perception to vision may be part of the problem. Sight is a unitary capacity that does not require explicit training to function successfully, at least for most people. Developing a compassionate and just moral vision requires a number of skills, few of which are natural endowments. Comparisons to sight also give the impression that, short of blindness, problems of moral vision can be easily corrected. When we discover that our eyesight is getting worse, we go to an optometrist to get eyeglasses or to change our present corrective lenses. If our vision has gradually become clouded, we may need cataract surgery to remove the interior lens of the eye, which has become opaque.

Moral myopia, however, is not so easily corrected as near-sightedness. Most of us do not suffer from a generalized problem of perception comparable to myopia or complete color blindness. We are afflicted by a selective blindness that resembles glaucoma, which occurs when high pressure of the fluids in the eye leads to blank spots of vision. Nothing registers in these zones, even though the rest of the lens functions adequately. Persons with glaucoma often do not notice these gaps in vision until it is too late; even more ominously, glaucoma is irreversible.

Analogously, we often suffer from selective moral blindness to certain types of people and certain varieties of problems. We tend to be morally alert in those areas where we have developed some virtue and less so in other areas. Good habits can be quite compartmentalized, as we see in people who are loving with family members and ruthless toward their competitors in the business world. Empathy tends to be localized to groups of people or problems with which we can identify. If challenged about leaving certain groups out of our range of concern, we might be surprised at the oversight, or we might justify the omission by saying that they deserve to be left out. They do not count in our moral community for reasons we can rarely articulate.

Once I was giving a church workshop on forgiveness. I pointed out that New Testament writers from a wide range of community situations repeatedly insist that Christians have to forgive their enemies. Perhaps they realized that anyone who tries to form a community or live in a committed relationship eventually discovers enemies. The mandate to forgive is relevant because we continue to have enemies in close and distant relationships. A woman came up after the talk and said, "I liked your talk but it doesn't apply to me. I haven't had any enemies since I accepted Jesus." Somewhat puzzled, I asked whether there wasn't anyone in her life that she was separated from. She replied, "Well, there's my son—but he doesn't count!"

The challenge, therefore, is not merely replacing one point of view with a more adequate one but becoming able to see the invisible. This calls for transformation of basic moral dispositions as a precondition to widening one's perspective. What would it take to expand a self-absorbed person to become alert to the independent reality of others? How could a defensive person become tolerant of those who have different values? Until recently, moral philosophers have offered few constructive suggestions on this point. Martha Nussbaum proposes that engaged and reflective encounter with serious literature can expand customary moral horizons by immersing the reader in the experience of others.[5] Political theorist Roberto Unger advocates penetrating emotional defenses by "experiments in vulnerability" that will force us to confront situations and problems that we usually shun.[6] Marilyn Friedman describes the friendships that feminists from different races and social classes have forged as "socially disruptive possibilities."[7]

To some extent we can be educated to notice what we have been accustomed to ignore. New categories like racism and sexism can help us see the unseen. These new moral categories gain authority from hearing the voices of those who have suffered from discrimination. They demand that the rest of society wake up to what it has perpetrated upon them. The comfortable majority is unlikely to welcome these claims because they indict the present arrangements of power and respect. I cannot acknowledge these grievances to be valid without some painful self-assessment and repudiation of past practices and my own privileges.

Education cannot heal all moral blindness because it is more than just ignorance. Moral obtuseness can be "a conspicuous not seeing."[8] We shield our sight and willingly screen out people who make us uncomfortable. Liberation theologian Jon Sobrino argues that the opposite of truth is not ignorance but a lie. While ignorance is a mere fact, a lie is a positive action, a counterposition that distorts reality to fit certain interests and needs. We are usually glad to have knowledge replace our ignorance, but we bristle at any suggestion that we have been living a lie. The resistance provoked by uncomfortable truths indicates that we have a stake in maintaining the illusion. Profitable deceptions prefer to remain hidden. Here a greater degree of transformation is needed, perhaps even removing oneself from the systems that thrive on these ideological deceptions.

Conversion: Radical Transformation

Religious traditions, unlike most philosophies, have often insisted that radical change is required to remedy moral blindness and narcissism. The New Testament supports two paths to transformation: the more dramatic way is articulated in the hard sayings of the Gospels and exemplified in Paul's experience, the other is a more gradual way taken by disciples in the Gospels.

First let us examine the more dramatic variety of conversion. Theologians of the dialectical imagination call for radical personal transformation by God. This side of the Christian tradition stresses the reality of human alienation and the need for explicit religious conversion before there is any prospect for moral renewal. Moral blindness is a symptom of "the heart turned in on itself," a condition that cannot be reversed by the human agent.[9] Transformation is required because the self-centered person is caught in an infinite loop, where every effort to cure only deepens the problem. Augustine and Luther framed human life with New Testament metaphors that highlight the need for profound change. Augustine himself described his own long struggle to come out of darkness into the light in his classic *Confessions.* He wrote, "Our whole business in this life is to restore to health the eye of the heart whereby God may be seen."[10] Luther, an Augustinian monk, struggled to break free from the anguish of living according to the law in order to accept the free gift of grace. His experience of conversion became paradigmatic for spiritualities of the Reformation. Like Augustine, he read Christian discipleship through a particular interpretation of Paul that emphasized human impotence and the need for radical transformation.

Does the narrative of the Gospels support the Pauline paradigm of dramatic reversal, a clear "before" and "after" in discipleship? Certainly repentance is an integral dimension of Jesus' proclamation of the reign of God. It is breaking into "occupied territory" where other allegiances hold sway. Only those who renounce final allegiance to family, wealth, status, and violence can see the dawning of the kingdom. If parables such as that of the workers in the vineyard subvert the ordinary world, many of the sayings of Jesus drive home the lesson in uncompromising terms. A. E. Harvey captures the urgency of these "strenuous commands" of Jesus for God's reign:

> "God is king"—that is certainly true here and now; but it is also true that God will be fully king, his kingship will be fully manifested, only when a different state of affairs obtains on earth. . . . his Kingship becomes an all-pervasive reality only when people freely acknowledge it and direct their lives towards the worship and service of their heavenly king.[11]

Jesus calls his disciples to strive to enter the reign of God, because they will embrace it only by putting aside their old ways and accepting God's ways.

The "hard sayings" of Jesus imply that disciples must make a radical break with their conventional way of life. Old ways cannot contain the exuberance of the gospel's new wine; they will burst asunder like dried-up wineskins, ruining the skins and spilling the wine (Matt. 9:17). When one of his disciples asks for leave to go and bury his father, to perform one of a son's most sacred obligations, Jesus replies, "Follow me, and let the dead bury the dead" (Matt. 8:22). The old rules have lost their urgency in comparison to the breaking in of the reign of God. Family, the all-important social and economic location of life in that culture, will be supplanted by the surrogate family of the children of God. Status, whether based on power or religious respectability, is reversed when the master endorses the paradigm of servanthood. Wealth, particularly in Luke-Acts, is not a sign of God's favor but an obstacle to perceiving the needs of others compassionately.

The Synoptics draw analogies that point to radical transformation. Matthew drives home the lessons of the Sermon on the Mount by invoking the image of root and fruit: "You will know them by their fruits. Are grapes gathered from thorns, or figs from thistles? In the same way, every good tree bears good fruit, but the bad tree bears bad fruit" (Matt. 7:16–18). We cannot expect good actions to come from a twisted character. In the Synoptics the "hard sayings" of Jesus force his disciples to contrast the values of the kingdom with those of their society. In John's Gospel, these contrasts become more cosmic and theological in the dual metaphors of darkness and light, falsehood and truth, blindness and sight. There is no middle ground between these regions, and no one can straddle them.

The Johannine polarities echo Paul's stark metaphors for human existence. Every person lives under the bondage of death in self-centered existence (flesh) or in allegiance to life in Christ (spirit). Everyone lives in bondage or is liberated by grace, condemned or justified. Sin plays a more prominent role in Paul's drama of salvation than in the Synoptics, where the disciples are slow learners but not enthralled by sin. In Romans and Galatians especially, sin is portrayed as a player on the world stage, a cosmic contagion and social force. A radical break has to be made from sinful existence in order to live in freedom. The pattern for human transformation and the power to accomplish it are located in the death and resurrection of Jesus. Paul is blunt: "The death he died, he died to sin, once for all; but the life he lives he lives to God. So you also must consider yourselves dead to sin and alive to God in Christ" (Rom. 6:10–11).

Dialectical theologies and spiritualities have fastened on these stark contrasts to insist on the need for radical conversion at the beginning of Christian life. Discipleship begins with a death to self-centered existence and the beginning of a qualitatively new way of life through the grace of God. The hymn "Amazing Grace" classically expresses the resulting change in perception: "I once was lost but now am found, was blind but now I see."[12]

Conversion: Continuous Transformation

The narratives of the Gospels present a different scenario for conversion, one that is less stark. I will focus on the reactions of the disciples to the call of Jesus, because the narrative sets them up as paradigms for us to identify with. We recognize ourselves in their hopes and fears, blunders and generosity. Even though the disciples are called to leave all to follow Jesus, they do so in stages. As they watch and listen to their master, they are alternately confused, eager, reluctant, and obediently willing, just like subsequent hearers of the Gospel story. The disciples, however, are not presented as radically corrupt or as having been reprobates prior to responding to the call of Jesus.

In Mark they are slow to believe and even slower to get the point of Jesus' parables and miracles. Yet their deep resistance to his ways becomes manifest only when Jesus begins to speak of his impending crucifixion. The three predictions of the passion in Mark 8:22–10:52 follow the same pattern: Jesus predicts his death. Then the disciples do or say something that shows they do not understand Jesus at all. Finally, Jesus corrects them by instructing them that, as disciples, they must accept their share in his fate. Mark frames this pivotal section with two miracle accounts of Jesus healing the blind in order to highlight the disciples' dramatic need for insight. At the end of the second healing, Mark comments that the now-sighted Bartimaeus "followed him on the way" (10:52). Those who can see truly are those who are willing to follow Jesus in the journey that by this point is obviously leading to the cross. In chapters 14 and 15, the disciples fail their calling by fleeing the capture and execution of Jesus.[13]

Matthew also describes the disciples undergoing a gradual rather than a dramatic conversion. As in Mark, their reaction to the impending passion of Jesus reveals how little they have learned from listening to the lengthy discourses of their master. They are to be helpers of Jesus, but they are dogged by fear, lack of faith, and reluctance to understand. They gradually recognize Jesus as the Messiah and the Son of God and are welcomed as members of God's family, on the condition that they "do the will of my Father in heaven" (12:50). When they flee the cross, attention focuses on Peter's betrayal, which is ironic since he was the one singled out by Jesus for a special role of leadership. Nevertheless, the risen Lord moves past their weakness and betrayal, addresses them as brothers, and makes them the ones who will henceforth make disciples of all people.[14]

Luke paints a more positive portrait of the disciples, particularly in the second half of his Gospel, the Acts of the Apostles. In the Gospel he lays the foundational pattern of the power of the Spirit, the inclusive nature of Jesus' ministry, and the universal scope of the message, which will be replicated in Acts. The call of discipleship is radical and costly, imitating Jesus in unconditional obedience to God, daily taking up of the cross, and opting for the poor and marginal. For Luke, Paul is the archetypal disciple. His conversion from persecuting the church is a personal landmark which he recounts on three separate occasions in Acts. Nevertheless, the emphasis is not on Paul's sinfulness but on the power of the Spirit, which empowers the apostles to do what Jesus had done.[15]

In John, the first disciples recognize Jesus as the Messiah and immediately follow him in faith. Conversion comes through learning who Jesus is through the signs that he does. The crisis in the narrative comes in the sixth chapter after the multiplication of loaves. Many who wanted to declare him king find his explanation of the bread of life scandalous and abandon him. The disciples continue their familiar role of being foils to the teaching of Jesus right up to the end of Gospel, when Thomas doubts the others' testimony that Jesus has been raised from the dead. The final chapter of John counters Peter's triple denial of Jesus during the passion with Jesus' triple commissioning of Peter to feed his sheep.

Although both the dramatic and more gradual paths of conversion are present in the New Testament, the Gospel narratives do not portray the disciples as "totally depraved" and morally impotent to change. Instead, they seem only too human in following Jesus by fits and starts. Only gradually do they come to realize that his message cannot be accommodated to their usual way of seeing the world. Jesus returns to confirm their faith, which had been shattered by the scandal of the cross, but at no point are they dramatically transformed. Although the dramatic healing of Paul's blindness has become paradigmatic for one stream of Christian spirituality, the more pedestrian route of Peter and the other disciples seems to represent the path most Christians will take. Their blindness is not total and they do not recover their sight in a miraculous instant.

II. THE MEANS OF GRACE:
PRACTICES THAT SHARPEN PERCEPTION

What can Christians do to sharpen moral perception? Two ordinary spiritual practices play an important role in correcting our moral myopia. The Eucharist and intercessory prayer are ordinary "means of grace" widely practiced by Christians through the ages. Before discussing them in some detail, two cautions should be mentioned. First, the impact of intercessory prayer and sharing the Lord's table cannot be restricted to moral perception alone. Although I am concentrating on their formative role in moral perception in this chapter, these practices also profoundly influence the other two dimensions of moral psychology we will consider in subsequent chapters, namely, moral dispositions and identity. Eucharist and intercessory prayer tutor moral dispositions by engendering gratitude, forgiveness, justice, and many other distinctively Christian affections. Furthermore, they confirm the practitioner's corporate identity as children of God's family and members of the Body of Christ.

Second, we need to recall the familiar paradox about moral and spiritual practices. They confer their benefits indirectly. Christian theology shares with virtue ethics the conviction that growth in moral insight and virtue comes as a side effect of living for what is worthwhile. Christians do not commit themselves to spiritual practices in order to become experts at them but in order to deepen the mysterious relationship with God. The regular disciplines of intercessory prayer and meditation are components of a life of deepening friendship with God. We do not focus on God in order to see our neighbor more clearly, though if we do focus on God with committed love, we will see our neighbor in a new way.

For example, Christian prayer for enemies does not primarily aim at cultivating the virtue of forgiveness. It is done for the sake of reconciling with them and being obedient to God. If cultivation of the virtue were the main concern, it would not be a Christian practice—and it probably would not lead to true forgiveness. As praying for our enemies gradually establishes a disposition of reconciliation in us, we can begin to see these people less as enemies and more as children of God, fellow travelers on the way to God. We begin to see that we have more in common with them than we thought because all of us need God's mercy and healing. Seeing them in this new light, we should treat them accordingly. In this whole process, sharpening moral perception is not the goal; it occurs when reconciliation in Christ is the goal.

Looking around the Table of the Lord

The most important spiritual discipline for correcting perception is also the most common Christian public practice: coming together in worship. Although we will consider the eucharistic meal at length in the chapter on Christian identity, it is important to begin with it here. Every dimension of Christian moral formation flows out from community worship and congregating around the Lord's table.[16] Every spiritual practice done in private prepares Christians for the liturgical assembly, so none of them can be considered individualistic.

Paul's admonitions in 1 Corinthians show how worship ought to shape moral perception. The community was split into two factions, "the strong" and "the weak." The former saw themselves as strong in faith because their consciences could tolerate eating meat that had been offered to idols. They looked down upon those who had scruples about doing so as "the weak," those who worried that they would be contaminated by eating meat that had been sacrificed at the temples. Since the meat in Corinthian butcher shops came from the pagan temples, this meant that the scrupulous had to avoid all meat. This presented enormous problems when the entire community assembled for the liturgical meal of the Lord's Supper. If part of the community could not eat what was set out, were they actually sharing one common meal or were they reinforcing their divisions?

Paul does not tell the strong to change their convictions but to change their

way of looking at their opponents. He agrees that idols cannot contaminate anything. Rather, they should not flaunt their liberty if it means that others will be
scandalized. "But take care that this liberty of yours does not somehow become
a stumbling block for the weak" (1 Cor. 8:9). The "weak" might be tempted to
go against their consciences, and that would be disastrous. "So by your knowledge these weak believers for whom Christ died are destroyed. But when you
thus sin against members of your family, and wound their conscience when it is
weak, you sin against Christ" (8:11–12). Paul exhorts the "strong" to look at
these people in a different metaphorical frame. They must be "seen as" something quite different from the derogatory terms of "weak" and "scrupulous." Do
not look at them as "weak," but look at them as Christ does. He thought enough
of them to lay down his life for them. Don't think of them as dimwits clinging
to outmoded convictions about impurity; they are members of your own family. See them as so identified with Christ and Christ with them, that when you
sin against them you sin against Christ.

The strong have to look at the people they see as their opponents and see
them through a different set of metaphors. Paul realized that the divisions in the
community contradicted the meaning of sharing in the Lord's table, which
ought to have been a sign of unity and reconciliation rather than a theater for
disputes. He tells the "strong": look at your opponents in a new way and you
will have to treat them in an entirely different manner. This challenge seems
pertinent for Christian communities today, which disagree over numerous political and ecclesiastical issues. How do we look at our opponents? Does the unity
of the Lord's table and the family of God take precedence over our disagree-
ments over the ordination of women or the acceptance of gays and lesbians? The
challenge to Christian unity is harder to recognize when local churches have
become balkanized along the lines of race and class. Then "the others" are literally invisible since they worship in another denomination and in another part
of the city. It is difficult to imagine how the Body of Christ can be recognized
in churches where everyone looks alike.

Intercessory Prayer

The practice of petitionary or intercessory prayer is the second common spiritual practice that shapes moral perception. Christian worship services almost
always include a time for prayers that place the needs of the congregation and
the world before God. This practice locates Christian worship in the world and
instructs all the members of the congregation to expand their horizons to
encompass that world in concern and hope. The community is not shirking its
moral responsibility by turning the world's problems over to God. In fact, peti-

tionary prayer is a self-involving statement, since it commits the congregation to do something about these issues. Praying for peace should make them recognize their own hostility and try to uproot it. Praying for justice should alert them to the injustice in their own relations.

Prayers of petition seem to violate the caveat that practices are not techniques geared to produce external results. The one who intercedes is asking for God to do specific things for specific people. On the other hand, anyone who has tried to sustain this practice knows that it does not often produce the results intended. As one retort has it, "God always answers prayers; and often the answer is no." I want to argue that the practice of candidly and persistently making our needs and the needs of others known to God is not merely a technique. It is an activity that is worthwhile in itself because it deepens basic attitudes of faith and trust in God and encourages those who pray to see human needs in the context of God's care.

It is not easy to give a fully persuasive rationale for prayer of petition.[17] In fact we regularly engage in profoundly important human practices, such as friendship, without being able to give a full explanation of what they are about. For some, intercession implies an infantile, manipulative relationship to a provider deity. For others, it seems a pointless exercise in informing God of what God already knows we need. For many who accept the Newtonian view of the cosmos, prayer of petition seems to violate the autonomy of a world that follows its own laws without divine intervention. Nevertheless, prayer of petition remains a mainstay of popular religion to such an extent that some surveys show that more people in the United States pray than believe that God exists. Prayers of intercession or petition are nearly universal parts of the regular worship of every Christian community and have been so since the time of the apostles. These liturgical practices train the imagination to locate experience in the context of God.

They inculcate a different metaphorical frame that does not see life's events unfolding in a context of indifferent nature or mechanical fate. When seen *in* this framework, these events are seen *as* happenings that affect God and become the medium through which God touches us. The God to whom Jesus prayed was intimately involved in human life. This was not the string-pulling deity of predestination but One who companioned those on life's journey and ultimately led them through death to life.

The New Testament combines a commitment to intercessory prayer with complete confidence in God's providential care. Jesus commands his disciples to ask God for what they need with confidence. This theme runs through all of the Gospels and much of the rest of New Testament literature. In the Sermon on the Mount, Jesus states that God is well aware of our concerns about food and clothing (Matt. 6:32). Yet a few lines later, Jesus urges his disciples, "Ask, and it will be given you; search and you will find; knock, and the door will be opened for you. For everyone who asks receives, and everyone who searches finds, and for everyone who knocks, the door will be opened" (7:7-8). Paradoxically, God desires to be asked for the things God already knows we need. Jesus then offers a classic *a fortiori* argument about God's practical care. If we humans, who are morally ambiguous, would never give a stone to one of our children who asks for bread, "how much more will your Father in heaven give good things to those who ask him!" (7:11). Luke reworks Matthew's account by stating that what God is most willing to grant is the Holy Spirit (Luke 11:9-13). It seems that the "good things" received through prayer are signs of the fuller gift that God desires to give, divine self-communication, which is expressed in Matthew as "the kingdom of God and his righteousness" (Matt. 6:33) and in Luke as the gift of the Spirit, the intimate and empowering presence of God.

The final discourse in John underscores the role of intercessory prayer. Having assured his forlorn disciples that they are no longer servants but friends, Jesus urges them to petition God for fruitful lives, a somewhat curious departure from the vine-branches metaphor that structures the passage. Life passes from vine to branch by the longing of the disciples, not by an automatic organic process (John 15:17). A little later Jesus chides them for not taking him at his word: "Very truly, I tell you, if you ask anything of the Father in my name, he will give it to you. Until now you have not asked for anything in my name. Ask and you will receive, so that your joy may be complete" (John 16:23-24). Prayer of petition does not signify infantile faith; on the contrary, their reluctance to ask signifies that their faith is small. Ordinarily, asking for help indicates a solid relationship. We do not dare ask people for assistance unless we have a certain degree of confidence in the relationship. We don't want to risk rejection, and we are anxious about imposing too much on someone who might not be that good a friend. Jesus assures the disciples that they are no longer merely servants, who would be afraid to ask God for what they need. They are now his friends, because he has taken them completely into his confidence. Consequently they should be free to ask God for what they need. God's response will prove that they have a right to ask and will not be rejected.

This all seems quite paradoxical: God knows their needs but wants them to ask. God desires to give to them, but desires them to ask first. They need to seek earnestly the very gifts that God desires most to give them, namely, the justice of the reign of God and the Holy Spirit. This makes no sense if we think that petitionary prayer is a commercial transaction or a conduit of information to God. Prayer is a component of a deepening relationship with our Creator and Redeemer. Bringing our concerns to God places them in a different context. Once placed before God, they are now interpreted in a different context from our own anxious frame of reference. God's concern for them is more important than ours. We need regular practices to situate our recurrent worries in God's hands. When we daily pray, "Give us this day our daily bread," it helps us place that vital need in the scope of God's concern. When we pray a blessing over our meals, we are thanking the One who has provided the daily bread. These simple practices help us perceive our needs as signs of dependence on a gracious God.

This paradox of divine freedom and human initiative underlies Jesus' teaching about the reign of God. It is a confluence of God's activity and earnest human desire. This reign grows with God's energy in God's time, as inevitably as grain planted in springtime (Mark 4:26-29). The reign of God comes when it will, but the disciples are to be awake and watching for it, like the servants whose master is absent. At least they should be prepared to welcome it like the bridesmaids awaiting the bridegroom (Matt. 24:45-51; 25:1-12). At the same time, Jesus calls for active engagement and cooperation. He teaches his disciples to pray "Your Kingdom come, Your will be done, on earth as it is in heaven" (Matt. 6:10). God's reign extends where God's will is being done. This self-involving request implies a willingness to remove the obstacles to the coming of that reign, obstacles like human division, exploitation, and indifference to suffering. Prayer surrenders our constant anxiety to the One who actually is divine, so that we let God be God in all our affairs and burdens. Christian prayer of petition is not mechanical nor craven, since that would not fit the One whom it addresses.

Presenting our world's needs to God in trust reminds us to relate to all things in a manner appropriate to their relation to God. It helps us to endure the "not yet" of absence by bringing it up against the faith that God has "already" begun to reign. By consciously bringing all things into God's sphere, we begin to relate to them in new ways: with the patience that knows they are in God's care; with the freedom and "indifference" that appreciates them for what they are to God and not primarily what they are for us; with the generosity of spirit that sees our own capacities and wishes as finite and not the final answer; with gratitude for God's goodness, which makes us ready to be grateful for whatever seems to be God's response to the needs we perceive; even with hope against hope when we have to relinquish control over our lives and accept our impotence to prevent the suffering of those we love. Many times, after not receiving an answer to specific prayer, all we can do is to place the need in God's care and relinquish our specific desires in favor of a more radical trust that God knows and cares. That change of perspective may be the most profound answer we will receive.

Once we have asked earnestly for something, we will be looking for it. We will be attentive to some response on God's part when we have sought it earnestly, like the aggrieved widow who keeps pounding on the door of the judge until he gets up to hear her out (Luke 18:1–8). Perhaps we will not get what we asked for; nevertheless asking will make us more alert to the initiatives God will take in our lives. It will help us perceive in the unfolding of circumstances not just coincidence but the hand of God. When we do discern God's response in and through the actions of others, we will be drawn closer to God and respond with thanksgiving and greater trust.

That sort of faith has a vision that glimpses the hand of God in events that would otherwise be chalked up to coincidence. I know one family that had to find a nursing home for their ailing mother in an area where few convalescent facilities would accept patients suffering from Alzheimer's disease. They combined earnest prayer with a good deal of research, investigation, and networking. When one of these contacts turned up an open bed in an excellent facility run by a religious order of women, the eldest son remarked: "This is a Godsend!" For him, the opening was "sent" by God, a gift that was not diminished by the hard work his family had done to bring it about. To someone without their faith, finding the opening would have been interpreted as a lucky break and no more. Their prayer enabled them to see that what had been done was the action of God in and through their own action.

Certainly nothing would prevent the God that Jesus describes from acting without their petition. In that case, however, they might not have recognized the gift that drew them closer to God. They discerned the hand of God in the mix of events because they were looking for it. Praying for it made them more perceptive. When it happened, they saw something beautiful. It bore traces of the One who sent it, so they gave credit where credit was due. This gift became a memory that sustained them to look for God's continuing companionship in the years of suffering that followed. If God's gifts are meant to draw us closer to God in trust and loyalty, then we have to be able to recognize them *as* God's gifts. The gift bears some analogy to the Giver. So the practice of intercessory prayer tutors the Christian analogical imagination to see the world as the arena of God's care and action.

The practice of petitionary prayer begins in the life of common worship and reinforces the ties of Christian community. Some communities honor a regular "ministry of prayer" that continuously intercedes for people in need. In times of special crisis, they mobilize "prayer trees" to enlist the rest of the congregation to pray. Often they will gather at the home of a sick person to pray together for light and healing. Whether the healing comes physically or through the resurrection, the faith of those who come to intercede often has a profound effect on the sick person and family. They experience God's companionship in the fidelity of those praying. This solidarity plays the same role that medieval monasteries and convents did in praying and fasting for the whole Body of Christ. Recently I told a colleague that my wife and I were going to Guatemala on a peacemaking delegation sponsored by our university. He asked me for the dates of the trip and then said that his family would remember us every night in their "blessing prayer" before dinner. Their Presbyterian piety included the practice of explicitly commending those in need to God's care. Knowing that they were praying for us deepened the meaning of our time in Guatemala. Finally, even the solitude of times of silent retreat can become intensely social when supported by the promise of prayers from others and nourished by prayerful gratitude and intercession for them.

Fundamentally the practice of intercessory prayer locates all the events of life and all the happenings of our time within the space of God's reign. It affirms that nothing great or small falls outside the compassion of "the One in whom we live and move and have our being." It helps us perceive traces of the dawn of God's reign. The practice of intercessory prayer brings what we need into the scope of what God wants, relating all things to the friendship that God has for us. As such it may be the least infantile of spiritual practices.

In conclusion, there is no conversion without a change of sight. Every profound change of heart entails a different way of looking at the world; and paying attention to experience in this new way will deepen that change of heart. Correction of moral vision is central to human transformation. For some Christians the transformation of vision occurs in a dramatic healing of blindness; for others, it comes more gradually, as their myopic field of vision expands beyond habitual fears and self-concern to see the world with compassionate sight. Whichever path of deepening conversion we find ourselves on, we learn to see the reality of God's emerging reign by taking on the new lenses offered in the New Testament.

In the next chapter we consider the dispositions that empower Christian transformation and morality. We move from the metaphorical frames of perception to the specific images and stories that shape moral disposition and action. Within the framework of the reign of God life should be guided by the paradigmatic stories of the gospel, particularly when we learn to enter them appreciatively through the analogical imagination.

CHAPTER 6

Emotions and Dispositions

W E NOW TURN TO THE SECOND major focus of Christian virtue ethics and spirituality: emotions and dispositions. How do the paradigms, the normative patterns, of the life of Jesus empower the moral life? The kingdom of God frames perception for the Christian, because every encounter, event, and issue is grasped within the conviction that God is definitively setting the world straight. A metaphorical frame, however, does not immediately determine how to respond appropriately to specific situations. Negative rules set the outer limits of behavior but do not offer much further instruction. Specific metaphors guide the way we see particular persons: they are no longer strangers, but brothers and sisters for whom Christ died; they are like the man in the ditch on the road to Jericho. When "seen as" these figures, they should evoke an appropriate response, especially compassion and loyalty.

In this chapter we will examine how the moral dispositions of Christians are shaped by biblical images and stories. Virtue ethics and cognitive psychology will help analyze how affectivity is shaped by the imagery of the psalms and typical stories of encountering Jesus. Finally we will turn to the spiritual practice of meditatively reading scripture, which "schools the affections." Through spiritual practices biblical images and stories become affective paradigms for moral dispositions. They tutor the basic emotional tendencies so that Christians are disposed to respond in a manner that is consonant with the story of Jesus. Story-shaped dispositions sharpen perception and help Christians determine what to do. Religious convictions are not held primarily as abstract propositions. They are embedded in images and metaphorical frames for viewing and assessing the world. Paradigmatic biblical stories are prototypes for recognizing an emotion and indicating appropriate responses.[1]

This aspect of spiritual formation was central to the apostolic communities and should be a primary moral function of Christian communities today.[2]

Attending to the images and stories of scripture is necessary because the moral content of the kingdom cannot be determined simply by looking to the rules and principles of the New Testament. There is no dearth of normative material. Jesus reaffirms the Decalogue and other fundamental commands of Torah; however, they do not chart the full path of discipleship, as the dialogue with the young man in Matthew 19:16–22 makes clear. When asked what he must do to inherit eternal life, Jesus reminds him of the second table of the Decalogue. When pressed for more guidance, Jesus tells him to sell everything, give it to the poor, and come follow him as a disciple. The commandments are the first step but not the whole journey. In Matthew's Sermon on the Mount (chapters 5–7) the major collection of Jesus' explicit moral teaching is found, although much of it is couched in imagery and brief parables rather than in abstract moral principles. Rules set the outer limits of Christian behavior, but the actual content of the life of discipleship is derived from the stories and person of Jesus.

Before investigating the biblical images and stories, however, it will be necessary to specify what we mean by some key terms. Emotions engage us with our surroundings and with other people. They are produced by the cognitive evaluations we make about the import of events, people, and possibilities. Emotions should not be confused with *sentiments*. Sentiments are self-referential, not other-regarding. Emotions dispose and incline us; they "make us lean" toward an appropriate response. Emotions are the more conscious expressions of *dispositions*, which are habitual character dynamics that become motivations for specific actions. Virtues have an emotional component because they are inclinations as well as abilities to act in certain ways. Courageous people have the ability to act bravely in the face of danger; they also are inclined or disposed to do so. Dispositions connote a readiness to act in certain ways, where sentiments entertain the subject but do not engage the situation in any effective way. Emotions and their dispositional substrata are often structured by social expectations. Language, paradigmatic stories, and significant memories guide our dispositions. In this chapter we will consider how biblical images and encounter stories of the Gospels engage our dispositions and shape them.[3]

--- I. IMAGES THAT TUTOR THE EMOTIONS ---

The Names of God

The Psalms and the Lord's Prayer have been the basic "primers" for schooling the emotions and dispositions of Christians since the beginning. We learn about God by learning how to pray in a community that gives us the vocabulary of prayer. The images we use in prayer disclose who God is and who we are. They also help us discover what is going on in daily life. Garret Green writes, "The Scriptures are not something we look *at* but rather look *through*, lenses that focus what we see into an intelligible pattern."[4] To paraphrase, the vocabulary of scripture is not something we pray about but rather pray through, images that help us enter into conversation with the living God. Even when the believer turns to God in her own words to speak intimately, she will likely use images and terms of address that have been learned through scripture.

The names that we use to address God have perhaps the most basic impact on our affections. The language of prayer is direct address, not about God but to God. Intercession and thanksgiving naturally take the form of direct address, and the language of praise moves easily from second to third person address and back again. Prayer speaks to God through a variety of names, titles, and images. The customary terms that we use to address God speak about the character of the divine Other and convey specific assessments about God. Scripture teems with poetic images to invoke God, because no single term can possibly name God. The scope of our relationship with God is greatly expanded by the intense language of the psalms and the blunt way in which Moses and the prophets prayed. Their laments, complaints, anger, jealousy, intense joy, sexual and family references, and so on, make room in prayer for emotions which do not get voiced in official benedictions.

Addressing God under a certain image evokes the corresponding affect and the affect gradually colors the image. When we address God in a specific way, we take up a definite stance; and when particular emotions arise, we have a vocabulary of prayer to articulate experience in relation to God. The stance becomes less deliberate and more habitual as that language becomes a regular part of our life through practices of common worship and private meditation. The practice of prayer sharpens our perception to see the world in a new way. According to Don E. Saliers, "prayer in all its forms, particularly in its communal forms, both shapes and expresses persons in fundamental emotions. It shapes and gives utterance to the Christian affections, and in so doing provides us with emotional capacities whereby the world may be perceived as God's."[5] For example, to pray seriously "The Lord is merciful and gracious, slow to anger and abounding in steadfast love" (Ps. 103:8) is to take up a stance of gratitude, humility, and confidence. Do we feel these emotions every time we use these words? Obviously not, but the stance and disposition can be deepened even when feelings are not noticeable.

The Psalter's Rich Emotional Range

The Psalms provide a rich vocabulary for prayer for the Jewish and Christian traditions.[6] As an observant Jew, Jesus would undoubtedly have prayed the Psalms several times daily. When we use the same words he used, we enter into the same relation with God. As we grow in familiarity with the images and affections of the prayers of Israel, our own hearts are formed in a living tradition. The Psalms have been the primer of Christian affections since the beginning of Christianity. In the fourth century, Athanasius describes how different Psalms are meant for suffering, gratitude, endurance, joy, and the like. As we engage the Psalms, we learn to make them personal statements: "And the one who hears is deeply moved, as though he himself were speaking, and is affected by the words of the songs as if they were his own songs."[7] The one praying uses the images to identify her emotions and also to evoke them. We make the prayers of scripture our own by letting them give voice to our deepest concerns and longings.

The Psalter tutors the heart by moving from image to the appropriate affect and back again. The Psalms rarely say anything once: the poetic doublets are means to deepen the emotion by savoring it from another aspect. We also savor the meaning through the range of related images in the same psalm. Through repetition and personal endorsement the affect saturates the image and the image shapes the affect. Psalm 91 intones, "O God, you are my refuge and my fortress," and then expresses the affective response, "My God, in whom I trust" (91:2). The image states the grounds of the affect, and direct address endorses that affect. The assertion of trust does not report an emotional state; it takes up a stance. It intends or "stretches toward" God in the specific posture of trust. The believer naturally brings to mind times when God has been experienced as a refuge and a fortress, times when the person knew a powerful protection from threat. Images of protection tumble out as the psalm progresses: God delivers you from "the snare of the fowler," covers you under wings like an eagle; God's faithfulness is a shield so that "you need not fear the terror of the night, or the arrow that flies by day" (91:3, 4, 5). These images will probably trigger an awareness of present dangers and seek renewed confidence in God. The connections in this affective logic happen spontaneously as the Psalm becomes familiar.[8]

The Psalms rectify the emotions by articulating fear, sadness, and abandonment and then leading them back into the presence of God. The progression of several Psalms redeems the most abject affective states by reframing them within the care and presence of God. The original emotion is not repressed but gradually transformed into an emotion that unites the person with God. In

William F. Lynch's terms, the plunge goes far enough down to plunge back up with new meaning. In Matthew 27:46, the crucified Jesus cries out to God the opening verse of Psalm 22: "My God, my God, why have you forsaken me?" As the Psalm continues, the cry of abandonment moves into the language of terror and persecution, but then becomes a prayer for deliverance and ends with thanksgiving:

> For he did not despise or abhor
> the affliction of the afflicted;
> he did not hide his face from me.
> but heard when I cried to him. (Ps. 22:24)

Does Matthew presume that his audience would have known the rest of Psalm 22? If so, they would have heard a cry of abandonment but not of despair. At any rate, it seems likely that Jesus, who prayed the language of the Psalms for a lifetime, would have invoked their language at the end.

All the ways we address God have moral consequences, including praise. "Doxology" leads to the imitation of God's ways. We cannot celebrate God's holiness and powerful reign without being committed to bringing that holiness into the world through acts of justice. Praising God for certain attributes makes a moral claim: these are praiseworthy attributes, that is, ones we should emulate. It would be hollow praise if the worshipers ignored those same qualities in their lives and conduct.[9] Understanding the connotations of a term like "king" may help to recapture how holiness and justice are integral to Israel's notion of kingship.[10]

Our Father

The "Lord's Prayer" forms the dispositions of Christians in a preeminent way. It contains the most characteristic mode of address to God that Jesus used, namely, "Father." His disciples had asked him to teach them a prayer as John the Baptizer had taught his followers. Jesus begins it with language that confirms them as God's daughters and sons (Matt. 6:9-13; Luke 11:2-4). What will mark them as his disciples? They will be able to pray in the same language that Jesus does, because they are now members of the same family with him. This term of address—"*Abba*" in Mark and "Father" in Matthew and Luke—will come to replace the name Yahweh for Christians. It suggests "childlike trust, intimacy, and readiness of access."[11] Although referring to God as "Father" is problematic for many because of its patriarchal connotations, it does represent the teaching of Jesus and his way of praying.

> [This] imagery is primarily problematic when it is understood as exclusively paternal or male imagery that may be used to express the parental image. But that is a misunderstanding of the force of the image in its original and present context. The issue is the intimate, caring, personal image of a parent.[12]

In Matthew, which has the version of the Lord's Prayer that became standard for Christians, the prayer is minimally about God's "gender" and maximally about longing for and responding to the distinctive reign of God.

Matthew's version has probably been expanded by liturgical use over Luke's more terse language. Matthew brings out more clearly the framework of the kingdom. The first three petitions request that God inaugurate the reign definitively. This prayer develops out of Jewish tradition and longing for the kingdom to come. It also shows how Jesus reinterpreted the kingdom as morally engaging, marked by God's daily care, and based on forgiveness. "Hallowed be your name" repeats the promise of Ezekiel 36:22–32, where the gift of a new heart and spirit for Israel will sanctify God's name. "Your kingdom come" is strictly parallel to "Your will be done on earth as in heaven." God's reign will be on God's terms; that means doing God's will, which is preeminently justice and peace (Rom. 14:17).[13] God will reign fully when God's ways pervade the earth, an eschatologically future event that is already dawning now.

The next three petitions detail God's reign in terms of human response. "Give us this day our daily bread" asks for mundane sustenance and the messianic banquet. The return from exile will be the great time of national forgiveness, and it begins in the reconciling acts that are within human scope: "And forgive us our debts, as we also have forgiven our debtors." Unless we show mercy, we cannot understand who God is nor participate in the reconciling action that is central to the reign of God. In the final chapter we will consider the practice of forgiveness at length. Finally, the deliverance of Israel will occur in a great time of testing, so the disciples are instructed to pray that they may not succumb to this end-of-time testing, "And do not bring us to the time of trial, but rescue us from the evil one" (Matt. 6:9–13). Those who prayed this prayer were already becoming true Israelites and focusing on the vindication of God's covenant. This context of the reign of God and human longing for definitive forgiveness and justice should give a richness to the term "Father" that extends beyond gender. The father of Jesus is the Deliverer and Vindicator of Israel, and of the cosmic "Israel of God." Even though Jesus addressed God as *Abba*, he would also have used the whole range of images taught by daily praying the Psalms. Some of those images are more feminine, some more nature-based than *Abba* or King, and they should be used in Christian piety as necessary imaginative and affective complements of the masculine images.[14]

Images and Dispositions

Virtue ethics and recent cognitive psychology are highlighting the centrality of images in moral experience.[15] Their insights can help us understand why images play such a central role in the formation of religious dispositions. Neurobiologists argue that human cognitive, affective, and volitional functions are unified in brain function. The brain registers experience in neural images that are associated chemically and electrically with certain feelings. The mind is aware of these neural representations through mental images. Our long-term memory stores knowledge in the form of images that are emotionally nuanced. Stories and scenes are retained with the emotions associated with them. That is why recalling certain scenes evokes a particular emotion and why certain emotions call forth corresponding thoughts. Depression often triggers bleak thoughts and conjures up the worst consequences, while happiness stirs up optimistic thoughts.[16] Thoughts, in turn, can generate specific emotions because mental images have a feeling component. Although we cannot summon most emotions on cue, dwelling on certain thoughts can generate habitual emotional reactions, as rehearsing old grievances can work up a fine state of resentment.

Timothy O'Connell uses the work of neurobiologist Antonio Damasio to explain how a memory reappears in the brain laden with affect:

> And when it does, the image generates the same electro-chemical reactions as did the initial experience. Thus the feelings are felt once again. Damasio refers to these images as "dispositional representations." That is, they are representations that tend to "dispose" us to experience once again the particular feelings that were associated with the previous experience.[17]

The ethical power of the Psalms and other biblical images is captured in the term "dispositional representation." The image is stored in association with emotions that dispose us to feel and act in certain directions. The images of the Psalms and the language of Jesus "tutor" the emotions by associating them with images that point them in specific directions. These "habits of the heart" are not merely sentimental but dispositional in the sense that they ready us to engage the world.

Spiritual practices reinforce the association of image and disposition. When the image is recalled, some of the stored emotional richness and impetus naturally recur; and when certain emotions are experienced, specific images naturally come to mind to direct the emotions. For instance, the image of "turning the other cheek" may spontaneously come to mind with the first stirrings of anger. Or someone who has read the New Testament for years may find that resentful feelings are quickly accompanied by recollections of Jesus' parables of forgiveness.

Emotions are produced by the evaluations we make of the situations, persons, and so on, to which the mental images relate. Feelings are the experienced awareness of these evaluations. Emotions resist systematic treatment, since some are primitive and others more structured.[18] There is emerging agreement that *emotions* are dynamic structures that refer to some object, invoke a felt degree of subjective engagement (salience), usually involve some interpretation by reference to beliefs or paradigms, and, finally, dispose the subject to a particular type of action. Some of the beliefs that interpret emotions are fusions of previous experience and affect that are stored in the agent's memory, while others are culturally conditioned patterns of evaluation and response. Emotions can target a single aspect of a situation (their "object") or, more typically, they hold several aspects in tension. "Unalloyed joy" is the exception, since joy is often mixed with gratitude, elation, relief, surprise, or any other compatible emotion.

II. ENCOUNTERS WITH JESUS

The encounters that Jesus had with particular persons in the Gospels are paradigms for the way people continue to meet, follow, and respond to the risen Lord. I use the term *encounters* to refer to the events where Jesus engages particular individuals. At the same time, they are the points where the return of Yahweh to Israel occurs. God's reign breaks into the world through specific conversations, confrontations, and decisions of actual people. Christian faith recognizes that God continues to encounter us today in Christ through the Spirit. These stories help inaugurate that conversation with God that deepens into friendship, service, and union.

The Gospels portray almost every possible response: the awe of the shepherds and the terrified cries of those possessed by demons, the fearful approach of Nicodemus under cover of night, the coldness of Simon the Pharisee and the shallow exuberance of Peter, the ambitious maneuvering of James and John, the bewilderment of Jesus' relatives, the resentment of his fellow villagers in Nazareth, the steadfastness of his mother, the curiosity of the crowds, the befuddled questions of Philip, the betrayal of Judas. We can find ourselves in this gamut of responses. These stories are "concrete universals" by which the story of Jesus becomes the story about disciples and would-be disciples through history: the same Lord calls us to follow and we resist and respond just as they did. The analogical imagination makes these encounters a window into the world of the disciples and a mirror that reflects back on the viewer.

Just as the progress of a Psalm "regulates" the believer's grief or trust, the encounters of the Gospels model the appropriate response to Jesus as people move from surprise and fear to faith. We learn how to respond by seeing how others respond; we follow their lead in discovering a similar urgent goodness that is summoning us. Virtues are skills and inclinations to live in a certain way. To understand them, we need to see specific people display in concrete ways how to respond with trust, love, and courage to Jesus and the announcement of the kingdom. These encounters do not merely illustrate the virtues; they enter into the very definition of these virtues.

The virtues in any tradition are narrative-dependent, as Alasdair MacIntyre and Stanley Hauerwas insist.[19] What makes Christian virtues distinctive is that they depend on the stories of Jesus. They also draw meaning from the whole narrative of his life, death, and resurrection because each encounter makes sense only as part of the whole story. For instance, Christian nonviolence is not defined by the single verse of Matthew 5:39: "Do not resist the evildoer. But if anyone strikes you on the right cheek, turn the other also." It also depends on the servant songs of Isaiah and the narratives of Jesus' passion, including the violent action of Peter, which Jesus rejects.[20]

The Call of the Disciples

The call of Peter in Luke 5 is a prototype and paradigm for responding as a disciple. It follows Jesus' anointing by the Spirit after John's baptism, his testing in the desert, and his launching of public ministry in his hometown. "Filled with the power of the Spirit" (Luke 4:16), he announces that the promise of Yahweh's mighty deliverance is being fulfilled in him. Luke's second volume, the Acts of the Apostles, opens with a deliberate parallel: after the trauma of Jesus' passion, the Spirit descends upon the apostles, who immediately begin to preach the good news boldly and launch their own public ministry. The disciple who preaches on Pentecost is appropriately the first one called in the Gospel of Luke: Peter.

After a long, frustrating night of fishing, Simon Peter and some others were washing their nets on the shore of the lake of Gennesaret. Jesus gets into Peter's boat and asks him to pull out a way so that he can speak to the crowd that was packing the shoreline. After teaching for a while, he tells Peter to get the nets, pull out into deep water, and cast once again. The weary Peter half complains but follows the suggestion. When the fishermen try to haul in the nets, they are loaded to breaking with fish. They call other boats and fill them with so many fish that they almost swamp the boats. Raphael's tapestry captures the moment when Peter recognizes the full truth of what has happened. In a boat teeming with fish, sea birds, toiling mates, and nets, Peter half turns and sees Jesus for the first time. He recognizes in the abundant catch the fulfillment of the prophecies of Joel and Zechariah: the astonishing harvests of grain and grapes that mark the day of the Lord.

Peter is at once fascinated and terrified. He knows that the day of salvation would also be the day of judgment, when the holiness of God would expose human compromise and corruption. "But when Simon Peter saw it, he fell down at Jesus' knees, saying, 'Go away from me, Lord, for I am a sinful man!' For he and all who were with him were amazed at the catch of fish that they had taken" (Luke 5:8-9). Peter's reaction to this glimpse of glory parallels that of Mary, the shepherds, and so many others in Luke: he is terrified. Jesus does not deny that Peter is a sinful man because that is irrelevant now that the day of the Yahweh's return and forgiveness has come. Jesus responds with an inviting command and a commanding invitation: "'Do not be afraid; from now on you will be catching people.' When they had brought their boats to shore, they left everything and followed him" (5:11-12).[21]

What else could they do? That is the question that the story sets up the reader to ask. Peter is Everydisciple and his reaction is one that is easy to identify with. We can relate to his initial grudging consent to this carpenter's advice on where to fish; then we are ushered into his surprise at finding his nets brimming with fish. The overwhelming surprise, wonder, and humility launch Peter and his partners on a new life. Caught up in the reign of God, they drop their old lives and follow this new rabbi.

What does the analogical imagination do with this encounter? As it plunges down into the details it listens for echoes in personal experience. It sees in the story a possible scenario for the believer to follow, a pattern for discovering a similar invitation today. It may recall times of abundance that broke in on fruitless and weary toil, times that in retrospect are freighted with more than just good luck. Or it may puzzle at Peter's instinctive recoil—is this just guilt or shame? Or does the approach of God's glory always expose our shadow side? Is it terror at being consumed by One who is absolute and utterly beyond our scope? Or are confidence and surrender surfacing under his protest? We may recognize that we kept a safe distance from this Lord who has come too close for comfort. Out of Peter's confusion comes the promise of abundant life that Jesus extends to Peter and his mates. In the gift lies the invitation: this could be your life too.

As the believer returns again and again to this encounter story, the scenario gets more deeply rooted in memory and imagination. The schooling of the affections is a matter of depth, insight that finds ever deeper layers of meaning in the incident. Preaching, meditation, visual art, and hymns gradually deepen the impression. Emotions that ordinarily are not associated get pulled together by the story. They form a new "concrete universal" that can be extended to other situations. Repentance is disconnected from self-absorbed guilt and linked to the holiness of God. Weariness and frustration are linked to abundant, teeming life and promise. "Fear of the Lord" does not paralyze; it becomes awe that disposes to obedience to the call. In a word, the encounter becomes a "dispositional representation," a scenario for action that is engraved in the heart's basic tendencies.

The call of the disciples has a political dimension since it marks their shift of allegiance from one reign to another. The call extends God's reign to those willing to welcome it. Jesus was calling people to forsake the normal obligations of family and work in order to follow him and support his mission. Compared to what he was inaugurating, these legitimate duties could hold one back from welcoming God's work. How would the people of Israel understand this wandering prophet gathering disciples? According to Wright, "The announcement that YHWH was now king, and the consequent summons to rally to the flag, had far more in common with the founding of a revolutionary party than with what we now think of as either 'evangelism' or 'ethical teaching.'"[22] The choice of the Twelve clearly signaled that Jesus was reconstituting around himself the original Israel, which had been broken up for centuries. A pietist reading of the call to discipleship sees only personal engagement with Jesus, but a more historical reading sees it as a summons to a distinctive new community. The political import of this movement was not lost on those who were the official leaders of Israel.[23]

Rejecting the Kingdom

Since not all welcome the call of Jesus, the Gospels have a number of encounter stories that are "dispositional representations" of rejection. They enable believers to recognize in themselves the tendencies that shrink from the reign of God. In Luke 5, the call of Peter and his partners is followed immediately by a story of resistance. Certain people object to Jesus' forgiving sins, since that is God's prerogative (5:17–26). Why do sinners welcome his message while the respectable are alienated by it? He compares himself to a physician who has come for the sick but not for those who are convinced they are healthy.

Luke 7:36–50 offers a classic scenario of acceptance and rejection. Simon the Pharisee and the woman who is a "sinner" play point and counterpoint in this drama. Simon invites Jesus to dine with him but pointedly omits the normal signs of welcome for an honored guest: no kiss of greeting, no water to wash his feet or oil to anoint his head. While they dine, they recline on couches, leaning toward the table while their legs are angled away. A local woman of dubious reputation comes into the open dining room. "She stood behind him at his feet, weeping and began to bathe his feet with her tears and to dry them with her hair. Then she continued kissing his feet and anointing them with the ointment" (7:38).

Simon is appalled by the woman's display and Jesus' willingness to let her touch him. We can imagine his thoughts: "This so-called prophet doesn't realize that he is being contaminated by the touch of such a woman, an unobservant, immoral sinner. This Nazarene will share table with people I would shun like the plague." So Jesus poses a question to Simon in the form of a parable. A man had two debtors, one who owed him five hundred days' wages, the other fifty. Since neither could repay, he canceled both their debts. "'Now which of them will love him more?' Simon answered, 'I suppose the one for whom he canceled the greater debt.' And Jesus said to him, 'You have judged rightly'" (7:42–43). Then Jesus holds up the mirror to Simon. He turns to the woman and recounts her lavish gestures of hospitality, which contrast sharply with Simon's chilly reception. Jesus then makes the obvious conclusion. "Therefore, I tell you her sins, which were many, have been forgiven; hence she has shown great love. But the one to whom little is forgiven, loves little" (7:47).[24]

The parable turns into a mirror of how Simon and the woman stand with God. Neither could repay the debt they owed, and the one released from the greater debt experiences the greater love. Simon's coldness indicates that he has been forgiven a minimal amount. Perhaps he needs only a little forgiveness; more likely, he has not welcomed the forgiveness of God into his life. She has been touched by the abundance of God and responds passionately to the herald of the kingdom; Simon sees her abundant display and is disgusted. The story forces us to identify with one or the other central character: Do I respond to Jesus as Simon did or as the woman did? One loose end remains: What connection is there between God's forgiveness and Jesus? He finally removes all doubt about the central role he plays. "Then he said to her, 'Your sins are forgiven.' But those who were at table with him began to say among themselves, 'Who is this who even forgives sins?' And he said to the woman, 'Your faith has saved you; go in peace'" (7:48–50).

How does this encounter story tutor Christian moral dispositions? It serves as a graphic warning about religious self-righteousness. Our assumptions of respectability are undercut by watching the first becoming last and the last becoming first. The outsider is welcomed to the reign of God while the insider excludes himself. The story subverts the meaning of sin because forgiveness changes sins from liabilities into assets: the more that is forgiven the greater the love. Finally, the story reverses our usual association of love and forgiveness. We would expect that someone who has loved much would not need much forgiven, but the parable turns this upside down. The less forgiveness we receive, the more tepid our love. We might think that if you have loved much, you will be forgiven much. The little parable makes it clear our love does not evoke God's forgiveness. Rather, forgiveness disposes us to gratitude and gratitude disposes us to love lavishly.

Healing Encounters

The healing of the sick and exorcisms are encounters with Jesus that parallel the stories of forgiveness. These events were seen less as "miracles" than as "deeds of power" that demonstrated that God was finally acting to restore Israel.[25] These signs authenticated Jesus as one sent by God as prophet and reformer of Israel. His exorcisms raise just this question at the outset of Mark: "They were all amazed, and they kept asking one another, 'What is this? A new teaching — with authority" (Mark 1:27). The deeds of power back up his words, unlike the teaching his audience was accustomed to.

Healings and exorcisms heralded the restoration of the full Israel, a key component of the return of Yahweh. Those who had been outsiders because of non-observance or physical disability would be healed and become insiders. The healing that Jesus brought to the marginal meant physical and social restoration, since it removed the obstacles between them and the community. They were relegated to the periphery of the chosen people so long as they were disqualified from worshiping in the Temple.[26] When he bid people to "go in peace" after the cure, that *shalom* meant physical and social wholeness. Jesus often sent them off to be inspected by the priests in order to validate their new status.

The healing encounters are paradigms for every person who approaches Jesus conscious of sin, exclusion, limitation, and pain. They model a whole range of behaviors from the not-to-be-denied Syro-Phoenician woman bantering with Jesus to heal her daughter (Mark 7:24–30) to the woman with the hemorrhage who is afraid even to admit that she has touched Jesus' cloak in the crowd (Mark 5:24–34).

Most of the healings are not complete until the person has recognized who Jesus is and what has actually occurred. He does not heal to show off his powers but because specific people need it. Yet the healing is a sign that a bond has been established between the person healed and Jesus as bringer of the reign of

God. When the person sees that in faith, he or she is then "healed/saved" and can "go in wholeness." When the ten men afflicted with skin diseases are cured but only one returns to thank Jesus (and that one a Samaritan), Jesus' disappointment is not over a breach of etiquette. The healings of the other nine were only skin deep, since they did not acknowledge that the power of God was behind their cure (Luke 17:11-19). Where people did not acknowledge this, Jesus' healing power was sharply curtailed. The Nazarenes showed no respect to the local prophet so "he could do no deed of power there, except that he laid his hands on a few sick people and cured them. And he was amazed at their unbelief" (Mark 6:5). Healings are either from faith or at least intended to elicit faith, since full healing means inclusion in the reign of God.

Exorcisms showed that the final battle had begun. According to Wright, "the exorcisms, in particular, were not simply the release from strange bondage of a few poor benighted souls. . . . For Jesus and the evangelists, they signalled something far deeper that was going on, namely, the real battle of the ministry, which was not a round of fierce debates with the keepers of orthodoxy, but head-on war with the satan."[27] Jesus saw himself joined in battle and pointed to the exorcisms as signs that he was gaining the upper hand. The enemy has taken a deadly blow, even if the struggle has not yet reached its climax. Jesus is the one through whom God has begun to exercise his sovereignty over the forces of death. Another powerful force already occupies Israel, and it is not Rome. As Yahweh returns to claim Israel, "the strong man" must be engaged and rendered powerless.[28] In Luke, Jesus insists, "But if it is by the finger of God that I cast out the demons, then the Kingdom of God has come upon you" (Greek: *ephthasen eph' hymas* [Luke 11:20]). God's return is not imminent; this manifestation of power means that it is already happening.

Does one have to adopt the full cosmic worldview of Second Temple Judaism to appreciate the power of the exorcism stories? I do not believe that scripture requires a univocal or iconic imagination but an analogical one. These stories are prototypes for believers to enter imaginatively. They illumine our lives and perhaps open us to dimensions of reality that normal secular perspectives ignore. Can every evil in the world be directly attributed to responsible individuals or dismissed as pathological? Can these rationales explain Hitler's Holocaust or Stalin's Gulag, persistent slavery, sexual exploitation of children, domestic violence, the culture of poverty, the captivity of addiction, and the blind pursuit of profit at human expense? In the face of inexplicable evil, biblical imagery of evil may seem appropriate. A Belgian priest who was working in Rwanda said during the genocide, "There are no devils left in Hell. They have all come to Rwanda."[29]

Liberation theology finds that the exorcisms of Jesus display the conflict between the kingdom and the anti-kingdom. It uses the "dialectical imagination" to point to forces of evil that operate in the world which transcend individual persons or choices. Christ may have taken the victory from these forces of evil, but they have not left the field of battle. The Letter to the Ephesians sees Christians locked in continuing combat: "for our struggle is not against enemies of blood and flesh, but against the rulers, against the authorities, against the spiritual forces of evil in heavenly places" (Eph. 6:12).[30] Liberation theologians from Africa, Asia, and Latin America, as well as feminist scholars, attribute oppression to larger structures and organized attitudes of racism, greed, sexism, and the like as the root causes of human misery.

--------------------- ENCOUNTER STORIES AND DISPOSITIONS ---------------------

What sort of "dispositional representations" are these various encounter stories in the Gospels? The terms of direct address for God are usually images with a single affective connotation. The Psalms take the original image of grief or longing and nuance that representation by a poetic progression of new images. So, in Psalm 42, the longing likened to a deer thirsting for running streams moves through tears and loneliness to remembered celebrations. The mood oscillates between the terror of great torrents of water and the calm of self-exhortation: "Why are you cast down, my soul, why groan within me?" The journey that begins in weary frustration moves through a series of images that register yearning, mockery, nostalgia, and deadly terror to emerge as a quiet but tested hope that one day it will be possible to praise God. Thirst for an absent God is not negated; it is named, embraced, and sequentially reshaped. The Psalm etches a new path that redefines hope, much like Paul's map of the path to hope: "we also boast in our sufferings, knowing that suffering produces endurance, and endurance produces character, and character produces hope, and hope does not disappoint us because God's love has been poured into our hearts throught the Holy Spirit that has been given to us" (Rom. 5:3–5). Those who have probed these texts know that wherever they are on this twisting and obscure path, they have some assurance of where it leads.

In the encounter stories the progression occurs through narrative rather than poetry. Instead of the poetic logic of associated images, we have plot: characters contact Jesus, interact with him, and some resolution occurs. They are called, healed, and come to recognize who he is. These are cameos of how the reign of God catches people up in it, drawing them from their needs and confusion into insight and trust in Jesus. These prototypes chart how every aspect of life can be drawn into the relationship of faith in Jesus which is the beginning of the world according to God. As the believer watches the characters turn toward Jesus, she is drawn along the same path. The encounter stories become paradigms for her to find Christ in her own way. These scenarios are not fixed scripts; believers improvise on them. They are open-ended like short stories; they start conversations and trains of imagination that can lead in surprising directions. As we shall see below, the practice of meditation or Bible reading is the ordinary practice by which these stories become our stories of encountering Jesus and returning to God.

Moral psychology is rediscovering the constructive role that images and prototypes play in structuring the emotions. Emotions and dispositions are shaped by a matrix of memories, beliefs, and stories that are inculcated by culture. The Christian moral life involves tutoring the emotions through altering some of the images that constitute them. The scenarios of scripture not only give a new context for moral dispositions; they enter into the dispositions and redirect them. For instance, the emotion of resentful anger loses legitimacy when it is depicted in the prodigal son's older brother. Matched with the compassion and joy of their father, the older brother's resentment is exposed as utterly inappropriate (Luke 15:25–32). The older brother's resentment simply doesn't fit here. Paul Lauritzen comments, "In this situation, the retributive emotion of anger is as unnecessary as it is out of place; anger simply doesn't have a home here."[31] This is how certain stories can play a normative role in relation to the emotions. They set a personal context in which some emotions are appropriate and others are grossly inappropriate. Certain religious convictions support this reimaging of anger. Namely, life is a gift, not an entitlement; we are not in charge of making the universe turn out right; and finally forgiveness rectifies offense better than retaliation.

Although I have not said much here on the role of religious convictions, they help authorize dispositional representations. Images and emotions are powerful to the extent that they accurately engage reality. These biblical images shape and confirm our experience of ultimate reality. They help us recognize and name what is deepest in our world. These traditional images, which resonate with our individual and communal experience, are conceptually supported by the convictions of faith and pragmatically validated by the quality of life they lead to.

The analogical imagination would have very limited effect if it were only an "imaginary" exercise. The analogical imagination views some aspect of reality "as" something else, not "as if" it were while knowing all along that it could not possibly be so. It is difficult to imagine how "as if" musings could evoke serious emotional transformation or effective action. Sentiments entertain us but do not engage the world. Emotions, by contrast, draw their force from their accurate evaluative grasp of what is happening or could happen, not from objects that are purely fictional. Authentic emotions contain an element of judgment: they are felt reactions to what we take to be salient in our situation. We are afraid *of*, we are delighted *about*, we are angry *at*. Take away the real world referent, or "object," and the emotion usually vanishes. If the reader thought that the worlds of the Psalms and the parables were merely fictional, they would generate only sentiment, make-believe feelings that go nowhere, not dispositions that lead to meaningful action.[32]

--------------------- III. THE PRACTICE OF MEDITATION ---------------------

Spiritual practices are the classrooms where emotions are schooled by the scriptures. The paradigmatic encounters of Jesus are incorporated into our emotions by regular disciplines of prayer, community, study, and action. By tutoring the emotions, the practices of Christian spirituality form the bridge between the text of the New Testament and the virtues needed to live out a Christian way of life. Many practices contribute to this gradual tutoring of the emotions: liturgy, retreats, Bible study, pilgrimage, committed service to the poor, spiritual direction, personal witnessing. A single dramatic insight into a biblical story or image may impress us for a lifetime. However, regular disciplines are the usual way that these dispositional representations become habits of the heart. I want to examine briefly one practice, *meditation on scripture*, which has been the traditional way to assist the imagination to enter into the stories and expressions of the biblical text.

The word of God is not meant merely to be read but pondered, digested, absorbed. Although the Psalms were originally recited communally, they became the staple of individual prayer for the Jewish people. Today, the Orthodox will recite the entire Psalter over the course of a month. Psalm 1 coaches the reader in how to meditate on the Psalter. It declares blessed and happy those whose "delight is in the law of the Lord, and on his law they meditate day and night" (Ps. 1:2). The Hebrew root *hgh*, which is translated "meditate," refers to the heart, not the mind. The heart interiorizes the meaning of the words by repetition and "murmuring" the sacred words (Ps. 35:20; Isa. 38:14).[33] It also deepens the emotions of thanksgiving and trust by remembering the great deeds of Yahweh and the particular benefits the person has received. *Meditatio* stresses the regular discipline of this reflective exercise. "This Latin word described meditation as an exercise or practice like an actor memorizing his lines or a soldier undergoing military exercises."[34]

The ancient practice of meditation read the text for transformation, not information. The sacred texts of every tradition have to be read with a listening heart, not at 350 words per minute. The early monks would hear the scripture read in common and commit phrases to memory so they could continue to be nourished by it in solitude. In the ancient practice of *lectio divina*, the Psalms or other parts of scripture were read slowly and attentively until something struck the believer who would then pause and dwell on the verse or image.

Medieval spirituality described the progression from meditation to contemplation. Meditation actively entered into the text, discursively using the mind, emotions, and will. It would usually lead in time to the grace of contemplation, a loving attention to God that was more receptive. As the sixteenth-century mystic John of the Cross wrote, "Seek in reading and you will find in meditation; knock in prayer and it will be opened to you in contemplation."[35] Protestant devotional literature developed its own vocabulary for "Bible reading," but many of the same elements of meditation recur.[36] Whether or not Protestant denominations formally described Bible reading as meditation, it remains a common practice in devotional reading of scripture, Bible study groups, and pastors probing the readings for the Sunday sermon.[37]

This transformational reading of scripture is never strictly private. It remains within the horizon of interpretation and a tradition of community insight into the meaning of the text. It proceeds, however, from a "hermeneutics of trust" rather than one of doubt or suspicion.[38] The practice does not stifle intellectual difficulties or questions about just what is going on in prayer. It moves to participation, which offers a different sort of resolution than analysis can offer.[39] These trusting dispositions are appropriate for conversing with God. When the Lutheran theologian and martyr Dietrich Bonhoeffer established the seminary of the Confessing Church at Finkenwald to counter the Nazi-dominated official church, he prescribed a half hour of daily meditation for the seminarians. He recommended that they approach the text with the same disposition Mary had at Gabriel's annunciation: ". . . just as you do not analyze the words of someone you love, but accept them as they are said to you, accept the Word of Scripture and ponder it in your heart, as Mary did. That is all. That is meditation."[40]

Like every established practice, meditation has procedures that have been developed over time. I want to focus here on a particular form of meditation, a type that actively enters into particular stories and scenes of scripture. The procedures mentioned here are not a formula to manufacture a certain kind of experience. Every practice, however, has specific disciplines and activities that

constitute it. Especially at the outset we have to pay attention to the funda-
mentals. Attending to them helps the practice become habitual so that they can
then be ignored.

1. *Focusing.* There are common elements for beginning the time of meditation, but what happens next depends more on individual temperament and
gifts. The structure of the practice gives a platform for spontaneity. A definite
time and a quiet, private place are necessary to pray freely and without inter-
ruption, as Jesus did when "he withdrew from there . . . to a deserted place by
himself" (Matt. 14:13). Bodily posture is relaxed and reverent. The time of
prayer begins with an explicit request to God for what is being sought; this
focuses the attention and affect. It enables us to pray out of what we deeply long
for rather than what we think we are supposed to ask for. Most importantly, the
person enters meditation receptively in the confidence that they are seeking
God only because God has already found them. We do not initiate prayer so
much as enter into the conversation that God is already having with us and with
all people.[41]

2. *Taking part in the story.* Meditation uses the imagination to plunge down
into the details of narrative, into the color and weight of things. The meaning
of a narrative is woven inextricably into the gestures, inflection, and movement
of characters. Entering the drama of the story helps us "cross over" into the
experience of the characters.[42] Meditation uses this capacity for empathy to
enter into parables and stories.[43] Every biblical story has room for one more
character: the believer whose story it is also. This is not a recent invention.
Matthias Grünewald's rendering of the crucifixion in the Isenheim Altarpiece
(1515) has a blank spot at the foot of the cross, a space for the viewer to enter
into the scene with the other worshipers.[44] Identifying with the scene can help
us pray out of emotions or aspects of ourselves that have been kept buried and
can strip away the posture of formality that often inhibits our relation to God.
It also gets us to improvise and to see how the Lord responds.

The five senses help the imagination bring home the actual details of the
scene and fill in what the terse language of the Gospels leaves blank. For
instance, in the three scenes that make up the parable of the Prodigal Son, we
could place ourselves in the pigsty with the younger brother and imagine what
he is experiencing. Or we could imagine the joy of the father when he first catches
sight of the son for whom he has waited so long; then we could shift to what the
son feels as he sees the father run out to meet him on the road. It should not be
difficult to taste the resentment that sours the older brother as he listens to the
bustle of preparation for the feast and smells the roasting fatted calf.

3. *Savoring the scene.* Repetition is an essential part of meditation. What satisfies the spirit is going into depth in a small section of the text rather than quickly moving through many passages. A medieval directive put it: *Non multa sed multum*—not many things but much. Meditation means chewing, savoring, and enjoying a word or phrase until the savor is gone; only then do we move on to another aspect. The point is to dwell in the image-shaped emotion and to pray from that place to God. This savoring is helped by recalling analogous situations from personal history and returning to them in unhurried fashion.

Ignatius Loyola recommended pausing after a time of prayer to note what has struck us, recalling moments of insight and points where we were moved positively or negatively. At the end of a retreat day that had several times of meditation, he often places an "application of the senses" to savor and deepen the impact of those times.[45] Ignatius is trying to get the person familiar with the typical emotions and movements of the Spirit as well as with the counter-movements of "the enemy of our human nature."[46] More broadly, he is training the person to be attentive to deep emotions, for they are the ties that link her to God: "A breakthrough of faith occurs when we recognize that our desire for God originates not in ourselves but in God. . . . What we feel as our desire is the effect of God desiring to be desired, knowing that our responsive desiring will bring us to life."[47]

4. *Conversing with God or silence.* Meditation probes the Gospel scenes in order to move to a deeper friendship with God and a closer discipleship with Jesus. It should lead to the uncensored conversation that friends have with one another. These scenes are scenarios for expression as well as action. They are not motivational tapes for self-improvement or exercises to lead directly to plans of action. Oftentimes a single phrase may hold our attention. We latch onto a particular phrase that locates a stance to pray out of: the peace of "Abide in me as I abide in you" (John 15:4), or the relief of "Come to me, all you that are weary and are carrying heavy burdens and I will give you rest" (Matt. 11:28). Sometimes a single phrase can occupy people for weeks or months. As the practice of meditation deepens, it often leads to contemplation, when words fail and a simple reverent attention to God is all that satisfies.[48] Here the presence of God is entered directly and simply, even though a certain amount of distraction may be occurring at a more superficial level.

Like every spiritual practice, meditation brings a certain amount of detachment about performance and results. The practice of meditation and Bible reading can fail to be entertaining even though it is leading us deeper into God. Sometimes this comes when we persist in a practice of prayer or service when it is no longer rewarding and even seems pointless. John of the Cross, the sixteenth-century mystical theologian, described the process of detachment that we do not choose. He wrote that almost everyone who begins to pray regularly eventually experiences the "dark night of the senses." The religious good feelings that invited the beginner to seek God fade away in a time of dryness and distraction. Its purpose is to detach the person from the consolations of prayer in order to seek God for God's sake. The person has to choose to seek God in faith in the absence of any sensible consolation.[49] Those who persevere in patience through this desert time often come to a quieter and more receptive form of prayer that John of the Cross called contemplation.

The regular practice of meditative prayer gradually frees us from judging our performance because we are less and less in charge. A committed life of prayer is not likely to lead to ecstatic or mystical states. The fruits of prayer are more likely to turn up in greater tranquillity in human relations, generosity, increased reverence for and acceptance of others, willingness to forgive, and the like. Progress in prayer comes in becoming detached from concern about making progress. As one old saying has it: "Quit trying to pray. Quit trying. Quit quitting."

A friend who had meditated regularly for thirty years described the course of his journey in prayer: "When I first started to pray as a kid I talked *at* God. Then after a while, I began to talk *to* God. Then a few years later I was talking *with* God. That went on for a while and I began to listen *to* God. Now I am listening *for* God." He may have started to pray as a technique for getting what he wanted, but gradually it became a practice worth doing for its own sake. Rich practices have a way of winning us over. Whether it was entertaining or not, the practice of meditation fostered a deepening familiarity with God, a growing friendship and intimacy, a greater openness to the divine life and direction of the Spirit. Meditation may also encourage a simpler, less cluttered life, a more focused existence, better self-knowledge, greater sensitivity to others, and a readiness to "cross over" to serve them. Nevertheless, meditation is not a technique to achieve these goods; they come as side effects. Supposing that prayer is intended for personal benefit would be like supposing that Michael Jordan plays basketball to keep his weight down. Nor is prayer a technique to get to heaven and avoid hell. One gradually realizes that the desire for God is not a longing for reward and self-satisfaction but simply to abide with God on God's terms.

The imagination and the affections are tutored by meditation, which engages them in the images that are the alphabet of God's revelation. Daily meditation on the scenes and language of scripture gradually inculcates a vocabulary of prayer and images. Regular exposure makes these images and affections the background music of life. The stories turn the emotions to God in faith through the paradigms that have been absorbed in prayer. We may not get what we want from turning to Jesus, but doing so may help us see that we do get what we most need, his companionship and assurance for the journey. Over time, we build up a repository of these scenes and the related emotions, which are stored together in memory. They enrich our appreciation of the Gospels and guide our emotions to live a life consonant with their script.

How does spirituality get practical? What relevance does it have for moral judgment and assessment? We now turn to these issues and the practice of Christian moral discernment. All the stories of the Gospels are parts of a single overall narrative, and all the emotions and dispositions of the Christian life are components of "the mind of Christ." Bringing that internalized norm to bear on relations and decisions is the aim of the practice of Christian discernment.

CHAPTER 7

Dispositions and Discernment

CHRISTIANS NEED TO BRING the dispositions shaped by discipleship to practical assessment and expression. Discernment is the name for practical moral wisdom in the Christian life. It is the capacity to bring the commitment to follow Christ into the stuff of everyday relations and situations. Discernment is not the prudent application of general principles to particular cases. Rules are important in the moral life, but they are no substitute for wisdom. Discernment seeks not merely the right action but the appropriate one, that is, the one that fits the Christian way of life and the particular leadings of the Spirit. The path of discipleship is indicated by the analogical imagination, which has been tutored by the stories of Jesus and the dispositions of the heart prompted by the person of Jesus Christ.

We will first look at two Pauline "master images" that capture the overall shape of the life of Jesus. Paul looks to the cross and resurrection as the paradigm for Christian life rather than to particular incidents. He highlights a unity that might otherwise be missed. In the Gospel narratives, the individual encounters and scenes that shape specific Christian dispositions are parts of a whole. They hang together in the overall structure of the story of Jesus' life and death. The Gospels were composed with the end of the story in full view. In fact, every book of the New Testament is dominated by the climax of the story, the cross and resurrection. That climactic moment summed up the meaning of Jesus' entire life for Paul. From his christological overview, Paul sees that discipleship means conformity to the destiny of Jesus more than imitation of particular aspects of his life.

Then we will turn to the practice of Christian discernment which is guided by the normative structure of the cross and resurrection, particularly as it is embedded in Christian affectivity. Christians ought to have "that same mind in you which was in Christ Jesus" (Phil. 2:5). They should operate out of moral wisdom shaped by his story. Sometimes discernment is more deliberate, sometimes more intuitive. It recognizes God's invitations and discovers practical insights that are prompted by the central Christian affections. We do not have to ponder our every decision because we rely on habits that intuitively and spontaneously lead to action. Honest people do not stop to consider whether to tell the truth or not, because the habit of honesty disposes them to tell the truth. Analogously, Christian compassion often discerns how to help those in need in an intuitive manner. Dispositions informed by the story of Jesus prompt appropriately Christian assessments and actions. That component of discernment complements its more deliberate processes of judgment.

Christian moral discernment relies on the reasoning heart, but not in opposition to the reasoning head. It respects general moral principles which articulate the habits of the heart. It also realizes when legitimate exceptions should be made to these principles. Even though discernment operates through informed intuition, it should be able to explain its priorities and decisions in terms that are intelligible to the community of faith. Christian discernment does more than prudently apply general moral norms. It recognizes the particular invitations that God makes. Jesus was not a sage who dealt with humanity "wholesale" by dispensing moral aphorisms; he called particular people to follow in distinctive ways. He demanded that the rich young man give up everything to the poor in order to become his disciple (Matt. 19:16–22). Yet he made no such demand on Lazarus, Martha, and Mary, whom John's Gospel presents as respected landowners. The New Testament authors are wary of riches, which can stunt compassion and make us believe that we are self-sufficient. Yet there is no blanket condemnation of material possessions.[1] People are called to serve in many different ways in the Body of Christ, and each one has a unique contribution to make to the world. That path cannot be reduced to a formula. Christians must continue to ask, "What is the risen Lord enabling and requiring of me today?" That is the classic case for religious discernment.[2]

--------------------- I. FROM STORIES TO THE MASTER STORY ---------------------

The Point of the Story

Is the story of Jesus sufficiently unified to serve as the norm for Christian life and community? The object of Christian faith, of course, is not the lowest common denominator of the four Gospel accounts. Faith looks to the risen Christ, who was and remains Jesus of Nazareth. Nevertheless, this historical individual charts the "way, truth, and life" for every generation of believers.

Does the story of Jesus have clear enough boundaries to be normative, that is, to determine which forms of Christianity are legitimate and which are not? Unless it has this critical edge, it cannot be the norm for Christian moral discernment. Consider two disparate examples. In 1755 Jonathan Edwards wrote that true Christian affections can be distinguished from counterfeit affections "in that they tend to, and are attended with the lamblike, dovelike spirit and temper of Jesus Christ; or in other words, they naturally beget and promote such a spirit of love, meekness, quietness, forgiveness and mercy, as appeared in Christ."[3] Peruvian theologian Gustavo Gutiérrez gives a different profile of discipleship, one colored by the Latin American struggle for liberation: conversion as a requirement for solidarity, gratuitousness as the atmosphere for effective action, joy as the victory over suffering, spiritual childhood, radical dependence on God as the requirement for commitment to the poor, and community born out of solitude.[4]

The barrios of Lima are a long way from the godly commonwealth of Puritan Massachusetts. Those different contexts required different dimensions of the Gospel: "the concrete forms of the following of Jesus are connected with the great historical movements of an age."[5] The spirituality of Puritanism would not fit Latin America today any more than liberation spirituality would make sense in colonial Northampton. Yet the two profiles of Christian affections are not entirely disparate. Edwards's and Gutiérrez's analogical imagination stayed faithful to the prototypical story of Jesus in the Gospels. Some interpretations, however, failed to stay even analogically faithful to that story. The nineteenth-century portrait of a purely spiritual Jesus who preached "the fatherhood of God and the brotherhood of man" without concern for injustice has not stood the test of time.[6] A private, sentimentalized Jesus cannot be reconciled with what we have come to know through historical investigation. Some versions are blind to specific features of the Gospels. Liberal Christianity in the United States appreciates a Gospel commitment to inclusion and justice. Because of its esteem for individual freedom and skepticism about authority, it cannot appreciate God's sovereignty and the corresponding biblical virtues of obedience and radical dependence on God.

The figure of Jesus cannot support any and every interpretation, because he was a particular person with a specific way of being human. The universality of his story has to be grounded in its concreteness. The Christian moral imperative is not simply "Be human," but "Be human in the way in which Jesus Christ is human."[7] Bland or culturally accommodated versions of Christianity have to hide the scandal of the cross. Change the ending of the story and you have a different story. If Jesus had been killed while leading a bloody revolution against the Romans, or died in bed at the age of seventy, the evangelists would have a very different story to tell. Just as the last act of a play determines whether it is a comedy or a tragedy, the final scenes of the life of Jesus define the whole. By focusing attention on the event that climaxed the story, Paul distills the meaning of the story. "The gospel of Christ" (Phil. 1:27) refers not to all the parables, encounters, and teachings that occurred on the way to Jerusalem but to what Jesus accomplished for humanity in his cross and resurrection. What this paradigm loses in narrative richness and detail it gains in starkness and clarity.

Each of the Gospels is structured around the journey from Galilee to Jerusalem, where Jesus must meet the fate of all the prophets. The passion narratives are most likely the oldest continuous literary units in the Gospels; they indicate that the earliest preaching centered on Jesus' passion and resurrection. Mark, who invented the literary form of "gospel," devotes over a third of his text to the passion narrative. Every encounter, every parable of Jesus leads to the final contest with the forces of death. The turning point of the drama of Mark's Gospel is the eighth chapter. The plot changes once the ending is predicted: Jesus is going to Jerusalem to suffer, be killed, "and after three days rise again" (Mark 8:31). When Peter balks, Jesus makes it utterly clear that every disciple must share his destiny. "If any want to become my followers, let them deny themselves, take up their cross and follow me" (8:34). As in the prediction of the passion, the promise of resurrection is only a glimmer of light cast from the wings: "For those who want to save their life will lose it, and those who lose their life for my sake, and for the sake of the gospel, will save it" (8:35).

The cross has the same theological priority in Paul, who wrote only two decades after the death of Jesus and at least two decades before the final composition of Mark.[8] The cross and resurrection are as central to Paul's theology as they are to the Gospel narratives. The cross of Christ becomes theological shorthand for the whole life and ministry of Jesus; it is the succinct norm of Christian discipleship. As the exodus from Egypt was "the classic Jewish metanarrative," so for Paul the cross and resurrection would be the normative Christian metanarrative.[9]

Paul prefers the language of cross and resurrection to language about the reign of God. In effect, he is replacing one metaphorical frame of Christian experience with another. Paul repeatedly uses the phrase "in Christ" because the Christian lives in Christ and must apprehend every experience within that horizon. Paul's Gentile converts might not have understood the symbol of the kingdom, since they had not shared Israel's centuries of longing for return from exile. He realized that Second Temple Judaism's expectations for the reign of God had been radically redefined by the cross. The real oppressor of Israel was not Rome but the forces of cosmic evil. God defeated evil not by violent resistance but by overcoming it in the death of Jesus. He absorbed the full impact of evil in his own body, and it destroyed him. But God proved faithful to his servant and raised him from the dead. Everything must be considered in reference to this event because it has inaugurated the final era of history.

This event is a paradigm for Christian life as well as the horizon in which everything must be situated. It shows that God reigns in a very paradoxical manner. The power of God breaks out in weakness and defeat, as the dying and rising of Jesus is extended in human experience. This event retains the tensive expectation of "already but not yet" as we await the fullness of the resurrection. Paul strives to make this event paradigmatic for every practice of the communities he founded. The cross manifests the pattern of faithfulness to God to which Christian life must be conformed, the standard by which all must be judged. Of course, patterning life on Christ requires exercising the analogical imagination. In almost every moral dispute Paul finds some analogy to the cross and resurrection of Jesus.

Discipleship and "following" Jesus are key metaphors in the Gospels for being a Christian. These terms are not found outside the Gospels and Acts, with the exceptions of Rev. 14:4 and 19:14. Perhaps these images connoted a direct access to the details of Jesus' manner that is no longer possible. Paul prefers the language of "imitation" to express the relation of Christians to Christ.[10] He embodies a number of attitudes that should be found in those who are "in Christ": radical trust in God, generosity, forbearance and gentleness, love, self-forgetful service, forgiveness, and steadfast courage. Paul points to his own life as an exemplar, or rather a visible embodiment of the prime exemplar. "Be imitators of me, as I am of Christ" (1 Cor. 11:1). If Paul refers to himself, it is because he is their father in Christ. Fathers and teachers in the Greco-Roman world had the duty to set a model for their offspring. However, since Paul's life has been stamped with the seal of Christ, the point of reference is not Paul but Christ, and more precisely the cross and resurrection of Jesus. That event encapsulates all that should be imitated; it is the embodied norm of Christian life.

Imitation of Christ is the touchstone for Christian moral discernment in Paul. Exhortations to imitate Christ punctuate Paul's letters; the imitation of Christ is the ethical subtext of all of them. It is most detailed in 2 Corinthians, where Paul presents his credentials as a true apostle. His experience manifests the attitudes and the peculiar pattern of power-in-weakness of the cross of his

Lord. We will focus on two major appeals to this master pattern: the exhortation to the Philippian community to imitate Christ and the argument in Romans 6 for individual Christians to model themselves on Christ, into whom they have been baptized.

Philippians 2: The Master Pattern for Community

The logic of Christian imitation stands out in Paul's Letter to the Philippians. There are three parties in this triangular reflection: the Philippians, Paul, and Christ. Each point of the triangle is connected to the other two by the dynamics of imitation and affection. The community is to imitate Paul, who imitates Christ; the community is to imitate Christ, who sets the standard for them and for Paul.[11] Deep emotions of loyalty, gratitude, and intense affection motivate all the relations of imitation. Paul has deep affection for the Philippians and expects their loyalty; Paul strives for union with Christ like a runner pressing to the finish line; Christ became their slave to the point of death. Clearly, Christ sets the pattern for the other relations. Paul must embody Christ's ways for the community, and they should relate to each other as Christ has acted toward them.

Paul recalls the deep bond he has with the community at Philippi and sees his present imprisonment as connecting him to Christ.[12] To found the church that was the beginning of his ministry on the European mainland Paul was arrested, flogged, and thrown in a prison, which that night was destroyed by an earthquake (Acts 16:11–40). Paul expresses a deep affection for the Philippians, who continue to share the grace and struggles of his ministry (1:3–11). He is troubled, however, by reports of divisions in teaching and leadership rivalries in the community. He exhorts them to recover the unity they should have in Christ with words addressed to the whole community: "Live your life in a manner worthy of the gospel of Christ . . ." (1:27).[13] What God has done for them in Christ sets the standard for their own behavior.

Paul urges the community to return to a loving unity, "being in full accord and of one mind." They must reject arrogance and ambition and begin to "regard others as better than yourselves. Let each of you look not to your own interests, but to the interests of others" (2:3–4). They must relinquish voluntarily their own position and become compassionate servants to their opponents.[14] Then he turns to the pattern of Christ's descent and ascent as the standard, urging the Philippians, "Let the same mind be in you that was in Christ Jesus" (2:5). By the Greek *touto phroneite*, "Paul calls on his readers to cultivate a habit of mind," which he then sketches out.[15] He cites a common baptismal hymn that expresses the parabolic curve of Jesus' radical emptying of himself to the uttermost nadir of the cross and then his exaltation by God in the resurrection:

> who, though he was in the form of God,
>> did not regard equality with God
>> as something to be exploited,
> but emptied himself,
>> taking the form of a slave,
>> being born in human likeness.
> And being found in human form,
>> he humbled himself and became obedient to the
>> point of death—even death on a cross.

> Therefore God also highly exalted him
>> and gave him the name that is above every name
> so that at the name of Jesus
>> every knee should bend, in heaven and
>> on earth and under the earth,
> and every tongue should confess
>> that Jesus Christ is Lord,
>> to the glory of God the Father. (Phil. 2:6–11)

Unlike Adam, who reached for equality with God, Christ freely let go of his Godlike, immortal condition out of concern for others.[16] He became powerless, emptying himself into human bondage and slave status, and in obedience lower still to its destiny of death.[17] Paul inserts the words "even death on a cross" to underscore this abasement: crucifixion was the lowest form of execution, reserved for slaves and those without any rights. At this point the descending curve bottoms out and begins to rise. God responds by vindicating this one who placed himself radically in divine care. Emptying is met with exaltation; the whole universe acknowledges and worships as the universal Lord the one who was a slave. The goal of this entire descent-ascent is reconciling all creation with the sovereignty and glory of God. As in the language of the kingdom, Jesus' mission is directed toward a single goal: that God may reign over all.[18]

Paul follows the same standard that he sets for the Philippians. In the following chapter he describes his own journey as analogous to Christ's self-renunciation and exaltation. He gave up the status of his Pharisaic upbringing, strict observance of the Law, and all the privileges that he once clung to. "More than that, I regard everything as loss because of the surpassing value of knowing Christ Jesus my Lord" (3:8). Imitation leads to intimacy because he is becoming like the one he loves. In relinquishing everything, he is becoming like Christ; in becoming like Christ he is coming closer to Christ. Suffering in the ministry further conforms him to Christ. He willingly participates in Jesus' sufferings so that he may be united with him in resurrection. Although he has not made it yet, he is striving like a runner for the prize. Only when the race is over will the judge call the victor to receive the crown. Paul's self-renunciation, like that of Christ, is not for the sake of a reward but so that he and others will be united with God.

The Philippians' rivalry and self-assertion are completely inappropriate. They clash with the example and spirit of Jesus and of Paul. They are as out of place as the anger of the elder brother of the prodigal son: rivalry and self-assertion do not have a home here. Discernment tests actions and attitudes against a way of life to determine whether they fit or not. The test is intuitive and aesthetic, a matter of harmony and disharmony. What does self-assertion have to do with self-renunciation? How can people whom Christ served as a slave demand that others submit to them? They should imitate Paul, who is imitating Christ, and also pay attention "to those who live according to the example you have in us" (3:17). There are others in the community who also are living witnesses to the same paradigm. Within the local church there must be people who are living analogues of the way of Jesus, so that others can learn from them.[19] Richard Hays sums up Paul's christological ethic:

> The distinctive shape of obedience to God is disclosed in Jesus Christ's faithful death on the cross for the sake of God's people. That death becomes metaphorically paradigmatic for the obedience of the community: to obey God means to offer our lives unqualifiedly for the sake of others. Thus, the fundamental norm of Pauline ethics is the christomorphic life.[20]

The impetus for this "Christomorphic" life comes from within, because the Spirit of Jesus is reshaping the identity of every Christian.

Romans 6: The Master Pattern in the Christian

The same shape of life that was being embodied in Paul is also being embodied in the lives of each Christian. Paul teaches that not only are believers "in Christ" but Christ is in them. Through baptism they have been plunged into the life of Christ and have been given the Spirit, which will shape them to resemble Christ more and more.[21] The deepest aspirations of each member of the community, therefore, should be disposed to embrace the master paradigm preached by Paul. More technically, the cross and resurrection of Jesus are exemplary because Christ's life has been given to Christians; they are members of his body and live by his life through the Spirit. Karl Rahner explains that each of us is personally involved in the life of Jesus:

> We should not reduce participation in the life of Jesus to some sort of moral relationship. Moral influence coming from Jesus is made possible by and based on an ontological influence. . . . The imitation of Christ consists in a true entering of *His* life and *in Him* entering into the inner life of the God that has been given to us.[22]

This is the deepest root of the capacity of Christian discernment. The call of Christ is recognized because it resonates with the life of Christ within us. The life of discipleship is not alien to our deepest dispositions and aspirations but unfolds our humanity, which has been joined to Christ. Imitation comes from participation: Christian love, service, and hunger for justice express the very life that is within those who have been plunged into Christ. They are not merely friends of Christ; they have become part of his living Body.

How did this profound connection with Christ happen? Paul locates this in the practice of baptism. The very pattern of the ritual recapitulates the event of the cross and resurrection. The converts are plunged down into the waters of death and chaos, into the descent of the cross; then they rise up out of the watery grave to new life, ascending with Christ. According to Paul, this baptismal event recurs in every moment of Christian moral life. Christians have to "walk in the newness of life" by conduct that welcomes the upward call of resurrection (Rom. 6:4). Paul explains in Romans 6 how baptism empowers the transition from the death of sin to new life in Christ.

Paul uses the practice of baptism to develop the connection between sin, death, and cross on one side and morality, life, and resurrection on the other. Baptism united the converts with the dying of Christ; where Jesus died physically, they have died morally to sin. "We know that our old self was crucified with him so that the body of sin might be destroyed, and we might no longer be enslaved to sin" (6:6). Since Christ is dead to sin, those who have been joined to him are also dead to sin: it has no dominion over them. But that is not the whole story. They have been baptized into the whole destiny of Christ, not just his death. "Therefore we have been buried with him by baptism into death, so that, just as Christ was raised from the dead by the glory of the Father, so we too might walk in the newness of life" (6:4). "Walking" is a standard metaphor for conducting one's life morally. Since Paul makes "walking in the newness of life" parallel to the resurrection, this means that the impetus for Christian morality comes from the resurrection of Jesus. "The newness of life" is the resurrected life, which is already in Christians and needs to be expressed in faithful living.

We might expect Paul to draw the parallel between the destiny of Jesus and the ultimate destiny of the Christian, and he does: "For if we have been united with him in a death like his, we will certainly be united with him in a resurrection like his" (6:5).[23] Baptism unites us to Christ like branches grafted unto a tree, so that we can expect the shape of his life to become visible in our own. By adding sin and morality to the master pattern of death and resurrection, however, Paul gives eschatological and christological import to moral life. Every moral act is a baptismal act, since it dies to sin and lives to God. In moral life, the life they participate in expresses itself in dispositions and relationships that are conformed to the prime exemplar: "So you also must consider yourselves dead to sin and alive to God in Christ Jesus" (6:11).

Baptism represented a radical transfer of allegiance from the dominion of sin to the dominion of God's grace. It meant entry into the life of the Body of Christ both ontologically and socially. An old way of life should have died in baptism, and the vocation of Christian morality is to live the Christ-life.[24] In an analogy there are usually four terms, as we have here. The terms of the prime analogate are already set; the other side of the analogy must be established by affirming God's grace through walking in the newness of life:

> As Christ is dead to sin   You are dead to sin
>   so likewise
> and alive to God   and alive to God

The analogy graphs the tension between the *indicative,* which states what has been done for us, and the *imperative,* which states what should be. This pattern of indicative and imperative is a familiar one in Pauline ethics.[25] It frames the moral question in new terms: You have already died to sin; now will you live to God? The mere posing of the question means that the indicative, the death to sin, is not a fait accompli but needs to be reaffirmed over and over again. It is ratified precisely by affirmatively embracing the new life. You will live to God only if your conduct identifies with the dynamism of the grace that God has given you in Christ. If you slip back into sin, you are letting yourself fall back into slavery, a condition that ends only in death. If you live in obedience to God, however, you follow the parabola of ascent, the upward call that is the new life of the resurrection. The indicative/imperative formula reflects the eschatological tension of living between the "already" and the "not yet," the tension between sin, which is not yet eliminated, and grace, which is not yet triumphant. "The transition from old age to new age is long-drawn-out and those in transit from one to another are caught 'with Christ' in the overlap."[26]

Paul is much more concerned about the power to live this new existence than about knowing what to do. Our problem is not ignorance but impotence and bondage. The gap between the indicative and the imperative is bridged by the power of the Spirit given by Christ. The power of the gift of salvation carries over into the moral call through the Spirit of Jesus, which works from within to conform them to Christ. The Spirit is the Christ-life which now animates the Christian, provided that that person lives it out in disposition and deed. The Spirit conforms Christians to the ascent-descent of the cross and resurrection. The inner patterning of the Spirit coincides with the historical pattern of the passage of Jesus.[27] The analogical imagination, therefore, is at the core of Christian discernment, because our lives are called to be analogies of the prime analogate, the life of Jesus Christ. We are not called to replicate the life of Jesus but to imitate it in different times and distinctive ways. Discernment tries to spot the rhyme between what we are doing and what Jesus did, between who we are becoming and the destiny of Jesus.

In sum, the master paradigm of the cross and resurrection epitomizes for Paul the humanity of Jesus that is narratively recounted in the Gospels. Christian ethics is "narrative-dependent" in two convergent ways. The full story of Jesus sets the norm for Christian dispositions and actions, not only as the external standard but also as the internal pattern of their emotional roots. Christian hope, service, generosity, and the rest are in the story of Jesus—and that story is constitutively in them. Jesus, therefore, is not an example of theocentric piety and affections but the revelation and definition in history of what that piety should be.[28]

II. THE PRACTICE OF DISCERNMENT

Christian moral discernment is the spiritual practice that brings together actions and ways of living with the normative pattern of the story of Jesus. It seeks practical ways to live in a manner appropriate to the gospel. In a narrow sense, discernment is a specific process of deliberating and testing specific options. In a broader sense it is the "discernment of spirits," a habit and gift of wisdom that listens to all the voices in experience to find the invitation and presence of God.[29]

There is no step-by-step procedure for successfully practicing discernment and acquiring the habit of "finding God in all things." There are some practical suggestions, but they do not do the real work. A piano tuner ought to know how to read music, strike the keys on the keyboard, work the pedals, and be able to tighten or loosen the piano strings to produce true notes. None of these skills will help if she does not have a good ear for pitch. The criterion for tuning pianos is internal. Only a very accurate sense of pitch will tell whether the notes being sounded are true or off. The skill lies in registering harmony so acutely that the slightest deviation is detected.

Analogously, discerning what to do or how to live in a manner appropriate to the gospel requires a religious "ear" that has accurately internalized the mind of Christ. This is evaluative knowledge, a judgment of what is worthwhile, not a simple matter of hearing marching orders from God. It can have greater or less degrees of clarity, in which our own immaturity and reluctance may cloud our perception. While some persons are born with perfect pitch, no one has an innate sense of Christian "pitch." In fact, the contagion of sin has damaged all our hearing, if not rendered us quite deaf to the values of Christ. Developing a good ear requires conversion, healing, and the gradual sanctification that comes from God's grace through a faithful community. It takes an openness to the advice of others within and outside the community of faith. Christian discernment engages every aspect of moral psychology with the life of grace, including moral perception, dispositions, and identity. "Finding God in all things" means knowing who it is we are seeking. It resists turning away from the problems and people where God might most readily be found, namely, the poor, the suffering, the unattractive, and the enemy.

Discernment relies on intuition that has been informed by mature emotional dispositions. In chapter 6 and the present chapter, I have tried to spell out how the stories and master story of Jesus evoke and shape Christian dispositions. Discipleship is not based on carefully calibrating actions to an objective standard as though discernment were some sort of surveying process. We become disciples by committing our lives to the Lord and taking seriously what Jesus took seriously. His attitudes take root in our dispositions and emotions: inclusive love, compassionate service, radical trust in God, gratitude, forgiveness, courage, a thirst for justice, nonviolence, freedom from anxiety, dependence on God, obedience. While the practice of meditation nurtures these dispositions, they have to be lived out in order to become deep habits of the heart.

For Paul we take on the mind of Christ, namely, the attitudes and qualities mentioned in the Beatitudes and the fruit of the Spirit: "love, joy, peace, patience, kindness, generosity, faithfulness, gentleness, and self-control" (Gal. 5:22). Christians led by the Spirit come to resemble the person of Jesus by having his attitudes and dispositions. This Spirit should also produce a life rich in good works, but without these qualities no good deed counts.

These dispositions together comprise a distinctive sensibility, rooted in the values of Jesus Christ, that is the basis of judgment for Christian discernment. It is the well-tuned "ear" for judging what fits with the person and mission of Jesus and what does not. Some discussion of the practice of discernment may be instructive, but it will mean nothing if I am tone deaf to the values of Christ. The spiritual practice of discernment, therefore, presupposes a heart that is being transformed by the gospel, a willingness to hear the call, and a community that is faithful to its calling to be the Body of Christ. As a Catholic who was experienced in the art of spiritual direction once said, "It is not hard to find the will of God. The hard part is wanting to find it."

Why not simply turn to scripture for the answers to our practical questions? Scripture has authority over discernment but cannot be the final word. In the first place, not every biblical institution sets a precedent for moral discernment, because some contradict God's intentions as revealed in Christ. God does not underwrite every arrangement in the cultures that produced biblical texts. The institution of slavery may have seemed inevitable to David or Paul, but it contradicts the freedom of the gospel. That disjunction became more obvious over time, so that even Paul's qualified acquiescence to the institution now seems inconsistent with his message. No child of God should own another; the practice does not fit the identity of Christians.

The presumption of male dominance in biblical texts is another accepted practice that contradicts Christian identity. Biblical patriarchy does not express the revelation or will of God; if anything, it reveals sinful attitudes and a repudiation of Jesus' mandate to mutual service and love. The incompatibility of male dominance with the gospel is not demonstrated primarily by reference to the trajectory of change in gender relations in the overall text; nor does it rest on a principle such as Gal. 3:28, which asserts that race, gender, and religious status do not define those who are in Christ. More profoundly, Christian feminists discerned the radical incompatibility between the attitudes of male dominance and the habits of the heart inculcated by the gospel. The cross cannot be assigned to one gender and resurrection to the other. It has become painfully obvious that male dominance cannot be squared with the master pattern of the life of Jesus.

In the second place, the stories of Jesus could not possibly contain solutions for the complex personal and social issues that arise in every generation. However, even when there is no normative precedent in scripture for *what* to do, the internalized pattern of Christian dispositions guides action by signaling *how* to act. This happens negatively and positively. Some motivations, actions, policies, and ways of relating are compatible with the mind of Christ and others are not. Any action or way of life that fosters the quest for dominance over others, the pursuit of material goods above all else, the thirst for recognition, the life of pleasure, or proud self-sufficiency does not harmonize with the Gospel portrait of Jesus. Christians should be acutely aware of the disharmony and reject them. The pattern of gospel dispositions should also serve as a tuning fork in a positive sense. Virtuous dispositions can prompt us in how to act appropriately. Humility should help one tell the truth; gratitude should prompt generous actions; compassion should suggest what to do practically for someone in trouble or need. Certainly we have to find out what the facts are to determine our options, but there are times when the virtuous inclination can illumine our path.

Three anecdotes may help to show the range of this practice of Christian discernment.

1. A few years ago I was on a delegation to El Salvador, not long after the bloody civil war had come to an end. The country was desperately poor, but the people seemed to have a hope that defied the hard economic and social odds against them. I was speaking with an American Jesuit friend who had volunteered to serve at the Universidad de Centro Americano in San Salvador after several Jesuits were martyred by the army in 1989. In a mixture of admiration and genuine puzzlement, I asked him how he could stand to live in such a bleak situation. He said, "When you first come down here, you can live off of anger for a while, but that anger eventually fades or you burn out. Then you idealize the people and their struggle, but after a while you realize they are just like everyone else; they too lie, steal, cheat on their wives, and the rest. Eventually you just despair. You go numb. But if you can hang in there, you sort of get to the other side. Then there is a quiet peace, and you can live and work out of that." I pushed him about the problems of living on the edge, being someone who would never be fully at home in that culture. He said, "I like living on the margins. That's where the Paschal Mystery seems to break out." That was where he found the dying and rising of Jesus going on in people's lives. He had an equanimity and good humor that made him credible. Five years later he is still doing very effective work in El Salvador.

My friend was describing a process of Christian discernment. He heard the call to stay in El Salvador as his path to follow Christ. It did not come in a peak moment or a mystical uprush. He recognized the call as genuine because it pulled him deeper into the dying and rising of Christ. Going through profound disillusionment to quiet trust brought him closer to God and closer to the people that Jesus was most concerned about. His shattered optimism was transformed into hope, which according to Gabriel Marcel is a decision made in the face of despair. The courage to follow a path that went into darkness reshaped his habits of the heart.

2. Another friend from graduate school dropped a very promising academic career to do pastoral work. The prospect of teaching and writing lost its appeal as she began to work as a pastoral associate in a Catholic parish. She found that

she liked to preach and work directly with people in times of crisis and preparing for baptism and marriage. Despite a natural reserve, she found increasing ability to exercise leadership and reconcile different factions in the parish. After a few years she taught at a university for a while. Her courses were well received but preparing them was sheer drudgery. She went back to full-time parochial ministry and became the de facto pastor of a Catholic parish, assisted by visiting priests who would preside at the Sunday Eucharist. Ten years later, she is an effective leader and gifted preacher.

Her discernment of a calling came through discovering what her gifts were. She placed herself in situations that demanded talents she did not know she had. Conversely, she paid attention to the inner resistance and heaviness that cropped up when she went back to teaching, the vocation she seemed ideally suited for. For eighteen years she has been faithful to a calling to serve in a denomination that cannot ratify her gifts by ordination but obviously needs what she can offer. A vocation has been described as "where your greatest gifts meet the world's greatest needs, and the community verifies your call." The local parishes have welcomed her gifts, but church officials are unwilling to ordain women. Her ministry is fruitful, even if constricted and at times frustrating.

3. I remember going to a Trappist monastery in California twenty years ago with some other young Jesuits to give the monks a workshop in Ignatian discernment. It said a great deal about their humility that they listened to us—also a good deal about us since we were unaware of the irony. Our basic message was that Ignatius of Loyola was only formalizing a process that Christians already followed in their lives. Most of us spontaneously test our options against our basic sense of who we are to see whether it fits. We use the reasoning head to ask questions and the reasoning heart to see whether it harmonizes with this basic sense of self.

We asked the monks to reflect on a recent decision they had made and see whether it had unconsciously followed the Ignatian pattern of discernment. When the time came to recount these experiences to the group, one of the older monks said, "You are probably right about discernment, but to tell the truth, I can't remember when the last time was that I made a decision. When you get to my age, ideas that are from the Lord are just easy to welcome and those that aren't from God just drop off; you just let them go without much fuss." I swallowed hard and wondered why we were giving a workshop on discernment to someone like this. I found out later that he had been Thomas Merton's spiritual director for several years at Gethsemani monastery in Kentucky.

This monk had such a well-tuned ear for the Spirit that he did spontaneously what the rest of us have to do reflectively and methodically. His intuition was so highly tuned to the values of Christ that it was just natural for him to brush aside distractions and cooperate with God's leading. He lived in an atmosphere of prayer and quiet union with God that had become second nature to him after a lifetime of fidelity. This wisdom ran so deep that he did not have to engage the reasoning heart on specific decisions: the path was obvious. It may be that he was temperamentally a more intuitive person than one given to step-by-step thinking, but there is a wisdom that comes from holiness whatever the temperament. I do not want to argue for this Trappist monk as an ideal for discernment, but he does give some clue about the virtue of wisdom to which the practice of discernment can lead. Mature docility to the influence of Christ is as ingrained as the awareness that some long-married couples have for each other's wants and needs. They know their spouse so well that they are more aware of the other's needs than of their own. Deep dispositions sharpen perception to a high degree.

Even for the mature Christian, however, there are difficult choices where duties conflict and inclinations pull in opposite directions. Should we end life support for Uncle Harry? What can we do about easing racial tensions in our school district? How do I reconcile with my cousin after all these years of not speaking? At these points more deliberation and careful discernment are called for, as well as consultation with others. There are many gifted people in the community whose wisdom and experience we need to profit from. Moral norms encapsulate the wisdom of the tradition and save us from having to start from scratch. We have to think about all the stakeholders in the decision and discover what our realistic options are. There is nothing mystical about doing the homework necessary for many times of discernment.

Character ethics emphasizes that most of the "work" of the moral life happens before we get to the moments of decision. The quality of our lives between decisions will determine what we see, how we are affected, how truthfully we examine our options, and consequently what we decide. The quality of our lives will determine our ability to discern. Experienced spiritual directors often say that there is no point in doing religious discernment with people who avoid prayerful reflection and seriousness in their lives. It is like trying to teach music appreciation to the tone deaf.

Christian discernment asks what God is enabling and requiring of us. Some principles behind it:

1. *The gift precedes the call; in fact, the call is contained within the gift.* By paying attention to God's "enabling," that is, to the direction of God's drawing, luring, and empowering, we can discover the inviting command and commanding

invitation of God. This means that we have to probe the promise and gift of God as it begins to dawn in our affective life. Values first surface in affectivity as something becomes "salient," leaps out at us. Whether the first impression is sound has to be tested out by reflection, but reason by itself will not produce longing and engagement. The ordinary way of Christian discernment is through paying attention to the movements of a heart that has been tutored by the gospel.

2. *Discernment pays special attention to emotions, because the call is always particular.* Emotions connect with the qualities of particular objects, assessing their salience and potential for us, in a more refined way than is possible for discursive reason. We need to pay attention to the affective clues to determine the fitting action. You don't need an argument to tell you that a new pair of shoes does not fit; if they pinch the side of your toes, you ignore that evidence at your own peril.

General moral principles can help determine what the *right* action would be; they cannot determine exactly what the *appropriate* action is here and now. The way of Christian discipleship for a specific person or community cannot be determined by moral generalities alone.[30] Jesus did not advertise for disciples; he called specific people. The judgment of appropriateness is rooted in specific relationships, conditions, and possibilities. It finds the particular act that is done "at the right time, toward the right objects, toward the right people, for the right reason, and in the right manner. . . ."[31] The appropriate action "fits" the whole interactive context. It fits like a *mot juste* in the middle of a conversation, the thoughtful response in a crisis, or the punch line of a story. The appropriate action fits the persons and the situation involved at a whole number of points, and it can be inappropriate by failing to do so at only one point. A familiar, affectionate gesture that would be appropriate among friends may be gauche if made to your employer.

3. *Discernment seeks clarity but cannot guarantee certainty.* Most of our muddling through of moral decisions consists in imagining whether a particular course of action will fit the specific challenges and potentials we are engaged in. Deliberation and discernment make judgments by the process of converging probabilities.[32] No single source of wisdom is sufficient by itself to settle matters, whether moral principles, memory, projection of consequences, advice of friends, or assessment of hopes and fears. Each of them weighs in and tends toward a specific direction which gradually converges with the drift of the other sources. At the point that they do come together, an act of judgment steps in to ratify the consensus. There is, however, one class of judgments that bypasses deliberation and speaks on its own authority. These are the intuitions that

seem to convey a direct command from God, a class of intuitions that has often given discernment a bad name.

4. *Not every powerful intuition is divinely inspired.* The simpler case of discernment is the immediate intuitive judgment of what is the appropriate thing to do. These judgments are intuitions, because they are direct apprehensions of a course of action, not simply hunches on the one hand, or apprehensions of the truth of a proposition on the other. They are immediate because they do not occur as the result of a process of discursive thinking. Having these immediate intuitions is not so much a practice as an event. All of us have had flashes of insight that clearly and effortlessly show us what to do. And since most of us have been wildly wrong about our clearest intuitions, we learn to become critical of them.

Some people take these immediate intuitions to be direct revelations from God. This can be quite tricky to address pastorally, since it is difficult to respond to the confident claim, "God told me to do X." In fact, claims like that often connote a further claim ". . . and don't you tell me otherwise!" Intuitions, however clear they may be, ought to be subject to some examination and possible revision. Their clarity and force are not proof of their validity. I do not mean to rule out the possibility that God does call individuals today as God called individuals in biblical narratives. The long tradition of Christian discernment has always held open that possibility of individual vocation—and it has spent even more time trying to help people sort out the genuine calls from the many counterfeits that crop up.

5. *You can trust your feelings, as long as they are virtuous.* Immediate intuitions in the moral life are often the products of well-developed emotional habits. So, a person of fairness and broad experience can often spot the course of action that will treat all parties in a complicated situation justly. They do not have to know about the theory of justice to do so. The problem is that habits prompt insights on both sides of the moral ledger. People who are mendacious are much better liars than those hampered by the habits of honesty and candor. They do not have to go against the grain of character to lie with aplomb.

Habits suggest what to do in an aesthetic manner, by inclination and taste. Just as a well-trained palate will suggest to a chef what ingredients are missing from a sauce, a well-developed habit of virtue spontaneously indicates what is "suitable" behavior. Virtues and vices have a felt tendency toward certain behaviors, because they are disposed to act consistently with ingrained preferences. According to Jonathan Edwards, a master at Christian pastoral discernment, the converted soul that has grown in sanctification operates in the same manner: "its holy taste and appetite leads it to think of that which is truly lovely, and naturally suggests it; as a healthy taste and appetite naturally suggests the idea of its proper object." The mature Christian "knows at once what is a suitable amiable behavior" because the dispositions of love and reverence seek to express themselves in appropriate actions.[33] These "habits of the heart" suggest appropriate words and actions more astutely than would a gifted intellect that lacked these virtues.[34]

These suggestions are not immediate directives from the Spirit; they arise from well-developed dispositions. If we are emotionally or spiritually immature, our dispositions may incline us to actions that should not be blamed on the Holy Spirit. Dispositions incline to actions that fit them. A benevolent person will have a sense of how to act toward a friend, while a self-centered individual is unlikely to notice or respond to the needs of others. The disposition of benevolence has a built-in tendency, a scenario, for helpful and considerate behavior. It knows this particular friend's likes and dislikes, genuine needs and particular sensibilities. Aristotle linked this guidance by virtuous inclination with practical wisdom, and Thomas Aquinas called it "knowledge by connaturality."[35] Charity produces its own wisdom, which is able to judge correctly, because it is attuned to divine realities.[36]

6. *Character determines the quality of the discernment.* Since the person's values and commitments are the norm against which the options are measured, the character of the person is crucial. A courageous, honest person will find that the right thing to do is "connatural"; it fits with the basic dispositions of her character. A manipulative person will find devious actions connatural; they harmonize with the sort of person that he is. Each will feel "comfortable" with the action that fits their characteristic dispositions, with one of them being quite content with actions that are morally dubious. In religious terms, a character oriented toward God is indispensable. Authentic conversion, ongoing repentance, self-knowledge about one's biases and blind spots are all necessary for accurate discernment. There has to be a fundamental attraction to God to serve as the "magnetic north" of the person's moral compass. The more a person is committed and drawn to God, the more astute they are likely to be in discernment.

Discernment seeks harmony between the qualities that are present in the available options and the fundamental values of character rooted in the person. God does not often give direct "marching orders"; more usually, God invites by evoking desires in us that echo God's desires for healing and reconciling the world.[37] Encountering the most authentic desires of your heart becomes an encounter with God when they echo God's intentions. Obviously, this does not happen on demand, and these judgments are not infallible. Commitment flows naturally from these deeper desires, since they resonate with what is central to the Christian's identity. Philip Sheldrake writes that in this discerning contemplation, "our desires are transformed, intensified, concentrated to the point where choice, commitment and action inevitably follow."[38]

7. *Prayer is the place where we can hear the harmony that discernment seeks.* The metaphor of harmony runs through the literature on discernment. There is a structural and valuational correspondence between a religious affection and its "proper object" that registers harmoniously. Edwards writes, "The soul distinguishes as a musical ear; and besides, holiness itself consists in spiritual harmony; and whatever don't agree with that, as a base to a treble, the soul rejects."[39] The practice of Christian discernment helps us develop that well-tuned ear. The tuning fork is the life of Christ as presented in the Gospels and present in faith. Prayer is the place where we can best hear the dominant tone of that tuning fork. No piano tuner has a radio playing while he is trying to work.

Sometimes we can enter into the presence of God by recalling a past experience when we were guided or graced by God. In the gratitude for that time, we may begin to sense that the same One who was present then is with us now. A confidence grows that God will continue to be faithful, even if we are being called to something quite challenging. There is a peace and a deep quiet that characterize the longing for God. It knows that beyond all the things we hope for lies God, who is greater than the sum of our hopes. Which of the options available to us resonates best with this longing for God that is at our core? Which of the attractions are self-centered, and which are centered on God and the genuine needs of others? Some attractive ideas will fall flat here, while another possibility may seem to carry and deepen that movement toward God. In prayer we turn to the One who is the end of our journey. Having the goal fixed in our heart, we can determine whether one path leads more surely to it than another does. We do so by seeing which of them harmonizes with our basic orientation to God which has been raised to conscious awareness in prayer.[40]

This testing of the options against our basic orientation to God does not usually yield insight the first time we come to prayer. In times when we are torn, or when the stakes are high, it may take weeks of prayer to sort things out. If no option is endorsed by religious experience, it probably means that we can find God equally in any of them.

8. *The reasoning head can help the reasoning heart.* Although the usual way of discerning focuses on testing the felt evaluations of various options, this is not to denigrate a more critical approach. Discernment is a process in which con-

siderable "cross-checking" goes on between mind, heart, memory, and imagination. There are times when we need to get some distance because all the options are equally attractive and none stands out. Or we may be overly invested in one course of action or terrified of another. That is the time to ask the hard questions in a deliberately rational and calculating way. What are the pros and cons? What sort of advice would I give someone who came to me faced with the same alternatives? Looking back from the end of my life, which route would I have wanted to have taken? This rational deliberation remains incomplete until it has been confirmed by an affective experience of divine consolation—in effect, until the richness of the reasoning heart endorses the prudent strategy of the reasoning head.[41]

We also need to step back and assess the outcomes of the discernment. What have been the fruits of following this course of action or taking on this new job? Has it deepened the sense of call? Has it evoked new gifts that are suited for the task or has the task overwhelmed me? Do my closest relationships show a deepening of the fruit of the Spirit? The discernment is confirmed when my decision in the long run harmonizes with the basic paradigm of loving God, which is found in the narrative of Jesus' passion and resurrection.

The dispositions of the Christian, in conclusion, are the places where the identity of being a true disciple is being worked out. From them come a wisdom and an inclination to follow the way of service and justice that Jesus took, even at the cost that he paid for such fidelity. The formal practice of discernment should engender a broader wisdom and deeper perception to recognize the traces of God's presence in daily life. "Finding God in all things" means that one expects not so much to have experiences *of* God as experiences *with* God. The daily fabric of existence becomes transparent to those whose focused intensity on God allows them to appreciate all things in God. This sensibility depends on a fundamental moral orientation toward God and commitment to God's purposes in the world. We now turn to the final dimension of moral psychology, identity, to examine how the character coalesces around the explicit commitment to be a disciple of Jesus Christ.

CHAPTER 8

Identity and the Lord's Supper

I N THIS FINAL CHAPTER we turn to the issue of identity, the most basic aspect of moral psychology. Our actions and relationships flow from who we think we are. Virtue ethics inevitably considers identity, since it asks about character, the integration of life into a relatively coherent unity. Insofar as this integrated self becomes conscious, it forms the identity of the person. Mature people have developed the virtue of integrity: they show the same face to every group. Their conduct reflects their convictions; they do not live compartmentalized lives. Immature people usually have fairly weak and unfocused identities, which are manifested in the vice of irresponsibility. Lacking a core, they are ruled by whim; they cannot be depended on.

First, we will discuss a Christian identity in the light of the biblical accounts that describe the Lord's table. Then we will consider some contemporary insights on identity from virtue ethics and psychology. Finally, we will examine the practices of forgiveness and solidarity as necessary components of Christian worship and identity.

Christian identity is relational rather than individualist. The relevant question is no longer *Who* am I? but *Whose* am I?[1] Christians have been claimed by God and by a community so that their destiny is bound up with others. Becoming a disciple of Jesus Christ changes the individual at the very core of her being. The New Testament's central images speak of this radically altered identity: people are born again, leave all behind to embark on a mysterious journey, pass from death to life, leave the old person behind to be part of the new humanity of Christ. Their individual identity is now bound up with the Master whom they follow as disciples. At the same time, they do not travel this way alone. As members of the local and extended Body of Christ, they use their gifts in concert with specific other people to witness God's love. So the question of Christian identity is also, Who are *we?* Christian spirituality promotes practices that effect and celebrate this passage from one identity to another, namely, the Lord's Supper and its practices of solidarity and forgiveness.

I will argue that the story of Jesus is normative for *who* we are to become as Christians, individually and communally. Here too we use the analogical imagination flexibly in relation to the patterns of the gospel. In each dimension of virtue ethics we have found that patterns derived from the life of Jesus function as norms for the Christian. Paradigms highlight certain features for moral perception to illumine *what* we should pay attention to. Story-based scenarios establish a distinctive set of dispositions that help us know *how* to act and to be. Finally, narrative forms the normative basis of the Christian's personal identity, of *who* we are to be. Committed action integrates these dimensions of moral psychology into character. The Letter to James bluntly warns that "if any are hearers of the word and not doers, they are like those who look at themselves in a mirror; for they look at themselves and, on going away, immediately forget what they were like" (Jas. 1:22–24). We become what we do: if we don't act as Christians, we won't identify ourselves as Christians.

───────────────── CHRISTIAN IDENTITY ─────────────────

The New Testament teaches that identity comes from commitment and identification with others as well as from God's care for each person. Instead of using the modern language of "self" and "identity," it points us in the opposite direction from the path of introspection. It also challenges the belief that identity is established by renouncing all communal ties and identifying with the self.[2] Christian identity comes from identifying with the person, cause, and community of Jesus Christ, which are inseparable. Disciples are committed to the person of the master and those whom he is concerned about; his cause is the reconciliation and healing reality of the reign of God. Belonging to this gracious Lord liberates us from self-centered existence: "We do not live to ourselves, and we do not die to ourselves. If we live, we live to the Lord, and if we die, we die to the Lord; so then, whether we live or whether we die, we are the Lord's" (Rom. 14:7–8). Christians belong to the Lord because he has first identified with them.

The New Testament has a rich vocabulary for following Christ. It portrays individuals as part of some larger relation. They are disciples of Jesus, sons and daughters of God, temples of the Spirit, members of the Body of Christ, a new creation, a royal priesthood, a holy people, friends of the Lord, firstfruits of the new creation, a people set apart, a light to the nations, servants of the Lord, those who have been set free from captivity, the lost who have been found—the list goes on and on. Personal identity, however, is not constituted by assimilation. God's providential knowledge and care for each person mean that each person is recognized, each called by name. That central relation is mediated through the communal relations without being reduced to them. All these terms identify us by what has been done for us, and at the same time each of them has implications for what we should do in response. What God has done for us becomes, through the faithful analogical imagination, the standard for what we should do for others.

Those who belong to Christ ought to feel and act as he does. Paul repeatedly exhorts the converts to "put on the Lord Jesus Christ" (Rom. 13:14). The metaphor derives from the stage: "the metaphor of immersion into Christ is equally close to the actor's total immersion in the character being played on stage."[3] Converts need to take off the old roles and loyalties that run counter to the way of Christ. Other aspects of who they are must now constellate around Christ as the center of gravity. Every social role, personal accomplishment, career, or group membership must conform to the way of Jesus. The primary identification with God in Christ supersedes even the most common terms of self-designation: "As many of you who are baptized into Christ have clothed yourself with Christ. There is no longer Jew or Greek, there is no longer slave or free, there is no longer male or female; for all of you are one in Christ" (Gal. 3:26–28).[4]

───────────── I. THE TABLE OF UNITY AND DISUNITY ─────────────

The Lord's Supper, or Eucharist, is the spiritual practice where this relational identification with Christ is regularly fostered.[5] A common meal signifies shared and sharing life. The bread and wine are shared with others and consumed. This sharing of life enacts and displays what the Body of Christ is in the world. When the New Testament describes this practice, however, there is almost always an undercurrent of disunity. A closer look at these descriptions will illumine worship and community today.

The Lord's Supper forms the paradigm for the community of faith, which is composed of those who share the life and table of Jesus. Their table fellowship echoes the meals of Jesus with sinners and outcasts as well as the climactic Passover meal he celebrated with the Twelve. This meal inaugurates and foreshadows the final messianic banquet at the culmination of history. It gathers

Jesus' followers into the rhythm of his continuous Passover, moving from death to life in the world. Those who identify with that Passover by sharing in the blessed bread and cup become implicated in its dynamics. They are identified with his way of ushering in the reign of God. They eat and drink his life into their own.

Unfortunately, these lofty meanings bear scant resemblance to most worship services this side of the eschaton. The actual gatherings at the Lord's table manifest our disunity and divisions as much as any unity we have in Christ. Denominational fissures, evangelicals quarreling with mainstream churches, fundamentalists who cannot recognize anyone outside their clique as Christian, congregations defined by race, class, ethnic origin, riven by sexual politics—who could imagine that their gatherings celebrate the unity of Christ in the world? I will argue that the scandal of division is entirely appropriate. It runs through the early communities' celebrations of the Lord's Supper, pervades the Gospel accounts of that fateful night, and warrants the practices of forgiveness and solidarity, which are necessary constituents of the practice of Eucharist.

Fractious Congregations: Paul and James

It seems that whenever the early communities gathered for worship their divisions came to the surface. Is this because the authors mentioned only congregations with problems? Though that is part of the story, I believe that Christians were called to the same table precisely to bring our their divisions.

Paul recalls his bitter confrontation with Peter in Antioch in his letter to the Galatians. Peter, "the apostle to the circumcised," initially joined the open meals where the community gathered, meals that presumably included the eucharistic blessing and sharing (Gal. 2:8). There, Jewish followers of Jesus set aside purity laws so they could eat alongside Gentile disciples. When hardliners arrived from Jerusalem, however, Peter "drew back and kept himself separate for fear of the circumcision faction. And the other Jews joined him in this hypocrisy" (Gal. 2:12-13). The hardliners believed that they could not sit at table with the Gentiles until they became fully Jewish. Paul upbraided Peter before the whole assembly in no uncertain terms. Separating from the common table meant severing the common life with the Gentiles Christians. It betrayed the gospel of Christ that grace qualifies people to come to the table, not the works of the law.

The table of unity was also a table of disunity at Corinth. The Jewish-Gentile rift did not divide that community, which was too busy fighting over other issues. The exasperated apostle chides every faction in the community and wonders why they even convene at all "because when you come together it is not for the better but for the worse" (1 Cor. 11:17). Nevertheless, the disputes bring sin and pretension into the open so that the chaff can be separated from the wheat. Divisions of class and wealth become obvious in the assembly in the lack of generosity and solidarity with the poor. Paul concludes from this that their liturgy is a sham. "When you come together, it is not really to eat the Lord's Supper. For when the time comes to eat, each of you goes ahead with your own supper, and one goes hungry and another becomes drunk. . . . Do you show contempt for the church of God and humiliate those who have nothing" (11:21–22)?

When the assembly is riven by dissension, however, they are not commemorating Jesus or receiving his life. Instead, their very "communion" reinforces their divisions. In the language of later theology, their ritual remains a sacrament that "effects what it signifies," only now it effects deadly division rather than the life of Christ. They do not discern the reconciled and reconciling Body of Christ. Paul concludes ominously, "Examine yourselves, and only then eat of the bread and drink of the cup. For all who eat and drink without discerning the body, eat and drink judgment against themselves. For this reason many of you are weak and ill, and some have died" (11:28–30). Absent forgiveness and solidarity with the poor, the banquet of life in Christ has become a ritual that breeds death.[6]

The Letter of James agrees that discrimination shown in the liturgical assembly calls into question the faith of the offenders:

> My brothers and sisters, do you with your acts of favoritism really believe in our glorious Lord Jesus Christ? For if a person with gold rings and in fine clothes comes into your assembly, and if a poor person in dirty clothes also comes in, and if you take notice of the one wearing the fine clothes and say, "Have a seat here, please," while to the one who is poor you say, "Stand there, or "Sit at my feet," have you not made distinctions among yourselves, and become judges with evil thoughts? . . . Has God not chosen the poor in the world to be rich in faith and to be heirs of the kingdom that he has promised to those who love him? But you have dishonored the poor. (Jas. 2:1–6)

Where the poor are discriminated against in favor of the rich, faith has disappeared and so has the Lord's Supper, because the ritual does not foreshadow the messianic banquet of God's reign. Solidarity with the poor is, in the view of Paul and James, not an optional good work that Christians should practice. It is a constitutive practice of the faithful celebration of the Eucharist. The practices of forgiveness to overcome social divisions and solidarity to break down economic barriers are necessary for a community to celebrate the Lord's Supper.

The Lord's Supper in the Gospels

The table fellowship of Jesus' ministry and the accounts of the Lord's Supper manifest the same paradox of unity and disunity. Every Gospel portrays that fateful night as shadowed by betrayal and division. Jesus demonstrates a love that is merciful and reconciling in the face of misunderstanding, enmity, and betrayal. The Lord's Supper not only manifests the return from exile, but forgiveness is extended even in the course of the banquet itself.[7] The earliest Christian liturgical formula of that event, the one that Paul invokes in 1 Corinthians, mentions the counterpoint of betrayal: "the Lord Jesus on the night when he was betrayed took a loaf of bread" (1 Cor. 11:23).

Above all, the love God shows in Christ reconciles, removes the obstacles to unity. Active mercy defines God's love and Jesus' compassion. God's love is tailored to its recipients, who need forgiveness and healing first of all. The meals that Jesus shared during his ministry did not make distinctions. They were subversive because he gathered around him the sinners and outcasts, those who knew they needed a physician (Mark 2:15-17). If there was unity at those meals, it was achieved by surmounting the divisions that were fragmenting the people of Israel. In effect, the meals brought the disunity of Israel out into the open in order to overcome it. What the Temple system and observance of Torah could not accomplish, the open table fellowship of Jesus did. These meals enacted the forgiveness of sins, the welcoming home of the exiled, lost sheep of the house of Israel.[8] Perhaps it was not only Jesus' opponents who were scandalized by this lowering of sacred standards. Were the observant disciples any less troubled by sharing bread with people they would have spent a lifetime avoiding?

The Gospel accounts of the night Christians celebrate as Holy or Maundy Thursday mention the same motifs that characterize Jesus' meals with outcasts, sinners, and prostitutes. This time, however, the misfits whom Jesus reaches out to are his own inner circle of disciples. When Judas is about to leave in order to sell him out, Jesus lets him know that he knows. Jesus says that his betrayer is one who makes the routine, intimate gesture of sharing a common life, dipping bread into the same bowl with Jesus (Mark 14:20). Peter's bravado, echoed by the others, rings a bit hollow to an audience that knows he will soon deny Jesus (Matt. 26:31-35).

Luke couches Jesus' reaction to Judas and Peter in terms of reconciliation rather than judgment. Though he could not dissuade Judas at the table, a few hours later in the garden Jesus keeps speaking the truth to him. He points out again that Judas is trading on intimacy to work betrayal: "Judas, is it with a kiss that you are betraying the Son of Man" (Luke 22:48)? When Peter boasts of singular steadfastness, Jesus prophesies his eventual conversion: "Simon, Simon, listen! Satan has demanded to sift all of you like wheat, but I have prayed for you that your own faith may not fail; and you, when once you have turned back, strengthen your brothers" (Luke 22:31–32). After the supper, all the Synoptics relate how his closest disciples offered no support and slept through his agonized wrestling with God over his impending death. The evangelists underscore what sorts of people Jesus was going to die for.

The New Testament accounts point also to the present assemblies of Christians: they continue to be a reconciling practice in the face of similar attitudes and divisions. Forgiveness and solidarity are not minor aspects of the Eucharist that are dispensed with in a hasty opening penitential rite or in taking up the offering. They are necessary components of the practice of the Lord's Supper. Today's commemorations of the Last Supper must replicate the divine love that convokes them. Christian unity is achieved by reconciliation, not homogenizing. It faces division and does not deny otherness. Mercy does not obscure the truth of judgment because judgment brings sin to the surface in order to heal and forgive. God does not love with a love of appraisal that celebrates the goodness of its objects. God loves with the love of bestowal, which gives them what they have no claim to. When asked for a short definition of worship, theologian Martin Marty replied simply, "Thanksgiving." When Christian liturgies celebrate the divine good taste in self-congratulatory ritual, they are not worship but parody.

Coming together for worship, particularly in the sharing of the Lord's Supper, shapes the identity of Christians. It names our hunger and our need for conversion. We do not only feed ourselves; we are fed by the Lord and we feed others.[9] It pulls us beyond individualism and defensiveness by having us identify with others and acknowledge that God has graciously identified with us in Christ. We come to realize whose we are by the very act of sharing the Lord's Supper. Before considering the practices of forgiveness and solidarity that unite believers in a reconciled community, we need to pause to consider the dynamics of identity and identification.

II. IDENTITY AND IDENTIFICATION

Identity is the conscious shape of character. It refers to the amalgam of interpreted memories, aspirations, relationships, and commitments that we have embraced as the core of who we are. It gives the sense of personal continuity that holds a life together. Many people today do not experience any continuity or core to their lives. They are a series of episodes and accidents that fit no pattern. They may be looking for a self rather than engaged in fashioning one. Personal identity is not innate but is an accomplishment that results from conscious commitments and deliberate fidelity to others. Identity comes from identifying ourselves with persons and values beyond the self.

At first glance, identity seems to be a matter of individual meaning, the person's sense of being an autonomous self. Erik Erikson coined the term "identity crisis" for some hospitalized veterans of World War II who "had through the exigencies of war [and] lost a sense of personal sameness and historical continuity."[10] Because they lacked a sense of personal reality, a vigorous sense of self, their thoughts and motivations were unfocused. They were incapable of initiating projects and sustaining commitments. Erikson detected an analogous condition in late adolescents who are unable to take their place in the world as self-directed individuals. Some young people suffer from "identity diffusion," where they wander aimlessly, drifting from one role to another without any personal focus. Others take the opposite tack and prematurely foreclose an identity by losing themselves in a role. They jump into a "ready-made" identity to resolve their ambiguities once and for all. Others pursue a more promising course by trying out different roles on the way to a more committed existence.[11]

Individual identity eludes direct knowledge because we cannot see it in the mirror. It is not a thing or categorically defined idea. Furthermore, identity always remains a work in progress. New decisions and new ways of interpreting the past can reconfigure identity. Those who expect a clear answer to the question Who am I? are doomed to frustration.

Social Identification

If identity comes from identification, however, we should look to the significant people, roles, commitments, and narratives in our lives. Who and what have we identified with? In moral experience, the significant persons that we identify with set an intuitive standard for us because we want to maintain and deepen those key relations. Others' expectations may be tyrannical, but they need not be. If they are knowledgeable and want the best for us, their expectations can encourage us beyond the ordinary. They can appeal to the very relationship as a norm and inspiration. My wife's mother would say to her daughters, "My girls aren't like that." She did not have to say, "I told you girls not to do that." They knew what she meant; and they knew that was the end of the discussion.

The great photographer Gordon Parks, who worked for *Life* magazine in its heyday, said that his mother was the most important figure in his life because she taught him right from wrong. He also admired his father, a hardworking "dirt farmer" on their meager farm in Kansas. Although his mother died when

Parks was only thirteen, she remains his point of moral reference. Even in his seventies he keeps a picture of his parents on his dresser. "Whenever I have to make a decision," he says, "I look at that picture." It holds him to the values and standards that she personified. She is a point of reference for his own identity and moral character. Not simply an echo of a child's superego, she has become an abiding feature of his adult conscience. We identify with our parents or with those who raised us, even when we reject what they stood for. We identify with them because much of who we are comes from them, genetically, psychologically, and ethically.

Social psychologists have discussed the issue of identity largely in terms of roles. The specific roles that we have define who we are, and the task of identity is to integrate those roles around some consistent personal core. More recent research has pointed out that the roles that count are always connected to significant relationships. The generic role of father and spouse is specified: you are father to these children and husband to this wife. Significantly, your commitment to them makes those roles central in your identity. All the other roles you play—as lawyer, citizen, environmentally concerned activist, and so on—are secondary to being father and husband. Identity combines commitment to a relationship with commitment to a role. Timothy E. O'Connell writes that "the more relationships I have that depend on my being a teacher, the more I am committed to that identity. And the *more important* to me the relationships that depend on my being a teacher, the more committed I am."[12] And the more committed I am to this role, the more likely that I will behave in a way that is consistent with that role.

In Paul's theology, individual calling and social role are integrated in the notion of "charism." God gives everyone a gift to contribute to the common good of the Body of Christ (see 1 Corinthians 12; Rom. 12:3–8; Eph. 4:7–16). The list of these gifts is open-ended, implying that all sorts of talents and occupations can become charisms. Many will be exercised not in ecclesial ministries but in working for justice and healing in the world. The Body of Christ remains immature until all recognize their gifts and work interdependently. No one needs to shoulder every task, because other gifted people can be relied upon. Every gift builds up the community as the embodiment of Christ's love and service; at the same time, the gift configures personal identity. We are called individually by name to fulfill a corporate mission.[13]

The communities that I identify with shape my personal identity in many ways. They define, set limits, and configure personal identity by the ideals they present and the symbols and vocabulary they provide for interpreting life. More vividly, other members of the community show how to live those ideals. A vital community of faith is indispensable in shaping Christian identity. The notion that "you can be a good Christian without going to church" would have been absurd to the writers of the New Testament.[14] Why? Because conscious personal identity almost always has reference to significant other persons with whom we are socially linked. Identity comes from conscious identification with them and with what they represent.

Identification becomes more problematic when we are faced with many competing roles and different groups that we could belong to. We have to choose particular frameworks, communities, and projects. Even if I have been raised in a community with a well-defined tradition or grown into a specific adult role, I will have to ratify those identifications at some point. Most likely I will adopt the tradition selectively, since I will identify with what has value for me. "A person who cares about something, is, as it were, invested in it. He *identifies* himself with what he cares about in the sense that he makes himself vulnerable to losses and susceptible to benefits depending upon whether what he cares about is diminished or enhanced."[15] We constitute our identities not from scratch but by investing in certain sources of meaning so that our destiny is connected to them for better or worse.

Knowing what we stand for also means knowing what we will not stand for.[16] An articulate framework clarifies what we do not identify with. Many basic moral principles, like the second table of the Decalogue, are prohibitions. They contributed to Israel's identity as a people by setting the outer limits of behavior.[17] I know a theoretical physicist who worked for a major research facility during the 1980s. As a Christian, he was increasingly troubled by the prospect of working on high-energy satellite laser weapons for the Reagan administration's Strategic Defense Initiative. He decided to transfer to a project that was working to improve seismic devices that monitored nuclear testing around the world. It was an important vocational decision for him to acknowledge that no matter how exciting and "cutting edge" science the laser research was, it was not something he could do with integrity.

The Common Cause

Identifying with others always implies some common cause. Friends have interests in common; spouses commit themselves to each other in intimate common life. The promises we make to others shape our future to specific goals. Promises coalesce the agent's transient experiences into the personal consistency of selfhood. They also forge the links to others that stabilize personal identity. We trust ourselves or portions of our lives to others, and they entrust themselves in return.[18] At the same time, every cause pulls people together.

Causes always involve companions with whom we have common cause and to whom we are accountable for being faithful to or betraying our common cause.[19] These social bonds breed conscience and sense of integrity. Accountable to others, I become responsible to myself because these social commitments now guide responsible choice and action.

No one can claim the identity of "Christian" without in some way identifying with the message of Jesus. Yet no one can identify with the message of Jesus without identifying with his person and the people he calls to be disciples. If the message of Jesus were primarily about how to act, how to be a good person, the Gospel could be read as good advice. We could identify with it as a plan of life. Jesus would function as a sage, and we could become wise by following his direction and keeping our distance from the unenlightened. The message of Jesus, however, is that God is now claiming us for God's own, that the reign of God is breaking out and pulling us into it. This cause cannot be joined by an individual who will not associate with others in some level of committed community. When we take on a cause as our own, a community always comes with it. There are others loyal to the same cause, and we find ourselves accountable to them as soon as we pledge ourselves to the common cause.

No community ever lives up to the ideal that draws it together. I know someone who was raised in a completely secular environment and in a family that had nothing but contempt for religion. As a sixteen-year-old, he came across the Bible and was fascinated by it. After reading from Genesis to Revelation, he came to two conclusions. First, if this story was true, there had to be a group of people somewhere who was actually living it out. Second, these people would be imperfect, or in biblical terms, "sinners." Eventually he was baptized and, after thirty years of ministry in various Christian communities, he has not had to revise his opinion on either count.

The Common Story

Finally, personal identity is shaped by identifying with the narrative of a community. Every culture and religion has a founding myth that somehow includes the present members of the community. A tradition literally "hands over" its shared meaning to the next generation through stories that convey basic beliefs about the world.[20] A narrative locates people in space and time, often to an ultimate framework. Myths define origin and destiny so that the members of the group can understand where they came from and where they are going. They grasp their personal story within the framework of the larger narrative. When cultures change and diversify, however, no single narrative gets passed down.

Individuals have to choose which narrative makes sense, or they may pick and choose among them. The result is often a kaleidoscopic, shifting identity or a self without clear boundaries or bearings.

Narrative theologians and literary critics have shown that story is the appropriate vehicle for human experience because both unfold over time and through choice and suffering. Human identity seems to require a temporal framework. A blueprint or program will not do; we need some structure with selves at the center who progress through a beginning, middle, and end. In other words, we need a story. No other imaginative device can synthesize our diverse moments of experience into a coherent whole.[21] The analogical imagination is stocked with models, metaphors, scenarios, and roles, but they do not hang together without narrative structures, which supply "the most comprehensive synthetic unity that we can achieve."[22]

Dramas, novels, and films involve us because we see ourselves in them. They travel the universal road from birth to death, center on characters who unfold in unexpected ways as they interact with a succession of persons and events in the developing plot. In the most significant stories we see an image of what our experience is or could become. Part of the experience of religious conversion is to see ourselves as part of a new narrative. No longer spectators or audience, we now identify with it. The words spoken on Sinai are spoken to us as well; the call of the disciples includes us; the cross becomes our destiny as well. The practices of spirituality depend on this imaginative identification with the stories. They may have been presented to us as authoritative, but they gain authority over us when we begin to see ourselves in them. After that, spiritual practices like meditation and Bible reading deepen the experience of participating in the story. We commit ourselves to let the full story of the Gospels become our story too. Narrative theory does not always mention the most persuasive transition: the One who speaks and acts in this story is recognized as speaking and acting in our own.

The story of Jesus is not so overdetermined that we cannot make it our own analogically. Although we are separated from it by time, space, culture, and gender, the path of discipleship still moves from call to cross, from confusion through betrayal to reconciliation for us just as it did for Peter and the others who first walked with Jesus. One cannot fashion a full personal identity around a creed or a set of doctrines, although these are useful synopses of the grand story. Identification with the God who calls us by name is crucial. Christian salvation comes through a particular human story that enables individuals to accept the healing of their fragmentation and betrayals, to see their present as linked with others committed to the future of God's reign, where all will be reconciled in justice, peace, and communion with God.

──────────── III. THE PRACTICE OF EUCHARIST ────────────

The central ritual practice for Christians from the first generation has been the commemoration of the Lord's Supper, or Eucharist. Baptism is necessary for initiation into Christ and the community. Preaching the Word and witnessing through service are also consistent practices of communities of faith. Nevertheless, the regular celebration of the Lord's Supper responds to the dominical command "Do this in remembrance of me," which is enshrined in the most ancient formula of Christian worship (1 Cor. 11:24-26).[23] We have looked at common practices of Christian piety to see their role in moral formation. In this final section we are examining how the regular celebration of the Lord's Supper is a practice that has profound moral implications for the identity and behavior of Christians. Wayne Meeks writes that, along with baptism, the Eucharist meal was a prime occasion of moral formation in the early communities: "Because it was celebrated more frequently than baptism, it provided more occasions on which the implications of that special identity for appropriate modes of behavior could be impressed on the participants."[24]

Contemporary Tensions in Worship

Present-day celebrations of the Lord's Supper have just as many tensions as did those of the early church. Although circumcision and purity laws no longer divide us, we have other issues. Arguments over ordaining women divide some churches, others fight over ordaining homosexuals living in committed, public unions. The socially progressive church members cannot abide the spiritual types, who tend to return the favor. Some prefer unchanging ancient rituals; others push for contemporary language and music. Biblical readings have to be couched in sexually inclusive language in many congregations; others condemn that innovation as tampering with the Word of God. On a given Sunday, a single Catholic church will house English, Spanish, Tagalog, and Korean Masses without one group ever meeting the others.

A more serious threat to the authentic practice of Eucharist comes from treating worship as a means to an end. The practices of Christian piety, just like the practices of friendship, marriage, and art, are often reduced to techniques. That temptation seems nearly irresistible in a therapeutic and consumerist culture. Intercessory prayer can fall into attempts to manipulate God; Bible meditation can seek sentimental satisfaction; discernment can pretend to have a direct line to the Almighty. Not surprisingly, then, assembling for worship can run the same risk. The Lord's Supper has two components, which should prevent it from being reduced to a technique: forgiveness and solidarity with the poor. These parts of the practice move us beyond our own needs.

Initially, we do come to worship to have our needs met—needs for security, fellowship, childrearing, even spirituality. Beginners usually approach practices as though they were techniques. If they commit themselves to worship, service, and prayer, however, they are drawn into the values that are inherent in the practices and begin to do them for their own sake. But if the activity is primarily structured to meet the needs of the customers, its full meaning may never emerge. Using worship to meet my needs will leave those needs unchallenged and untransformed. Eucharistic worship is a practice that reveals its true value only to those who give themselves to it. Committed participation in the Lord's Supper expresses and deepens who we are, whether or not it happens to be entertaining.[25]

Forgiveness

The downside of a relational identity is that we are related to people we do not want to be related to. It means that those I have hurt are still part of my life, and that I am still connected to those who have done wrong to me. The web of human relations is not tailored to include only people we like. The spiritual practice of forgiveness addresses negative relations as Jesus did. Since Jesus himself practiced it at the Last Supper, forgiveness cannot be absent from any eucharistic worship. Not that it ends in church. The community that shares Christian worship enacts forgiveness ritually so that it can perform forgiveness away from the table. The reconciliation of the world with God that Jesus proclaimed in the kingdom is an integral part of the authentic practice of the Eucharist. Every practice has inherent values to it, and these values become the criteria of whether it is being done well. Forgiveness is one of the inherent values in the celebration of the Lord's Supper and in every Christian service. It provides a measure by which we can tell whether the practice is being done well or poorly. Let us take a look at Jesus' mandate to forgive and see how it is enacted in the practices of Christian reconciliation.

Forgiveness holds a central place in the Lord's Prayer. Only one obligation is articulated in the basic Christian prayer: "Forgive us our debts as we also have forgiven out debtors" (Matt. 6:12). The verb "have forgiven" is *aphēkamen*, the perfect tense, which means that the action has taken place prior to the prayer. The perfect can also connote action initiated in the past that continues into the present. This is expressed in the common translation, "as we forgive those who trespass against us." This request sets a fearful standard for God's mercy toward us: we are asking that it follow the pattern of our mercy toward others. To emphasize the point, Matthew editorializes: "For if you forgive others their trespasses, your heavenly Father will also forgive you; but if you do not forgive others, neither will your Father forgive your trespasses" (6:14–15).

Does this mean that we have to fulfill the duty of forgiveness in order to qualify for God's mercy? Then God's forgiveness would be conditional on our compliance with the command to forgive. Matthew explains the proper relation of human and divine forgiveness in the parable of the unforgiving servant in chapter 18. Peter sets it up by asking how many times he has to forgive his brother, up to seven times? This phrase connotes a virtually unlimited number. Jesus responds, "seventy-seven times," or to paraphrase, "Multiply unlimited by unlimited and you will get the right number" (see Matt. 18:22). The parable that follows develops this open-ended requirement. The unforgiving servant is forgiven a staggering amount but demands repayment of a minor amount from his fellow servant. Although the man repeats the same plea he had made to his master, the servant ignores him and throws him into debtor's prison.[26] Hearing of this ruthless act, the master then reverses himself and throws the unforgiving servant into debtor's prison "until he would pay his entire debt," which would be completely impossible (18:34). Again, Matthew drives home the lesson: "So my heavenly Father will also do to every one of you, if you do not forgive your brother or sister from the heart" (18:35).

God's forgiveness is an offer that can be refused. All are debtors to God, but only some accept its remission. Hard-heartedness and resentment toward our equals negates the divine mercy. Those who truly receive God's forgiveness are changed by the gift, they will be merciful to others. If they are not merciful to others, it means they never received the gift of forgiveness—they merely got off the hook. L. Gregory Jones writes that "while repentance and confession are not *conditions* of receiving God's forgiveness, they are indispensable means of acknowledging our *need* for forgiveness and hence embodying that forgiveness in our relations with others."[27]

Forgiveness and the Worshiping Community

The practice of forgiveness imitates and extends God's forgiveness by being proactive. It takes the initiative to remove the barriers that separate people. It does not wait until the offender comes and asks for it. Indeed, in the Sermon on the Mount, Jesus commands us to suspend our rituals of worship in order to first forgive others. "So when you are offering your gift at the altar, if you remember that your brother or sister has something against you, leave your gift there before the altar and go; first be reconciled to your brother or sister, and then come back and offer your gift" (Matt. 5:23–24). It does not say "if you have something against your brother or sister," only "if you remember that your brother and sister have something against you." Note that nothing is mentioned about whether the other's grudge has any basis in fact. This saying traces back to the time before 70 C.E., when the Temple was destroyed. It continued to have meaning for Matthew's audience as they came together. Although they were mostly a Jewish community that had not broken completely from the synagogue, the priority of forgiveness over ritual would have applied to their own assembling for the Lord's Supper. Reconciling, even with those who have unfounded complaints, is a precondition for approaching the Lord's table.

The companion saying in the Sermon on the Mount underscores this initiative to forgive. "Come to terms quickly with your accuser while on the way to court" (Matt. 5:25). The Greek used is *eunoia,* which comes closer to "make friends" with your adversary. Settle at the courthouse door if you can. It does not seem to matter whether the accusation against you is warranted or not. Setting this aside silences the protest of resentment: "I have been wronged and it is someone else's fault." Whose fault it is, who is right and who is wronged, does not matter. Healing the breach is far more important than determining who is at fault.

Christian worship services typically honor this injunction of Matthew by some rite of reconciliation. A prayer of confession and a declaration of forgiveness usually follow the opening hymn in a Protestant service of the Word. Catholic Eucharists begin with a general confession and prayer for mercy or, during Lent and Advent, a ritual of sprinkling blessed water as a sign of the baptismal cleansing from sin. Since the Christian life begins with repentance and God's forgiveness, it is appropriate to open Christian worship in the same way. Some churches formalize the practice of reconciliation in a sacrament where sins are confessed privately, while others favor a communal confession of sin and declaration of God's forgiveness. The latter practice can help keep the community aware of the common need to forgive and be forgiven by others in the community. Reconciliation with God may be "cheap grace" compared to the difficult work of asking forgiveness from a relative or member of the church.

What happens when the other person refuses the offer of reconciliation? People can deny any fault or claim that their racist attitudes or sexist behavior do not matter. Forgiveness cannot be accomplished if offenders deny any need for it. The community of Matthew worked out procedures for reconciliation within the community, later referred to as the practice of "fraternal correction" (see Matt. 18:15–20). If one person's plea is ineffective, then others in the community should become involved. If even this fails, the last resort is separation. Every community has boundaries, and there are times when they need to be invoked to reject behavior that would destroy the community. Some closely knit churches have fairly elaborate practices of fraternal correction that can end in "shunning" and excommunication—always with the hope of eventual reconciliation, as Paul counseled in 1 Corinthians 5. Excommunication is possible in other churches, but people are rarely called to account. Even when it is impossible to remove the obstacles and reconcile, however, Christians are still called to love their enemies and pray for those who persecute them (Matt. 5:44). They will find that it is difficult to hate those they regularly bring before God.

Forgiveness is necessary to sustain any committed love and genuine community life. Christian love does not simply cancel out hatred, but overcomes it while acknowledging its reality. The hatred that alienates us from others is pulled into love by the process of reconciliation.

Sometimes the community itself makes forgiveness necessary. We have to forgive these people for failing to live up to what we expect. There are too few or too many of them; they don't look or act as they ought to; they have the wrong sort of politics; and they are led by people we wouldn't follow anywhere. It will take a good deal of forgiveness for these ordinary Christians to welcome a critic with such high standards, and that critic will have to forgive them. There is no denying the objective limitations of institutional churches and specific communities, but that is not the whole story. Christian community emerges in the journey toward reconciliation, which is never complete this side of the eschaton.

Forgiveness: Reconciliation over Time

Forgiveness is also an integral part of establishing a coherent identity over time. As Bishop Desmond Tutu remarked during the South African Truth and Reconciliation Commission, "Without forgiveness, there is no future." He was referring to the need to acknowledge and forgive those on all sides who had committed crimes during the decades of apartheid. His words are equally true for the lives of communities and individuals. The lack of forgiveness undermines the quest for justice, as is obvious in the intractable ethnic divisions of Bosnia, Kosovo, and the genocide of Rwanda. The future becomes unimaginable when the present has been mortgaged to past grievances and offenses. When the past is burdened with the memory of suffering and ill treatment, it dominates the present with anger, guilt, and resentment. The victim remains defined by the past and fears a future that can only repeat the old wounds. With forgiveness, however, a future becomes possible. It opens us to the healing of God, who is not bound by time. The images of scripture, from the exodus to the cross, point to God's ways of deliverance and new life where it is least expected. Hope does not come as cheap denial of the past; forgiving those who hurt us, whether they are willing to acknowledge their fault or not, makes space for hope.[28]

In order for the present self to make sense out of its past and to direct itself to the future, it needs a community and a truthful narrative, a story large enough to make my own. This task requires a vocabulary and images that can incorporate a past without deceit or denial and produce a future that can sustain faithful commitments. Trust and loyalty help integrate discrete experiences into a unified life, one of grateful memory and realistic hope. They unify the work of memory and interpretation. Trust retrieves the wrongs and slights that we have endured out of the fog of denial. Loyalty directs the self to a worthwhile future in continuity with our promises and the ones we have pledged ourselves to. The celebration of the memory of the Last Supper grounds a life of renewed hope, until we drink from the cup at the messianic banquet.

Solidarity

The second practice of the worshiping assembly that touches on identity is solidarity. Solidarity looks to a broader circle than the practice of forgiveness. I will use the term *solidarity* to refer to the union of compassion and justice that overcomes economic and cultural divisions. It is a different side of reconciliation from the practices of forgiveness, but just as closely related in the life of Jesus and his disciples.

Solidarity challenges any tendency to establish our relational identity by identifying exclusively with a finite community. If we overidentify with one community, even a particular church, we tend to become defensive about rival communities. This misplaced devotion leads to inner division and social defensiveness. When a finite community becomes the exclusive source of value and meaning, a limited portion of reality has been inflated to stand for the whole. That is how idols are made; the loyalty that should be directed to the One God is concentrated on one group. Loyalty that fails to be sufficiently inclusive eventually becomes exclusive. The rights of my group are pitted against the claims of all others. Militant nationalism, racism, and a host of other "evil imaginations of the heart" proceed from defensive loyalties.[29] Over against all parochial enclaves stands the reconciled totality that Jesus called "the reign of God," that is, the world according to God. Solidarity with those outside our circle will counter the defensiveness that crops up even in the best of our commitments.

The term "solidarity" entered current political vocabulary from the banners of the Polish labor movement during the 1980s, which proclaimed *solidarinosc*. The party that emerged played a key role in liberating Poland from Russian communist domination. The movement was cultivated by John Paul II, the Polish pope who repeatedly invoked the term as an alternative to the Marxist "class struggle."[30] He uses solidarity as a combination of justice with compassion, a willing identification with the suffering of others, which takes practical form to rectify the structures of injustice.[31]

> In the light of faith, solidarity seeks to go beyond itself, to take on the *specifically Christian* dimension of total gratuity, forgiveness and reconciliation. One's neighbor is then not only a human being with his or her own rights and a fundamental equality with everyone else, but becomes the *living image* of God the Father, redeemed by the blood of Jesus Christ and placed under the permanent action of the Holy Spirit. One's neighbor must be loved, even if an enemy, with the same love with which the Lord loves him or her.[32]

John Paul II calls for solidarity between the developed countries of the earth and the great masses of struggling and starving people. Even though he has expressed suspicions about aspects of Latin American liberation theology, the pope's notion of solidarity has considerable affinity to their "preferential option for the poor." Both put a human face on the struggle for justice and add an important affective component to it. Both call for a positive identification with those who struggle, not merely support from a distance, but direct engagement that shares the sufferings and joys of the poor. Both condemn the consumer mentality of North America and Europe as the diametric opposite of solidarity.

How is solidarity enacted in the Lord's Supper? It begins with the willing identification of Jesus with the hunger of his disciples, a hunger not only for a meal but for the final liberation to which the Passover seder pointed. Those who share in the life of Jesus are pulled into his mission. They have to feed others, wash their feet, be the servant at table rather than the ones sitting at the head table. These are the obvious implications of the practice of feeding on the blessed bread and cup, which represents the most intimate expression of union with the life of Jesus. Solidarity is better enacted when Christians feed each other from the one bread blessed in Jesus' name. Then they are practically recognizing the hunger of others and doing something about it.

Instead of endlessly debating quite how Jesus is present in the bread and wine (through commemoration, transubstantiation, real presence, etc.) theologians should have paid closer attention to the practice itself. What kind of gift is Jesus making? He is giving his whole self as bread for the life of the world. What does he ask? That his disciples "take and eat." Those who take the blessed bread become his "body for you." By receiving his life they are by that act committing themselves to strive to give themselves, to become bread for the life of the world. Those who drink from the cup enter into the new covenant with him and each other to pour out their own lives in reconciling service. These actions have inescapable moral implications for the practice of the Eucharist, not accidental additions.

Solidarity in the Lord's Supper implies practical solidarity with those who are oppressed. The scandal of rich Christians feasting at the Corinthian gatherings while others went hungry so violated the solidarity intrinsic to the Eucharist that Paul told them they were performing a travesty. The scandal is more subtle in the formalized "communions" of Christian churches today, where no actual meal points out the haves and the have nots. It is also less obvious because many churches who talk about diversity are actually rather homogeneous in terms of race, class, ethnic group, educational level, gender preference, and so on.

Although the first Christian communities had different forms of economic solidarity, the Acts of the Apostles presents an idealized vision of the Jerusalem community: "All who believed were together and had all things in common; they would sell their possessions and goods and distribute the proceeds to all, as any had need" (Acts 2:44–45). The community attracted such a number of the dispossessed, such as widows, that eventually a separate ministry of deacon had to be established to oversee the distribution of goods to them (Acts 6:1–6). The spread of the Way in the great cities of the Roman world was due in no small part to the safety net that the community provided to its needy members.[33]

This sharing of goods stressed solidarity within the community of faith while recognizing a duty to go beyond it. Paul captures the tension in his command, "So then, whenever we have an opportunity, let us work for the good of all, and especially for those of the family of faith" (Gal. 6:10).[34] The community was an *oikos*, an extended family household, which supplanted the patriarchal family, the basic social unit in their world. Christians transferred their allegiance and to some extent their resources to this new unit. What analogous structures would be appropriate in a contemporary postindustrial economy? New "intentional communities" are attempting to update ancient practices of shared goods and the voluntary poverty which religious orders have practiced. However, the dominant individualism of a consumer culture makes it difficult even to raise the question of economic interdependence in most churches.

Solidarity beyond the local community is equally important. Paul labored to get the Gentile communities to support the Jerusalem collection as a sign of the unity of the whole Body of Christ (2 Corinthians 8 and 9). Many local church communities today announce that a fixed percentage of each Sunday's offering is going to local or international charities. The prayers of intercession in the liturgy, usually prayed right before the collection is taken up, stretch the concerns of the community to the needs of the world.[35] Movements like Sanctuary and CISPES for El Salvador relief and the "twinning" of American congregations with poor churches in Mexico and Latin America can help to foster this kind of solidarity. Central to all these projects is the face-to-face involvement with the recipients. Solidarity does not mean checkbook philanthropy, but actual personal contact with others to share their lot. Dana W. Wilbanks, who writes about the Sanctuary Movement, which supported undocumented refugees fleeing persecution in Latin America, states that the most important factor in transforming individuals and church communities is direct involvement with particular people who were refugees and asylum seekers.[36]

A final way of engaging in the practice of solidarity is immersing oneself in a situation of oppression. This may represent a revival of the old practice of Christian pilgrimage, where people left their secure homelands and made arduous journeys to a holy place, often fasting and living celibately in order to express penitence and complete dedication. The travel was often more transformative than any experience at the shrine of destination. In thirteen years of teaching at an ecumenical consortium of seminaries, I noticed that an increasing number of those coming to study for the ministry had spent some time in service to the poor in Latin America and Asia. Instead of journeying to a holy place, they had journeyed with the poor in struggling for justice and peace; they never "arrived" but the arduous and compassionate journey transformed them. Some students and parishioners have been sent as delegates of their local community to work in areas like Chiapas, Cheletenango, San Salvador, and Mindanao. In the United States groups such as the Catholic Worker and programs such as "the urban plunge" immerse middle-class people in the lives of the homeless and street people, often with great impact.[37] These concrete actions of solidarity make the local communities part of the experience of suffering Christians in other cultures as part of the interdependent Body of Christ.

Hospitality to strangers, financial commitments, pilgrimage, the option for the poor: all of these may be necessary practices to prevent the local community from closing in on itself or being unfaithful to their calling. They can also bring the human face to the struggle for justice. The specific practices of solidarity can also disclose the dimension of reconciliation in the practices of justice. The poor and the well-off need to be reconciled at the table of the Lord, both by repentance and by forgiveness. The divisions of the comfortable from the poor may have to be bridged by voluntary divestment and renunciation of both fear and envy.

Christian identity does not come at once through baptism. Paul and the other New Testament writers strove to bring out the implications of the practice of baptism for every day of the Christian's life.[38] Likewise, the practice of celebrating the Lord's Supper in thanksgiving becomes a place where Christian

identity is enacted and rehearsed. The very rhythms of confession and proclamation, taking and eating, are performances. They perform in the liturgical
setting the practices that identify Christians and set the agenda for their performance in the world. The practices of forgiveness and solidarity are integral
to the celebration of the Lord's Supper, as self-renunciation and "walking in the
newness of life" are integral to baptism. The task of preaching and scholarship
is not to use the stories and rituals of faith to motivate Christians to do the right
thing in the world. That would make worship and prayer into techniques for living right. Rather, faithful living is already an inherent part of the practices of
the faith. Those who engage in the practices of intercessory prayer, meditation
on scripture, discernment, baptism, and Eucharist do so in order to deepen
their friendship with God. As they do, they will see that these practices necessarily imply "a life worthy of the gospel." Like Southern Christians who realized
that praying "Our Father" did not fit with segregation, those who share the
Lord's table have to be in solidarity with the hungry of the world or they should
stop coming to the table. Sharing the Lord's Supper commits them to go and
do likewise.

Conclusion

IN THE PRE-VATICAN II CATHOLICISM in which I was raised, the person of Jesus played an important role in devotional life while being largely ignored in Catholic moral theology. Eucharistic piety was complemented by ecclesial devotion to "the Mystical Body of Christ"; the sacraments integrated Christ's saving work into the major events of life; Catholics prayed the Stations of the Cross and focused on Jesus' birth at Christmastide and his passion during Lent. The sanctuary of every parish church was dominated by the crucifix behind the altar, which vividly displayed the crucified body of Jesus. By contrast, moral theology bracketed specifically Christian religious experience; that was relegated to "ascetical" and "mystical" theology. Natural law looked to the "proper end of man" and derived objective moral principles to guide the journey toward human fulfillment. The closest ally of moral theology was not the New Testament but the intricate system of obligations and regulations calibrated in canon law. Catholic moralists showed great skill in resolving the conflicting obligations that created "cases of conscience." However, the discipline of moral theology had become so isolated from its religious roots that the Second Vatican Council singled it out for renewal, calling for moral theologians to pay more attention to the person of Jesus and the biblical roots of the Christian vocation.[1]

The three decades since the council have witnessed a historic renewal of moral theology. The expansion of biblical studies has challenged the discipline to attend to the life and person of Jesus. Unfortunately, his witness has often been cited to illustrate and motivate conclusions that have been arrived at on other moral grounds. Often those moral presuppositions are untouched by the challenge of the gospel. A richer appreciation of the role of Jesus would have been gained from examining the practices of Christian spirituality. These have

185

implications for behavior and community that cannot be ignored. They engage us with Jesus Christ as both the norm and the empowering motivation to live as Christians. These practices have themselves become more attentive to the person of Jesus. New Testament studies, examination of Jesus' social context, and the challenge of feminism and liberation theology have expanded attention beyond his birth and death to encompass the whole story of his life.

The Christian moral life is grounded in the person of Jesus through regular practices that shape the lives of committed believers. I have concentrated on ordinary spiritual practices, mandated by the New Testament, that have always drawn Christians into the life of Christ. Baptism and Eucharist, intercessory prayer, biblical meditation and discernment, forgiveness and solidarity are the ordinary paths by which Christians connect with the person of Jesus Christ. This list should be supplemented by other practices that constitute the Christian way: witnessing to the gospel, nonviolence, serving the needy, living simply so that others may simply live. I have argued that certain spiritual practices make for a specifically Christian way of life. More abstractly, this argument has not been about justification and initial conversion but about sanctification, the gradual development of attitudes, habits, and relationships that are conformed to the Gospel story of Jesus.

Christian ethics aims to have believers take seriously what Jesus took seriously. Too often it has concentrated on moments of decisions and policy-guiding principles. These are necessary components of a workable ethics, but they do not go deep enough. Virtue ethics challenges the discipline of Christian ethics to move to the roots of vision, emotion, and character. Unless we are engaged with the reality of Christ at these levels, specific decisions are unlikely to be appreciated in terms of the gospel. Spiritual practices are the ordinary means by which Christians become engaged with the person of Jesus and learn the wisdom to follow his call. I have not offered summaries of what Jesus took seriously because abstraction does little for engaged appreciation. Love, justice, compassion, gratitude, hope, repentance, and the like gain distinctively Christian content from the particular ways that Jesus spoke and acted. They can too easily drift away from their proper anchorage in the stories of the Gospels and the testimony of faithful communities. Spiritual practices temper the universality of these terms by the concreteness of Jesus' life and manner.

Jesus of Nazareth lived a particular human life that has universal meaning; the analogical imagination recognizes how to be faithful to Jesus in ever new situations. If space allowed, I would have examined how communities of faith instruct, test, and inform the analogical imagination and keep it honest. Unfortunately, such reflection is limited by the fact that our churches only rarely become communities of serious moral discourse and personal challenge. Traditional Christian spiritual practices are accountable to the community, often through particular persons. "Spiritual directors" represent the community's wisdom in many people's path of prayer and discernment. Ministers and pastors are trained to articulate the wisdom of Christian history. Prophetic voices in the community challenge us to repentance and solidarity that we might prefer to ignore. Many of today's rootless New Age spiritual practices are prone to self-deception because they are not accountable to anyone else and lack the critical resources of a tradition.

Finally, the sort of moral formation and reflection proposed here is not primarily an academic enterprise. The New Testament writings should be engaged by specific communities to discern what they call for in their situation. Books about Christian ethics cannot substitute for actual communities who bring the story of Jesus to bear on the pressing needs of their society. Certainly they will need to do their homework to discover what can be done, and should think critically about past experience, moral principles, and consequences. But to spark the analogical imagination, they will need to "put on the mind of Christ" through engaging the story of Jesus. That story is not confined to the canonical text; it continues in their communities today through the presence of the risen Lord and the guidance of the Holy Spirit.

On a recent delegation to Guatemala, a group of us met with the poet and theologian Julia Esquivel. Although from a privileged background, she had committed herself to working to change that deeply divided and oppressed society. Threats from the death squads drove her into exile for many years. She has returned to Guatemala in the aftermath of the 1996 peace accords that ended thirty-four years of conflict. She told us that she can no longer afford to divide the world into rich and poor, left and right, good and evil. Deeply committed to working with the poorest of the poor, she has had to renounce anger and hatred for the privileged class. She meets regularly for Bible study with a group of women that she grew up with. They discuss Matthew's Gospel against the background of the socioeconomic conditions of Jesus' time. After they discussed Herod's slaughter of the innocents, one of the women took her aside and asked, "How did we not know what was going on here? How did we blind ourselves to what was being done in our name?" A community of struggling believers engaging the story of Jesus finds it to be, once again, a word of judgment and grace, the word of life. The Jesus who is present peels away our defenses and calls us to discipleship: "Go and do likewise."

Notes

Introduction

1. See Jon Sobrino, *Spirituality of Liberation: Toward Political Holiness* (Maryknoll, N.Y.: Orbis, 1988), 130. When referring to Jesus, I intend what John P. Meier does: "The object of Christian faith is a living person, Jesus Christ, who fully entered into a true human existence on earth in the first century A.D., but who now lives risen and glorified, forever in the Father's presence. Primarily, Christian faith affirms and adheres to this person—indeed incarnate, crucified, and risen—and only secondarily to ideas and affirmations about him" ("The Historical Jesus: Rethinking Some Concepts," *Theological Studies* 51/1 [1990]: 22).

2. See Franz Bockle, *Fundamental Moral Theology* (New York: Pueblo, 1977), 119.

3. "To the extent that the word of revelation does contain individual precepts of the law of Christ, it probably intends to help people out at those points where they have not yet managed to apprehend moral precepts on their intrinsic grounds. Even if human beings should never manage to dispense with this assistance totally, they should strive to require it as little as possible" (Bruno Schuller, S.J., "A Contribution to the Theological Discussion of Natural Law," in *Readings in Moral Theology, No. 7: Natural Law and Theology*, ed. Charles E. Curran and Richard A. McCormick, S.J. [Mahwah, N.J.: Paulist, 1991], 89).

4. William Wimsatt describes "the concrete universal" as a work of art or literature that presents "an object which in a mysterious and special way is both highly general and highly particular" (*The Verbal Icon: Studies in the Meaning of Poetry* [Lexington, Ky.: University of Kentucky Press, 1954], 71).

5. As the Epistle to the Hebrews states, "In times past, God spoke in fragmentary and varied ways to [us] through the prophets; in this, the final age, God has spoken to us through his son . . . . This Son is the reflection of the Father's glory, the exact representation of the Father's being" (Heb. 1:1–3).

189

6. Confessional claims can have an appropriate validity and truthfulness, even if they are not demonstrable to any observer. See Martin L. Cook, *The Open Circle: Confessional Method in Theology* (Minneapolis: Fortress, 1991).

7. See, for example, the discussions of nonviolence, divorce, abortion, homosexuality, and so on, in Richard B. Hays, *The Moral Vision of the New Testament: A Contemporary Introduction to New Testament Ethics* (San Francisco: HarperCollins, 1996). I agree with Hays that any constructive proposal needs to be tested by its adequacy to the "pragmatic task," but cannot do so in the present volume.

8. See H. Richard Niebuhr, *The Responsible Self: An Essay in Christian Moral Philosophy* (New York: Harper & Row, 1963).

Chapter 1: Ethics and the Word of God

1. Marcus J. Borg, *Jesus, A New Vision: Spirit, Culture, and the Life of Discipleship* (San Francisco: HarperCollins, 1987).

2. John Paul II makes this claim in his encyclical on moral theology, *Veritatis Splendor*, grounding Catholic moral teaching in the response of discipleship as portrayed in the dialogue between Jesus and the rich young man in Matt. 19:16-22 (John Paul II, "The Splendor of Truth," *Origins* 23/18 [October 14, 1993]: 298-334). Unfortunately, he restricts the source of Christ's call to the ecclesiastical "magisterium," which has been invested with the task of continuing the moral teaching of Jesus (see nos. 25-27, 30, and 110). See William C. Spohn, "Morality on the Way of Discipleship: The Use of Scripture in *Veritatis Splendor*," in *Veritatis Splendor: American Responses*, ed. Michael Allsopp (Kansas City, Mo.: Sheed & Ward, 1995), 83-105.

3. Jon Sobrino, *Spirituality of Liberation: Toward Political Holiness* (Maryknoll, N.Y.: Orbis, 1988), 130.

4. See H. Richard Niebuhr, *The Meaning of Revelation* (New York: Macmillan, 1960), 44-54. I agree with Niebuhr that the knowledge of engagement is qualitatively different from the knowledge of the detached observer.

5. See Timothy E. O'Connell, *Making Disciples: A Handbook of Christian Moral Formation* (New York: Crossroad, 1998) for a complementary approach that draws on more psychological and sociological sources than the present volume.

6. Some scholars prefer the term "Hebrew Bible" to "Old Testament." However, the earlier sacred texts also constitute "scripture" for Christians and form part of their Bible and normative identity. The New Testament is unintelligible apart from the history of Israel. Writing as a Christian theologian, I will retain the term "Old Testament."

7. Thomas Ogletree argues that consequential considerations play virtually no role in biblical ethics in *The Use of the Bible in Christian Ethics: A Constructive Essay* (Philadelphia: Fortress, 1983), 15-45. Although it is true that teleological justification of social policy is not prominent in the canon, rewards and punishments are not insignificant—unpalatable though this may be for contemporary ethicists.

8. I will use the terms "virtue ethics" and "character ethics" interchangeably to refer to "the ethics of virtue and character."

9. See John Kekes, *Moral Wisdom and Good Lives* (Ithaca, N.Y.: Cornell University Press, 1995).

10. See the work of Don E. Saliers for holding the balance between moral development and spiritual practices, particularly liturgy and prayer. See, e.g., Saliers, "Liturgy and Ethics: Some New Beginnings," *Journal of Religious Ethics* 7/2 (1979): 173–89; idem, *Worship as Theology: Foretaste of Glory Divine* (Nashville: Abingdon, 1994).

11. See William C. Spohn, "Spirituality and Ethics: Exploring the Connections," *Theological Studies* 58/1 (1997): 109–23.

12. There are of course other concerns of Christian ethics that will not be the focus of this work: developing the connection to common human ethics, analyzing particular moral issues, examining the relation of church and social policies, exploring the logic of justification, and so on.

13. See Sandra M. Schneiders, *The Revelatory Text: Interpreting the New Testament as Sacred Scripture* (San Francisco: HarperSanFrancisco, 1991); J. I. H. McDonald, *Biblical Interpretation and Christian Ethics* (New York: Cambridge University Press, 1993); Anthony C. Thistleton, *New Horizons in Hermeneutics: The Theory and Practice of Transforming Biblical Reading* (Grand Rapids, Mich.: Zondervan, 1992), 621–61 (comprehensive bibliography).

14. Paul Ricoeur, *The Symbolism of Evil* (Boston: Beacon, 1969), 349. See also idem, *Figuring the Sacred: Religion, Narrative, and Imagination* (Minneapolis: Fortress, 1995).

15. Ibid., 19. See Thistleton, *New Horizons in Hermeneutics*, 359, 372 on post-critical naivete.

16. On the need for an engaged exegesis, see Walter Wink, *The Bible in Human Transformation* (Philadelphia: Fortress, 1973).

17. See Bruno Schuller, S.J., "A Contribution to the Theological Discussion of Natural Law," in *Readings in Moral Theology, No. 7: Natural Law and Theology*, ed. Charles E. Curran and Richard A. McCormick, S.J. (New York: Paulist, 1991), 72–98. The position is less restrictively argued in Josef Fuchs, S.J., *Christian Morality: The Word Becomes Flesh* (Washington, D.C.: Georgetown University Press, 1987); idem, *Moral Demands and Personal Obligations* (Washington, D.C.: Georgetown University Press, 1993).

18. See Vincent Macnamara, *Faith and Ethics: Recent Roman Catholicism* (Washington, D.C.: Georgetown University Press, 1985). I agree with Macnamara that one can support a modified form of common human morality or natural law without sealing off moral content from motivation. See also Edward Collins Vacek, S.J., *Love Human and Divine: The Heart of Christian Ethics* (Washington, D.C.: Georgetown University Press, 1994).

19. The literal reading of scripture was complemented by the search for broader meanings: spiritual, allegorical, analogical, mystagogical, and so on. See Robert M. Grant and David Tracy, *A Short History of the Interpretation of the Bible* (Philadelphia: Fortress, 1984); Karlfried Froelich, *Biblical Interpretation in the Early Church* (Philadelphia: Fortress, 1984); D. K. McKim, ed., *A Guide to Contemporary Hermeneutics: Major Trends in Biblical Interpretation* (Grand Rapids, Mich.: Eerdmans, 1986).

20. Tobias Wolff, unpublished lecture, delivered at Herbst Hall in San Francisco on

December 10, 1997, as part of "City Arts and Lectures Series." See Wolff, *This Boy's Life: A Memoir* (New York: Atlantic Monthly Press, 1989); idem, *In Pharaoh's Army: Memories of the Lost War* (New York: Alfred A. Knopf, 1994). See H. Richard Niebuhr's insistence on the need for "internal history" to complement the chronicle of "external history" (*Meaning of Revelation*, 44–54).

21. Schneiders, *Revelatory Text*, 14; also Mark O'Keefe, O.S.B., "Catholic Moral Theology and Christian Spirituality," *New Theology Review* 7/2 (1994): 60–73.

22. See Elisabeth Schüssler Fiorenza, *Bread Not Stone: The Challenge of Feminist Biblical Interpretation* (Boston: Beacon, 1984), xxiii.

23. See Sandra M. Schneiders, "The Bible and Feminism," in *Freeing Theology: The Essentials of Theology in Feminist Perspective*, ed. Catherine Mowry La Cugna (San Francisco: HarperCollins, 1991), 48–49.

24. Walter Wink, "Jesus and the Domination System," in *Society of Biblical Literature 1991 Seminar Papers*, ed. Eugene H. Lovering (Atlanta: Scholars Press, 1991), 266.

25. Ibid., 267.

26. See McDonald, *Biblical Interpretation*; also Elisabeth Schüssler Fiorenza, "The Ethics of Biblical Interpretation: Decentering Biblical Scholarship," *Journal of Biblical Literature* 107/1 (1988): 14–15.

27. See Ben Witherington III, *The Jesus Quest: The Third Search for the Jew of Nazareth*, expanded edition (Downers Grove, Ill.: InterVarsity, 1997), 12.

28. See Bruce C. Birch, *Let Justice Roll Down: The Old Testament, Ethics, and Christian Life* (Louisville, Ky.: Westminster/John Knox, 1991), 21; also John R. Donahue, S.J., "The Challenge of Biblical Renewal to Moral Theology," in *Riding Time Like a River: The Catholic Moral Tradition Since Vatican II*, ed. William J. O'Brien (Washington, D.C.: Georgetown University Press, 1993), 59–80.

29. See Robert W. Funk, Roy W. Hooren, and the Jesus Seminar, *The Five Gospels: The Search for the Authentic Words of Jesus* (New York: Macmillan, 1993). The seminar's theological agenda and procedures are critiqued in Luke Timothy Johnson's *The Real Jesus: The Misguided Quest for the Historical Jesus and the Truth of the Traditional Gospels* (San Francisco: HarperCollins, 1996); and N. T. Wright, *Christian Origins and the Question of God*, Vol. 2, *Jesus and the Victory of God* (Minneapolis: Fortress, 1996), 29–41.

30. For discussion of the various quests, see Raymond E. Brown, S.S., *An Introduction to the New Testament*, Anchor Bible Reference Library (New York: Doubleday, 1996), 817–30; N. T. Wright, "Quest for the Historical Jesus," in *The Anchor Bible Dictionary*, ed. David Noel Freedman (New York: Doubleday, 1992), 3:796–802; Witherington, *Jesus Quest*, 1–41, 233–80; and C. J. den Heyer, *Jesus Matters: 150 Years of Research* (Valley Forge, Penn.: Trinity, 1996).

31. John P. Meier, *A Marginal Jew: Rethinking the Historical Jesus: The Roots of the Problem and the Person*, Vol. 1 (New York: Doubleday, 1991); idem, *A Marginal Jew: Rethinking the Historical Jesus: Mentor, Message, and Miracle*, Vol. 2. (New York: Doubleday, 1994); John Dominic Crossan, *The Historical Jesus: The Life of a Mediterranean Jewish Peasant* (San Francisco: Harper, 1992).

32. See Brown, *Introduction*, 106.

33. See Wright, *Jesus*, 89.

34. The Vatican has taken a similar stance. See Pontifical Biblical Commission, "The Interpretation of the Bible in the Church" *Origins* 23/29 (January 6, 1994): 524; also Donahue, "Challenge of Biblical Renewal," 60–61; and Joel B. Green, ed., *Hearing the New Testament: Strategies for Interpretation* (Grand Rapids, Mich: Eerdmans, 1995).

35. See James H. Charlesworth, "Jesus Research Expands with Chaotic Creativity," in *Images of Jesus Today*, ed. James H. Charlesworth and Walter P. Weaver (Valley Forge, Penn.: Trinity, 1994), 1–41.

36. E. P. Sanders, *Jesus and Judaism* (Philadelphia: Fortress, 1985).

37. For example, Crossan, whose wandering Cynic Jesus seems hardly worth the bother to proclaim, let alone being someone who could sustain a religious tradition for two thousand years.

38. N. T. Wright, *Christian Origins and the Question of God*, Vol. 1, *The New Testament and the People of God* (Minneapolis: Fortress 1992); and Ben F. Meyer, *The Aims of Jesus* (London: SCM, 1979).

39. See James D. G. Dunn, *Christology in the Making: A New Testament Inquiry into the Origins of the Doctrine of the Incarnation*, 2nd ed. (Grand Rapids, Mich.: Eerdmans, 1996); Marinus de Jonge, *Christology in Context: The Earliest Christian Response to Jesus* (Philadelphia: Westminster, 1988).

40. Wright states that the third quest for the historical Jesus is marked by taking the eschatological dimension of Jesus' proclamation and ministry seriously. See Wright, *Jesus*, 83–124.

41. See Rudolf Bultmann, *Jesus and the Word* (New York: Scribner's 1958).

42. See McDonald, *Biblical Interpretation*, 169–99.

43. See the important work of Wayne A. Meeks, especially *The Moral World of the First Christians* (Philadelphia: Westminster, 1986); idem, *The Origins of Christian Morality: The First Two Centuries* (New Haven: Yale University Press, 1993).

44. Lisa Sowle Cahill reviews current literature on the subject in "The New Testament and Ethics: Communities of Social Change," *Interpretation* 44/4 (1990): 383–95. See also Stephen E. Fowl and L. Gregory Jones, *Reading in Communion: Scripture and Ethics in Christian Life* (Grand Rapids, Mich.: Eerdmans, 1991). A good example of contextual criticism is Ched Myers, *Binding the Strong Man: A Political Reading of Mark's Story of Jesus* (Maryknoll, N.Y.: Orbis, 1988).

45. A good example of rediscovering the "world of the text" can be found in Kenneth E. Bailey, *Poet & Peasant and Through Peasant Eyes: A Literary-Cultural Approach to the Parables in Luke*, combined edition (Grand Rapids, Mich.: Eerdmans, 1983).

46. See, e.g., John S. Kloppenborg, "Alms, Debt and Divorce: Jesus' Ethics in their Mediterranean Context," *Toronto Journal of Theology* 6/2 (1990): 178–85; also Gerd Theissen, *Sociology of Early Palestinian Christianity* (Philadelphia: Fortress, 1978); idem, *The Gospels in Context: Social and Political History in the Synoptic Tradition* (Minneapolis: Fortress, 1991); and Sean Freyne, *Galilee, Jesus and the Gospels: Literary Approaches and Historical Investigations* (Philadelphia: Fortress, 1988).

47. David H. Kelsey argues that the terms "canon," "community," and "scripture"

are mutually interdependent (*The Uses of Scripture in Recent Theology* [Philadelphia: Fortress, 1975]).

48. See Brown, *Introduction*, 10–11. A hypothetical textual construct, such as "Q," the source of sayings that Matthew and Luke drew upon, may fascinate scholars, but it does not have the same normative standing as the four Gospels.

49. What is a Christian ethics to do when faced with the seemingly contradictory positions in the canon that cannot be reconciled, such as the attitudes of Romans 13 and Revelation 13 in regard to the state? Richard B. Hays argues that we must choose between these assessments or reject them both (*The Moral Vision of the New Testament: A Contemporary Introduction to New Testament Ethics* [San Francisco: HarperCollins, 1996], 187, 190).

50. Richard B. Hays starts with Paul in *The Moral Vision of the New Testament*.

51. In addition, ethicists almost always appeal to other sources of wisdom and pertinent data besides scripture: tradition, moral philosophy, scientific data, and relevant experience. How much the theologian will rely on each source will depend on the nature of the question and on the audience as well. The question of sources and ways in which theologians select and interpret scripture are addressed in William C. Spohn, *What Are They Saying About Scripture and Ethics?* rev. ed. (New York: Paulist, 1995).

52. I am indebted to Martha Ellen Stortz for this insight.

53. The transformed Paul still was driven, difficult to work with, oversensitive about slights, not crippled by modesty, and a firebrand who could provoke enmity and instigate riots.

54. James D. G. Dunn argues that the Spirit is the mode of the risen Jesus' personal presence to the Christians in *Jesus and the Spirit: A Study of the Religious and Charismatic Experience of Jesus and the First Christians as Reflected in the New Testament* (London: SCM, 1975).

Chapter 2: Virtues, Practices, and Discipleship

1. Lee H. Yearly, "Recent Work on Virtue," *Religious Studies Review* 16 (1990): 2.

2. See Robert Audi, "Responsible Action and Virtuous Character," *Ethics* 101/2 (1991): 304–21; also Jorge Garcia, who maintains that act assessment is more basic than character assessment in morality ("The Primacy of the Virtuous," *Philosophia* 20/1–2 [1990]: 82–85). On the importance of character in ethical method, see John Kekes, *Facing Evil* (Princeton, N.J.: Princeton University Press, 1990).

3. Some problems with virtue ethics are detailed in Julia Annas, *The Morality of Happiness* (New York: Oxford University Press, 1993); see also Pamela Hall, "The Mysteriousness of the Good: Iris Murdoch and Virtue-Ethics," *American Catholic Philosophical Quarterly* 64/3 (1990): 313–29.

4. Alasdair MacIntyre has forcefully argued for the diversity of traditions of virtue in *After Virtue: A Study in Moral Theory* (Notre Dame, Ind.: University of Notre Dame Press, 1981); idem, *Whose Justice? Which Rationality?* (Notre Dame, Ind.: University of Notre Dame Press, 1988). See also John Casey, *Pagan Virtue: An Essay in Ethics* (Oxford:

Clarendon, 1990). For a fuller discussion of virtue ethics in relation to moral theology, see William C. Spohn, "The Recovery of Virtue Ethics, *Theological Studies* 53/1 (1991): 60–75.

5. James M. Gustafson argues that biblical ethics is grounded in the imitation of God: see *Can Ethics Be Christian?* (Chicago: University of Chicago Press, 1975), 92–101.

6. See Gilbert Meilaender, *The Theory and Practice of Virtue* (Notre Dame, Ind.: University of Notre Dame Press, 1984). Philip L. Quinn argues that Aristotle's ethics is incompatible with Christianity in "A Response to Hauerwas: Is Athens Revived Jerusalem Denied?" *Asbury Theological Journal* 45/1 (1990): 49–57. See Stanley Hauerwas and Charles Pinches, *Christians Among the Virtues: Theological Conversations with Ancient and Modern Ethics* (Notre Dame, Ind.: University of Notre Dame Press, 1997).

7. See David W. Haddorff, "Can Character Ethics Have Moral Rules and Principles? Christian Moral Doctrine and Comprehensive Moral Theory," *Horizons* 32/1 (1996): 48–71.

8. Anti-Judaist readings have often used this contrast to denigrate the observance of Torah as merely external or the self-interested religion of "works righteousness." In fact, Jesus is calling on Israel's tradition to challenge its present.

9. See Gustafson, *Can Ethics Be Christian?*

10. Richard B. Hays, *The Moral Vision of the New Testament: A Contemporary Introduction to New Testament Ethics* (San Francisco: HarperSanFrancisco, 1996), 208–9, 293–96.

11. See MacIntyre, *After Virtue,* 116–19, 179–81.

12. "For our struggle is not against enemies of blood and flesh, but against the rulers, the authorities, against the cosmic powers of this present darkness, against the forces of evil in heavenly places. . . . Therefore, take up the whole armor of God, so that you may be able to withstand on that evil day, and having done everything, to stand firm" (Eph. 6:12–13).

13. John Henry Cardinal Newman, *Apologia Pro Vita Sua* (New York: Doubleday, 1962).

14. Wendy Kaminer, "The Last Taboo," *The New Republic,* October 14, 1996.

15. In fact, church membership peaked at 76 percent in 1947 and is now 68 percent; about 40 percent attend church weekly, as reported by Russell Shorto, "Belief by the Numbers," *The New York Times Magazine,* December 7, 1997, pp. 60–61.

16. "Both [the institutional dimension of religion and critical reflection] are sorely neglected in so many developments of spirituality today which tend to be overly subjective to the detriment of more objective and external consideration, as well as preoccupied with pragmatic results. . . . The result, as so many currents in contemporary spirituality manifest, is a highly individualized, indeed privatized approach to the sacred, devoid of any clear sense of belonging to a community, and a lack of a clear sense of critical social responsibility which any authentic awareness of the sacred demands" (Michael Downey, *Understanding Christian Spirituality* [Mahwah, N.J.: Paulist, 1996], 25). For a more historical treatment, see Mark O'Keefe, O.S.B., *Becoming Good, Becoming Holy: On the Relationship of Christian Ethics and Spirituality* (Mahwah, N.J.: Paulist, 1995).

17. See Wade Clark Roof, *A Generation of Seekers: The Spiritual Journeys of the Baby Boom Generation* (San Francisco: HarperSanFrancisco, 1993), especially the bibliography, pp. 269–85.

18. See Robin Maas and Gabriel O'Connell, O.P., eds. *Spiritual Traditions for the Contemporary Church* (Nashville: Abingdon, 1990); and Frank C. Senn, ed., *Protestant Spiritual Traditions* (New York: Paulist, 1986).

19. See Ignacio Goetz, "On the Impossibility of a General Spirituality," *Journal of Humanism and Ethical Religion* 4/1 (1991): 26–40.

20. See Ernst Troeltsch, *The Social Teaching of the Christian Churches*, vol. 2, trans. Olive Wyon (Louisville, Ky.: Westminster/John Knox, 1992), 700–703.

21. Marcus J. Borg, *Meeting Jesus Again for the First Time: The Historical Jesus and the Heart of Contemporary Faith* (San Francisco: HarperSanFrancisco, 1994), 15. See also Dorothee Soelle, *The Window of Vulnerability: A Political Spirituality* (Minneapolis: Fortress, 1990); Emilie M. Townes, *In a Blaze of Glory: Womanist Spirituality as Social Witness* (Nashville: Abingdon, 1995); and Oliver O'Donovan, "Evangelicalism and the Foundations of Ethics," in *Evangelical Anglicans*, ed. R. T. France and A. E. McGrath (London: SPCK, 1993), 96–107.

22. See Downey, *Understanding*, 14, and the various articles in Michael Downey, ed., *The New Dictionary of Catholic Spirituality* (Collegeville, Minn.: Liturgical Press, 1993).

23. Bernard McGinn, John Meyendorff, and Jean Leclerq, eds., *Christian Spirituality: Origins to the Twelfth Century* (New York: Crossroad, 1985), xv–xvi.

24. See Sandra M. Schneiders, "Spirituality in the Academy," *Theological Studies* 50/4 (1989): 676–97. Spirituality is still in the process of being defined as an academic discipline. See Walter H. Principe, "Christian Spirituality," in *The New Dictionary of Catholic Spirituality*, ed. Downey, 931–38.

25. See Sandra M. Schneiders, "Theology and Spirituality: Strangers, Rivals, or Partners?" *Horizons* 13/1 (1986): 253–74.

26. See Martha C. Nussbaum, *Love's Knowledge: Essays on Philosophy and Literature* (New York: Oxford University Press, 1990) 54–105; Owen Flanagan, *Varieties of Moral Personality: Ethics and Psychological Realism* (Cambridge, Mass.: Harvard University Press, 1991); William C. Spohn, "Passions and Principles," *Theological Studies* 52/1 (1991): 69–87.

27. See Bernard McGinn, *Anti-Christ: Two Thousand Years of the Human Fascination with Evil* (San Francisco: HarperSanFrancisco, 1994); also Donna L. Orsuto, "The Saint as Moral Paradigm," in *Spirituality & Morality: Integrating Prayer and Action*, ed. Dennis J. Billy, C.S.S.R., and Donna Lynn Orsuto (Mahwah, N.J.: Paulist, 1996), 127–40. Some liberal virtue theorists allow for a range that runs from cruelty to fairness and tolerance, but that seems a bit constricted compared to many spiritualities; see Judith N. Shklar, *Ordinary Vices* (Cambridge, Mass.: Belknap Press, 1984).

28. On the difficulties of conceptualizing sanctity in a strictly philosophical framework, see Susan Wolf, "Moral Saints," *Journal of Philosophy* 79 (1982): 419–39, and reply by Robert Merrihew Adams, "Saints," *Journal of Philosophy* 81 (1984): 392–401.

29. See Amelie Oksenberg Rorty, "Moral Imperialism vs. Moral Conflict: Con-

flicting Aims of Education," in *Can Virtue Be Taught?* ed. Barbara Darling-Smith (Notre Dame, Ind.: University of Notre Dame Press, 1993) 33-51. I do not believe that every assertion of faith can or should be ruled irrational simply because it cannot be fully translated into religiously neutral language. There are criteria of validity within religious traditions that demand rationality and truthfulness; some of those criteria are shared by nonreligious argumentation. Religious language can be "public"—so long as the "public square" has not been so narrowed as to exclude religious traditions.

30. Some authors connect the roots of morality and spirituality: Daniel C. Maguire cites "a sense of the sheer giftedness and sanctity of life. . . . From this primal awe, moral oughts are born; and from this primal reverence, religion emanates. The moral response pronounces the gift good; the religious response goes on to proclaim it holy" (*The Moral Core of Judaism and Christianity: Reclaiming the Revolution* [Minneapolis: Fortress, 1993], 41).

31. Increasingly theologians are substituting a list of constitutive Christian practices for the traditional "marks of the church" (one, holy, catholic, and apostolic). See Craig Dykstra, "Reconceiving Practice," in *Shifting Boundaries*, ed. Barbara G. Sheeler and Edward Farley (Louisville, Ky.: Westminster/John Knox, 1991), 35-66; and Nancey Murphy, "Using MacIntyre's Method in Christian Ethics," in *Virtues and Practices in the Christian Tradition: Christian Ethics After MacIntyre*, ed. Nancey Murphy, Brad J. Kallenberg, and Mark Theissen Nation (Harrisburg, Penn.: Trinity, 1997), 30-44.

32. See Richard J. Foster, *Celebration of Discipline: The Path to Spiritual Growth*, rev. ed. (San Francisco: HarperCollins, 1988). This Quaker author describes the gradual transformation from a life of self-interest and fear to one that welcomes God's abundance. This transformation is God's work, in which the person cooperates by committed practice of traditional spiritual disciplines. Foster describes four "inward disciplines" (meditation, prayer, fasting, and study); four "outward disciplines" (simplicity, solitude, submission, and service); and finally, four "corporate disciplines" (confession, worship, guidance, and celebration).

33. I will argue that the development of these capacities cannot be the main intention of entering into these spiritual practices; otherwise they would be reduced to techniques that could not produce the desired effect.

34. For a discussion of Aquinas's theory of habits in the context of contemporary psychological and physiological discussions, see G. Simon Hark, S.J., *Virtuous Passions: The Formation of Christian Character* (New York: Paulist, 1993). See also Timothy E. O'Connell, *Making Disciples: A Handbook of Christian Moral Formation* (New York: Crossroad, 1998), 39-53.

35. There are of course other legitimate concerns of Christian ethics that will not be treated in this work: developing the connection to common human ethics, analyzing particular moral issues, examining the relation of church and social policies, exploring the logic of justification, and so on.

36. Spiritual directors have played an important role in guiding Christian transformation since the desert monks of Egypt: see Lawrence S. Cunningham, "Cassian's Hero and Discernment: Some Reflections," in *Finding God in All Things: Essays in Honor of*

Michael J. Buckley, S.J. ed. Michael J. Himes and Stephen J. Pope (New York: Crossroad, 1996), 231–43.

37. Aquinas, for instance, distinguished sharply between virtues that are *acquired* by human effort and those that are *infused* by grace. This preserves divine freedom, but does not explain how grace is both "operative" and "cooperative." See Thomas Aquinas, *Summa Theologiae* I–II 63, 3 and 4, and I–II, 109, 6. See Joseph P. Wawrykow, *God's Grace and Human Action: 'Merit' in the Theology of Thomas Aquinas* (Notre Dame, Ind.: University of Notre Dame Press, 1995). For an integrated account of grace and personal experience, see Edward Collins Vacek, S.J., *Love, Human and Divine: The Heart of Christian Ethics* (Washington, D.C.: Georgetown University Press, 1994).

38. Don E. Saliers, "Liturgy and Ethics: Some New Beginnings," *Journal of Religious Ethics* 7/2 (1979): 173–89. This seminal essay is included in a festschrift honoring Saliers: E. Byron Anderson and Bruce Morrill, S.J., eds., *Liturgy and the Moral Self: Humanity at Full Stretch Before God* (Collegeville, Minn.: Liturgical Press, 1998).

39. Chapter 5 will expand on these distinctions. "Affections" is a term borrowed from Jonathan Edwards and his classic *Treatise on Religious Affections*. See Don E. Saliers, *The Soul in Paraphrase: Prayer and the Religious Affections* (New York: Seabury, 1980), 1–20.

40. See the seminal definition of practices in Alasdair MacIntyre: *After Virtue*, 175. A practice is both related to and distinct from *praxis*, the term often used in liberation theology for social action enhanced by critical reflection. *Practice* is almost always qualified by a definite or indefinite article and refers to a specific habitual activity. See also Dorothy C. Bass, ed., *Practicing Our Faith: A Way of Life for a Searching People* (San Francisco: Josey-Bass, 1997).

41. MacIntyre, *After Virtue*, 175.

42. Aristotle argues this in *Nicomachaean Ethics*, book 8.

43. Craig Dykstra emphasizes the historicity of practices. They cannot be made up on the spot. See his "Reconceiving Practice in Theological Inquiry and Education," in *Virtues and Practices in the Christian Tradition: Christian Ethics After MacIntyre*, ed. Nancey Murphy, Brad J. Kallenberg, and Mark Thiessen Nation (Harrisburg, Penn.: Trinity, 1997), 171.

44. The Christian practice of marriage adds further weight to the prohibition of adultery. See Nancey Murphy, "Using MacIntyre's Method in Christian Ethics," in *Virtues and Practices*, ed. Murphy et al., 39.

45. Lutheran theologian Reinhard Hutter distinguishes an inner circle of practices that constitute community life and an outer circle of practices of witness and service ("The Church as Public: Dogma, Practice, and the Holy Spirit," *Pro Ecclesia* 3/3 [1994]: 352–57).

46. "Unfortunately, much of the modern instrumentalist orientation has deformed christian asceticism, prayer, and piety . . . into techniques rather than the genuine practices they are meant to be" (Matthew Lamb, "Praxis," in *The New Dictionary of Theology*, ed. Joseph A. Komonchak, Mary Collins, and Dermot A. Lane [Collegeville, Minn.: Liturgical Press, 1987], 787).

47. Substituting "parent" for the term that Jesus used, "Abba," has some problems. Parents come gendered, not generic. Granted that masculine imagery for God causes significant problems to many Christians today, using gender-neutral language may not be adequate. Masculine terms need to be balanced by feminine terms for God. In addition, Jesus' image of God may be the corrective that is needed for negative experience of fathers. See Roberta Bondi, "Praying the Lord's Prayer: Truthfulness, Intercessory Prayer, and Formation in Love," in *Liturgy and the Moral Self: Humanity at Full Stretch Before God*, ed. E. Byron Anderson and Bruce Morrell, S.J. (Collegeville, Minn.: Liturgical Press, 1998), 153–67.

48. "Once in, you find that a practice has a certain internal feel and momentum. It is ancient, larger than you are; it weaves you together with other people in doing things that none of us could do alone. But each practice is also ever new, taking fresh form each day as it subtly adapts to find expression in every neighborhood and land" (Craig Dykstra and Dorothy C. Bass, "Times of Yearning, Practices of Faith," in *Practicing Our Faith*, ed. Bass, 7).

49. Saliers, "Liturgy and Ethics," 182–83.

50. See Allen D. Verhey, *The Practices of Piety and the Practice of Medical Ethic: Prayer, Scripture and Medical Ethics* (Grand Rapids, Mich.: Calvin College Publication, 1992), 17.

51. Saliers, "Liturgy and Ethics," 182. Saliers has expanded on this position in *Worship Come to Its Senses* (Nashville: Abingdon, 1996).

52. See Rembert G. Weakland, *Faith and the Human Enterprise: A Post–Vatican II Vision* (Maryknoll, N.Y.: Orbis, 1992).

53. Dykstra and Bass, "Times of Yearning," in *Practicing Our Faith*, ed. Bass, 8.

54. On the normative role of Jesus for Christian practice, see Luke Timothy Johnson, *Faith's Freedom: A Classic Spirituality for Contemporary Christians* (Minneapolis: Fortress, 1990), 28.

Chapter 3: The Analogical Imagination

1. See Michael Walzer, *Exodus and Revolution* (New York: Basic Books, 1985).

2. I take this formulation from David Tracy, *The Analogical Imagination: Christian Theology and the Culture of Pluralism* (New York: Crossroad, 1981), 88.

3. "But if we conceive of imagination as a more broadly based human operation involving intelligence and will as well as sense, imagination in itself can be seen as containing principles of association, judgment and discipline which are called to regulate the play of impressions in a productive fashion" (Philip S. Keane, S.S., *Christian Ethics and Imagination: A Theological Inquiry* [New York: Paulist, 1984], 86).

4. "An analogy in its root meaning is a proportion, and primarily a mathematical ratio, e.g., 2:4::4:X. In such a ratio, given knowledge of three terms, and the nature of the proportionate relation, the value of the fourth term can be determined. Thus analogy is the repetition of the same fundamental pattern in two different contexts" (Dorothy Emmet, *The Nature of Metaphysical Thinking* [New York: St. Martin's, 1945], 6).

5. See Richard B. Hays, "Scripture-Shaped Community: The Problem of Method in New Testament Ethics," *Interpretation* 44/1 (1990): 42–55.

6. See David B. Burrell, "Analogy," in *The New Dictionary of Theology*, ed. Joseph A. Komonchak, Mary Collins, and Dermot A. Lane (Collegeville Minn.: Liturgical Press, 1991), 15; also David Burrell, *Analogy and Philosophical Language* (New Haven: Yale University Press, 1973); J. S. Martin, *Metaphor and Religious Language* (Oxford: Oxford University Press, 1986); and Sallie McFague, *Metaphorical Theology* (New York: Seabury, 1983).

7. William F. Lynch, S.J., "Theology and the Imagination," *Thought* 29/112 (1954): 66. Lynch had a rich career as a classicist, literary critic, journalist, and interpreter of depth psychology. For an overview of his career and thought, see Gerald J. Bednar, *Faith as Imagination: The Contribution of William F. Lynch, S.J.* (Kansas City, Mo.: Sheed & Ward, 1996).

8. See William F. Lynch, *Images of Hope: Imagination as Healer of the Hopeless* (Notre Dame, Ind.: University of Notre Dame Press, 1987), 244.

9. Lynch's work was deeply influenced by his own struggle with mental illness and gradual recovery of hope through psychotherapy. His *Images of Hope* comes directly out of that experience.

10. William F. Lynch, *Christ and Apollo: The Dimensions of the Literary Imagination* (New York: New Modern Library, 1963), 23. This emphasis on the particular has its philosophical antecedents: "To use familiar examples . . . the finite is given metaphysical form in the concept of *haecceitas*, the pure and absolute *thisness*-and-not-thatness which the great Scotus saw in all things; in the 'inscape' which Hopkins, following in Scotus' footsteps, saw in everything; in the single farthing of the Gospel, which is the key to salvation; and in the little, sensible things which were the source of insight for St. Thomas" (ibid., 21).

11. Lynch, *Christ and Apollo*, 37–38.

12. Ibid., 28. His close scrutiny of literature and drama for its theological dimension was sparked by the belief that in the new creation, the life of Christ was beginning to reshape all things along the lines of "the one, single, narrow form of Christ of Nazareth. . . . To think and imagine according to this form is to think and imagine according to a Christic dimension. It would make every dimension Christic. However, like analogy itself, this would not destroy difference but make it emerge even more sharply" (ibid., 183).

13. Lynch, *Christ and Apollo*, 33.

14. See Mark Johnson, *The Moral Imagination: Implications of Cognitive Science for Ethics* (Chicago: University of Chicago Press, 1993), 185–203.

15. Lynch, *Images of Hope*, 246.

16. Tracy, *Analogical Imagination*, 454–55.

17. George Lindbeck criticizes Tracy's position as too individualist and unrelated to actual believing community practices and language (*The Nature of Doctrine* [Philadelphia: Westminster, 1984]). See Tracy's repeated insistence on the importance of community and tradition (e.g., *Analogical Imagination*, 322).

18. See Tracy, *Analogical Imagination*, 408.

19. Quoted in Gustav Niebuhr, "A Current Ring to an Ancient Story," *New York Times*, April 26, 1997.

20. Tracy, *Analogical Imagination*, 386.

21. Jon Sobrino, *Spirituality of Liberation: Toward Political Holiness* (Maryknoll, N.Y.: Orbis, 1988), 130; see also idem, *Jesus the Liberator: A Historical Theological View* (Maryknoll, N.Y.: Orbis, 1993), 36–40.

22. See Garrett Green, *Imagining God: Theology and the Religious Imagination* (San Francisco: Harper & Row, 1989), 73.

23. See Albert R. Jonsen and Stephen Toulmin, *The Abuse of Casuistry: A History of Moral Reasoning* (Berkeley: University of California Press, 1988).

24. For their definition of casuistry as based on paradigms and analogies, see Jonsen and Toulmin, *Abuse of Casuistry*, 41, and 257.

25. See H. Richard Niebuhr, *Meaning of Revelation* (New York: Macmillan, 1960), 113.

26. See the definitions worked out by Green in *Imagining God*; see also Harriet Crabtree, *The Christian Life: Traditional Metaphors and Contemporary Theologies*, Harvard Dissertations in Religion (Minneapolis: Fortress, 1991), 6–20.

27. Green, *Imagining God*, 94.

28. "Reason does not dispense with imagination but seeks to employ apt images and patterns whereby an inscrutable sensation becomes a true symbol of a reality whose other aspects, as anticipated in the image, are available to common experience" (Niebuhr, *Meaning of Revelation*, 71).

29. "Symbol" is sometimes used as an umbrella term for all language that is not literal or conceptual, a usage I will avoid.

30. Stephen Happel, "Symbol," in *The New Dictionary of Theology*, ed. Joseph A. Komonchak, Mary Collins, and Dermot A. Lane (Collegeville, Minn.: Liturgical Press, 1987), 997.

31. Paul Ricouer and Paul Tillich expanded on the religious import of symbols. See the discussion in Anthony C. Thistleton, *New Horizons in Hermeneutics: The Theory and Practice of Transforming Biblical Reading* (Grand Rapids, Mich.: Zondervan, 1992), 576–78.

32. See John B. Rawls, *A Theory of Justice* (Cambridge, Mass.: Harvard University Press, 1971).

33. See Hans Kvalbein, "The Kingdom of God in the Ethics of Jesus," *Studia Theologica: Scandinavian Journal of Theology* 51/1 (1997): 60–84.

34. "These are metaphors insofar as they involve understanding and experiencing a domain of a certain kind (e.g., the social, moral, legal, or religious institution of *marriage*) by means of structures and relations mapped from a domain of a different kind (e.g., a manufactured *physical object*, a *physical bonding process*, or a *physical journey*.)" (Johnson, *Moral Imagination*, 53). Like many others, Johnson uses "metaphor" where it would be more accurate to use "analogy."

35. I am avoiding the commonly used term "paradigm shift" for this change in scientific outlook because its original description by Thomas Kuhn is so confused. See

Kuhn, *The Structure of Scientific Revolutions* (Chicago: University of Chicago Press, 1970).

36. See Sobrino, *Jesus the Liberator*, 93–95.

37. See John R. Donahue, S.J., *The Gospel in Parable: Metaphor, Narrative, and Theology in the Synoptic Gospels* (Philadelphia: Fortress, 1988), 79–85.

38. Bruce Chilton and J. I. H. McDonald, *Jesus and the Ethics of the Kingdom* (Grand Rapids, Mich.: Eerdmans, 1987), 69.

39. Apartheid is an example of an evil imagination of the heart; see Niebuhr, *Meaning of Revelation*, 73.

40. See Freeman A. Dyson, *Weapons and Hope* (New York: Harper & Row, 1984).

41. See Lisa Sowle Cahill, *Love Your Enemies: Discipleship, Pacifism, and Just War Theory* (Minneapolis: Fortress, 1994), 119–48.

42. See H. Richard Niebuhr, *The Kingdom of God in America* (New York: Harper, 1959).

43. Don Lattin, "Baptists Say Wives Must Submit," *San Francisco Chronicle*, June 10, 1998, A 1.

44. See Lisa Sowle Cahill, *Between the Sexes: Foundations for a Christian Ethics of Sexuality* (Philadelphia: Fortress; New York: Paulist, 1985); also Phyllis Trible, *God and the Rhetoric of Sexuality* (Philadelphia: Fortress, 1978).

Chapter 4: Perception

1. See Allen Verhey, *The Great Reversal: Ethics and the New Testament* (Grand Rapids, Mich.: Eerdmans, 1984).

2. This formulation is gratefully taken from James M. Gustafson, *Can Ethics Be Christian?* (Chicago: University of Chicago Press, 1978).

3. N. T. Wright argues that we can discern the preaching of Jesus of Nazareth by moving in a pincer movement from two well-documented historical points. Jesus' understanding of God's reign is transmuted into the different understanding of the early churches through the "middle term" of the actual preaching of Jesus. See Wright, *Jesus and the Victory of God* (Minneapolis: Fortress, 1996), 215–20, vol. 2 of *Christian Origins and the Question of God*.

4. Wright, *Jesus*, 151.

5. There is little consensus on these terms. I am following Bruce Chilton: "In the interest of clarity, 'eschatology' should refer to an anticipation of divine judgment, while 'apocalyptic' should refer to the calendar of the end, as is presented in a literary document that styles itself as an 'apocalypse' (a revelation, the Revelation of John, for example" (*Pure Kingdom: Jesus' Vision of God* [Grand Rapids, Mich.: Eerdmans, 1996], 3); see also idem, "Kingdom of God," in *The Oxford Companion to the Bible*, ed. Bruce M. Metzger and Michael M. Coogan [New York; Oxford University Press, 1993], 408–9).

6. See Chilton, *Pure Kingdom*, 27–31.

7. See Daniel J. Harrington, S.J., "The Gospel According to Mark," in *The New*

Jerome Biblical Commentary, ed. Raymond E. Brown, S.S., Joseph A. Fitzmeyer, S.J., and Roland E. Murphy, O.Carm. (Englewood Cliffs, N.J.: Prentice-Hall, 1990), 623.

8. Wright, *Jesus*, 421.

9. Ibid., 423.

10. See Bruce Chilton and J. I. H. McDonald, *Jesus and the Ethics of the Kingdom* (Grand Rapids, Mich.: Eerdmans, 1987), 17–20, 110–24.

11. See Lisa Sowle Cahill, *Love Your Enemies: Discipleship, Pacifism and Just War Theory* (Minneapolis: Fortress, 1993); see also Richard B. Hays, who categorically rejects violence in defense of justice as a Christian option (*The Moral Vision of the New Testament: A Contemporary Introduction to New Testament Ethics* [San Francisco: Harper, 1996], 317–46).

12. Wright, *Jesus*, 257: "It came down to this: if the story which Jesus was telling by his words and actions was true, the climactic moment in Jewish history had arrived in person, and was behaving in a thoroughly unprincipled manner."

13. See Walter Wink, *Naming the Powers: The Language of Power in the New Testament* (Philadelphia: Fortress, 1984); idem, *Unmasking the Powers: The Invisible Forces That Determine Human Existence* (Philadelphia: Fortress, 1986).

14. See John P. Meier, *The Vision of Matthew* (New York: Paulist, 1979).

15. See Sharon H. Ringe, *Jesus, Liberation, and the Biblical Jubilee* (Philadelphia: Fortress, 1985).

16. See Bradford E. Hinze, "A Prophetic Vision: Eschatology and Ethics," in *The Praxis of Christian Experience*, ed. Robert J. Schreiter, S.PP.S., and Mary Catherine Hilkert, O.P. (San Francisco: Harper & Row, 1989), 131–46.

17. "Realized eschatology" is attributed to C. H. Dodd. See Raymond E. Brown, *The Gospel of John*, 2 vols., Anchor Bible Commentary 29, 29A (Garden City, N.Y.: Doubleday, 1966, 1970).

18. See Albert Schweitzer, *The Quest of the Historical Jesus*, trans. W. Montgomery (London: Black, 1910); Johannes Weiss, *Jesus' Proclamation and the Kingdom of God*, trans. H. Hiers and D. L. Holland (1892; Philadelphia: Fortress, 1971). Marcus J. Borg gives a noneschatological reading of Jesus (*Conflict, Holiness & Politics in the Teachings of Jesus* [New York: Mellen, 1984]).

19. William James, *The Principles of Psychology* (Cambridge, Mass.: Harvard University Press, 1983), 380–81.

20. Gustavo Gutiérrez, *We Drink From Our Own Wells: The Spiritual Journey of a People* (Maryknoll, N.Y.: Orbis, 1985), 35.

21. See Karl Barth, *Church Dogmatics II/2*, ed. G. W. Bromiley and T. F. Torrance (Edinburgh: T & T Clark, 1957), 584.

22. I am using the categories of Arne Johan Vetlesen, *Perception, Empathy and Judgment: An Inquiry into the Preconditions of Moral Performance* (University Park, Penn.: Pennsylvania State University Press, 1994), especially 153–79. See also Charles M. Shelton, *Morality of the Heart: A Psychology for the Christian Moral Life* (New York: Crossroad, 1990).

23. Compassion is an important component of *agapē* in the New Testament, espe-

cially in Luke. See Luke 15:20, where the father of the prodigal son is "filled with compassion" when he sees his returning son even while he is far off. "Compassion is that divine quality which, when present in human beings, enables them to share deeply in the sufferings and needs of others and enables them to move from one world to the other: from the world of helper to the one needing help; from the world of the innocent to that of the sinner" (John Donahue, S.J., *The Gospel in Parable: Metaphor, Narrative, and Theology in the Synoptic Gospels* [Philadelphia: Fortress, 1988], 132).

24. Stephen Post, *Spheres of Love: Toward a New Ethics of the Family* (Dallas: Southern Methodist University Press, 1993), 113. He cites Henry Sigerist, *Civilization and Disease* (Ithaca, N.Y.: Cornell University Press, 1943).

25. Robert Wuthnow, *Acts of Compassion: Caring for Others and Helping Ourselves* (Princeton, N.J.: Princeton University Press, 1991), 161.

26. Martha C. Nussbaum, *Love's Knowledge: Essays in Philosophy and Literature* (New York: Oxford University Press, 1994), 152.

27. Iris Murdoch, *The Sovereignty of Good* (New York: Schocken Books, 1971), 34.

28. Aristotle, *Nicomachean Ethics*, trans. Martin Ostwald (New York: Macmillan, 1962) 1107a 30–33, pp. 44–45.

29. Aristotle, *Nicomachean Ethics*, 1106b 21–23, p. 43.

30. Aristotle compares moral rules to a flexible leaden rule used on the island of Lesbos for measuring uneven surfaces (see *Nicomachean Ethics*, 1137b 30–32).

31. Lawrence A. Blum distinguishes seven steps in moving from a given situation to action based on moral principle (*Moral Perception and Particularity* [New York: Cambridge University Press, 1994], 58–59).

32. "By import, I mean a way in which something can be relevant or of importance to the desires or purposes or aspirations or feelings of a subject; or otherwise put, a property of something whereby it is of non-indifference to a subject" (Charles Taylor, *Philosophical Papers* [Cambridge: Cambridge University Press, 1885], 1:48; discussed in Vetlesen, *Perception*, 167).

33. "According to new psychological approaches to the mind, these appropriate emotions emerge because the good person's past deployments of attention and previous moral decisions ensure a good preconscious self-filtering system in the present" (Sidney Callahan, *In Good Conscience: Reason and Emotion in Moral Decision Making* [San Francisco: HarperSanFrancisco, 1991], 131).

34. See Blum, *Moral Perception*, 46–47; also Martha C. Nussbaum, "The Discernment of Perception: An Aristotelian Conception of Private and Public Rationality," in *Love's Knowledge*, 54–105.

35. Callahan, *Good Conscience*, 14.

36. "My discussion suggests that sympathy and empathy are in a sense not unitary phenomena but, rather, collections of at least somewhat distinct sensitivities to different aspects of other people's well-being (discomfort, physical pain, the hurt of injustice, the hurt of disappointment, and the like)" (Blum, *Moral Perception*, 47).

37. Diana Fritz Cates argues that compassion is learned from the practice of close

friendship (*Choosing to Feel: Virtue, Friendship, and Compassion for Friends* [Notre Dame, Ind.: University of Notre Dame Press, 1997]).

38. Aristotle, *Nicomachean Ethics*, 1143 b 14, p. 167.

39. Nussbaum, *Love's Knowledge*, 95.

40. See Martha C. Nussbaum, *The Fragility of Goodness: Luck and Ethics in Greek Tragedy and Philosophy* (New York: Cambridge University Press, 1986), 304.

Chapter 5: Correcting Perception

1. See H. Richard Niebuhr, *The Responsible Self: An Essay in Christian Moral Philosophy* (New York: Harper & Row, 1963), 149–60.

2. Thomas Ogletree discusses "pre-understandings" in the moral life in *The Use of the Bible in Christian Ethics: A Constructive Essay* (Philadelphia: Fortress, 1983), 15–45.

3. See ibid.

4. Translation by John R. Donahue, S.J., in *The Gospel in Parable: Metaphor, Narrative, and Theology in the Synoptic Gospels* (Philadelphia: Fortress, 1988), 82.

5. Nussbaum has advocated both Greek tragedy and nineteenth-century novels for this expansion of sympathy. See *The Fragility of Goodness: Luck and Ethics in Greek Tragedy and Philosophy* (New York: Cambridge University Press, 1986); eadem, *Love's Knowledge: Essays in Philosophy and Literature* (New York: Oxford University Press, 1994).

6. "It is in the interstices of mutual vulnerability that the experiences of faith, hope, and love have the best chance of taking hold" (Roberto Mangabeira Unger, *Passion: An Essay on Personality* [New York: Macmillan, 1984], 247).

7. Marilyn Friedman, *What Are Friends For? Feminist Perspectives on Personal Relationships and Moral Theory* (Ithaca, N.Y.: Cornell University Press, 1993), 248.

8. Arne Johan Vetlesen, *Perception, Empathy and Judgment: An Inquiry into the Preconditions of Moral Performance* (University Park, Penn.: Pennsylvania State University Press, 1994), 179.

9. See Waldo Beach and H. Richard Niebuhr, *Christian Ethics: Sources of the Living Tradition*, 2nd ed. (New York: John Wiley & Sons, 1973), 237.

10. Augustine, *Sermon* 88.5.5. Cited and expounded in Margaret Miles, "Vision: The Eye of the Body and the Eye of the Mind in Saint Augustine's *De trinitate* and *Confessions*," *Journal of Religion* 63/2 (1983): 125–42. See also Ronald H. Nash, *The Light of the Mind: St. Augustine's Theory of Knowledge* (Lexington: University of Kentucky Press, 1969).

11. A. E. Harvey, *Strenuous Commands: The Ethic of Jesus* (Philadelphia: Trinity, 1990), 163.

12. Virtue ethics has considerably less to say about dramatic reversals and conversions than it does about the regular development of virtuous and vicious habits. It may be a more effective instrument to interpret the habits of Christian sanctification than the more dramatic instances of repentance and conversion. While becoming changed may be the work of "amazing grace," staying changed requires human cooperation and commitment to regular practices and an actual body of Christians.

13. See John R. Donahue, *The Theology and Setting of Discipleship in the Gospel of Mark* (Milwaukee: Marquette University Press, 1983); also R. C. Tannehill, "The Disciples in Mark: The Function of a Narrative Role," *Journal of Religion* 57/4 (1977): 386–405; and Larry W. Hurtado, *Mark*, New International Biblical Commentary (Peabody, Mass.: Hendrikson, 1989)

14. See Jack Dean Kingsbury, *Matthew as Story* (Philadelphia: Fortress, 1988); and M. J. Wilkins, *The Concept of Disciple in Matthew's Gospel* (Leiden: Brill, 1988).

15. See Charles H. Talbert, "Discipleship in Luke-Acts," in *Discipleship in the New Testament*, ed. F. E. Segovia (Philadelphia: Fortress, 1985), 62–75; and Richard N. Longenecker, "Taking Up the Cross Daily: Discipleship in Luke-Acts," in *Patterns of Discipleship in the New Testament*, ed. R. N. Longenecker (Grand Rapids, Mich.: Eerdmans, 1996), 50–76.

16. Communities whose worship centers around a service of the Word rather than the Eucharist obviously share many of the same challenges that came up at Corinth.

17. Marjorie Hewitt Suchocki wrestles with these issues in *In God's Presence: Theological Reflections on Prayer* (St. Louis, Mo.: Chalice, 1996), especially 43–56.

Chapter 6: Emotions and Dispositions

1. "An emotional paradigm, such as the romantic ideal . . . can be likened to a set of blueprints or rules for the construction of behavior. The same rule or prototypic feature, however, can be instantiated in a variety of ways, depending on the person and the situation. . . . At the very minimum, the prototypic features serve as a guide, indicating the kinds of component processes that might be relevant and important" (J. Averill, "The Social Construction of Emotion: With Special Reference to Love," in *The Social Construction of the Person*, ed. Kenneth Gergen and Keith Davis [New York: Springer-Verlag, 1985], 98).

2. As historian Wayne Meeks explains, morality "names a dimension of life, a pervasive and, often, only partly conscious set of value-laden dispositions, inclinations, attitudes, and habits" (*The Origins of Christian Morality: The First Two Centuries* [New Haven: Yale University Press, 1983], 4).

3. See Robert C. Roberts, *Spirituality and Christian Emotions* (Grand Rapids, Mich.: Eerdmans, 1982); idem, "Emotions as Access to Religious Truths," *Faith and Philosophy* 9 (1992): 83–94; Paul R. Noble, "Reason, Religion and the Passions," *Religious Studies* 32 (1996): 513–17; Andrew Tallon, "Religious Belief and the Emotional Life: Faith (Love, and Hope) in the Heart Tradition," in *The Life of Religion*, ed. Stanley M. Harrison and Richard C. Taylor (Boston: Boston University Press, 1986) 17–38; Michael Hoffman, "The Structure and Origin of the Religious Passions," *International Journal for Philosophy of Religion* 8/1 (1977): 36–50; William M. Shea, "Feeling, Religious Symbol and Action," in *The Pedagogy of God's Image*, ed. Robert I. Masson (Chico, Calif.: Scholars Press, 1981), 75–94.

4. Garret Green, *Imagining God: Theology and the Religious Imagination* (San Francisco: Harper & Row, 1989), 107.

5. Don E. Saliers, *The Soul in Paraphrase: Prayer and the Religious Affections* (New York: Seabury, 1980), 36.

6. In a work that concentrates on the Psalms, Patrick D. Miller writes, "Most of the praying recorded and alluded to in Scripture is [in the Old Testament]" (*They Cried to the Lord: The Form and Theology of Biblical Prayer* [Minneapolis: Fortress, 1994] 2). See also Don E. Saliers, "Religious Affections and the Grammar of Prayer," in *Grammar of the Heart*, ed. Richard H. Bell (San Francisco: Harper & Row, 1988), 188–205; James M. Gustafson, *Theology and Christian Ethics* (Philadelphia: Pilgrim Press, 1974), 161–76.

7. Athanasius, "A Letter to Marcelinus," in *Athanasius: The Life of Antony and the Letter to Marcelinus*, trans. Robert C. Gregg, Classics of Western Spirituality (New York: Paulist, 1980), 109. Dietrich Bonhoeffer outlines a similar description of biblical prayer in *Life Together* and *Prayerbook of the Bible*, ed. Geffrey B. Kelly, trans. by Daniel W. Bloesch and James H. Burtness, vol. 5 of *Dietrich Bonhoeffer Works* (Minneapolis: Fortress, 1996), especially 51–66, 158–77.

8. For a detailed analysis of the structure and theology of prayer in the various types of psalms, see Miller, *They Cried to the Lord.*

9. See Gustafson, *Can Ethics Be Christian?* 82–116.

10. See J. David Pleins, *The Psalms: Songs of Tragedy, Hope, and Justice* (Maryknoll, N.Y.: Orbis, 1993), 106–32.

11. Benedict T. Viviano, "The Gospel According to Matthew," in *The New Jerome Biblical Commentary*, ed. Raymond E. Brown, S.S., Joseph A. Fitzmyer, S.J., and Roland E. Murphy, O.Carm. (Englewood Cliffs, N.J.: Prentice-Hall, 1990), 645. John Ashton cautions against giving *Abba* too childlike a connotation ("Abba," in *The Anchor Bible Dictionary*, ed. David Noel Freedman (New York: Doubleday, 1992), 1:7.

12. Miller, *They Cried to the Lord*, 329.

13. "The intent and effect of these petitions is to subordinate all prayer to the will and purpose of God. The starting point of Christian prayer on this model is the prayer for the effecting of God's purpose, not the prayer for our need. . . . Here therefore, Jesus teaches what he clearly practiced at Gethsemane" (Miller, *They Cried to the Lord*, 331).

14. The full story of Israel and Jesus can also reconfigure the meaning of Father and King so that the psychological template of human parents can be altered. Since no one has had a perfect relationship with a father, the experience of God should heal and correct the template that childhood has left us with.

15. See Mark Johnson, *The Body in the Mind: The Bodily Basis of Meaning, Imagination, and Reason* (Chicago: University of Chicago Press, 1987); Robert C. Solomon, *The Passions: The Myth and Nature of Human Emotion* (Notre Dame, Ind.; University of Notre Dame Press, 1983); Johannes A. van der Ven, *Formation of the Moral Self* (Grand Rapids, Mich.: Eerdmans, 1998). Images are not the only factor in the formation of emotions; cognitive psychologists describe how ideas tutor emotions and how combinations of emotions affect each other. See Sidney Callahan, *In Good Conscience: Reason and Emotion in Moral Decision Making* (San Francisco: HarperSanFrancisco, 1991). On the social construction of emotion, see James Averill, *Anger and Aggression* (New York: Springer-Verlag, 1982).

16. See Callahan, *In Good Conscience*, 105.

17. Timothy E. O'Connell, *Making Disciples: A Handbook of Christian Moral Formation* (New York: Crossroad, 1998), 168. See Antonio Damasio, *Descartes' Error* (New York: Putnam's, 1994).

18. Emotions "do not form a natural class," writes Amelie Oksenberg Rorty in *Explaining Emotions*, ed. A. O. Rorty (Berkeley: University of California Press, 1980), 104; see also her "Virtues and Their Vicissitudes," in *Midwest Studies in Philosophy*, Volume 13, *Ethical Theory: Character and Virtue XIII*, ed. Peter A. French, Theodore E. Uehling, Jr., and Howard K. Wettstein (Notre Dame, Ind.: University of Notre Dame Press, 1988), 136–47.

19. See Stanley Hauerwas, *A Community of Character: Toward a Constructive Christian Social Ethic* (Notre Dame, Ind.: University of Notre Dame Press, 1981); idem, *The Peaceable Kingdom: A Primer in Christian Ethics* (Notre Dame, Ind.: University of Notre Dame Press, 1983); also James E. Gilman, "Reenfranchising the Heart: Narrative, Emotions and Contemporary Theology," *Journal of Religion* 74/2 (1994): 218–39.

20. See Willard M. Swartley, ed., *The Love of Enemy and Nonretaliation in the New Testament* (Louisville, Ky.: Westminster/John Knox, 1992).

21. In the Greco-Roman world, the symbolism refers to teachers who lured students by their wisdom and then transformed their lives by education. "Peter will be catching men and women with the bait of God's word and thereby bringing them new life" (Robert J. Karris, O.F.M., "The Gospel According to Luke," in *The New Jerome Biblical Commentary*, ed. Brown et al., 692).

22. N. T. Wright, *Jesus and the Victory of God*, vol. 2 of *Christian Origins and the Question of God* (Philadelphia: Fortress, 1996), 2:301.

23. The initial call of the disciples can be seen as embryonic for the whole Christian life. According to Bonhoeffer, every crucial moment of faith bears the same "cost of discipleship" as the first moment of call. See Dietrich Bonhoeffer, *The Cost of Discipleship* (New York: Simon & Schuster, 1995), especially 86–93.

24. Although some New Testament manuscripts read that the woman was forgiven because she loved much, the sounder reading is that she loves much because she was forgiven so much. That lesson fits the parable of the two debtors, where the greater love was generated by having the greater debt forgiven. See Raymond E. Brown, *An Introduction to the New Testament*, Anchor Bible Reference Library (New York: Doubleday, 1997), 241.

25. See Wright, *Jesus*, 186–96; Marinus de Jonge, *Christology in Context: The Earliest Christian Response to Jesus* (Philadelphia: Westminster, 1988), 206–7; Borg, *Jesus A New Vision: Spirit, Culture, and the Life of Discipleship* (San Francisco: HarperCollins, 1987), 60–71; Edward Schillebeeckx, *Jesus: An Experiment in Christology* (New York: Crossroad, 1991), 180–83.

26. See Wright, *Jesus*, 191.

27. Ibid., 195.

28. See Ched Myers, *Binding the Strong Man: A Political Reading of Mark's Story of Jesus* (Maryknoll, N.Y.: Orbis, 1988).

29. For a scholarly reappropriation of this biblical material, see Walter Wink, *Unmasking the Powers: The Invisible Forces That Determine Human Existence* (Philadelphia: Fortress, 1986); idem, *When the Powers Fall: Reconciliation in the Healing of the Nations* (Minneapolis: Fortress, 1998).

30. See Heinrich Schlier, *Principalities and Powers in the New Testament* (New York: Herder & Herder, 1962).

31. Paul Lauritzen, "Emotions and Religious Ethics," *Journal of Religious Ethics* 16/2 (1988): 321.

32. James M. Gustafson seems to propose that traditional religious symbols can play an important role in religious experience even though they have no referent. It is difficult to see how religious affections could be nourished by symbols that are treated "as if" they referred to something, when we know that they do not. Prayers, hymns, and rituals would ring hollow if they were addressed to an imaginary deity. It seems unlikely that fictional objects could generate the deep senses of piety that Gustafson counts on to inspire and guide moral commitment. See his *Ethics from a Theocentric Perspective* (Chicago: University of Chicago Press, 1983), 1:317-25.

33. See Laurence Freeman, O.S.B., "Meditation," in *New Dictionary of Catholic Spirituality*, ed. Michael Downey (Collegeville, Minn.: Liturgical Press, 1993), 648.

34. Lawrence S. Cunningham and Keith J. Egan, *Christian Spirituality: Themes from the Tradition* (New York: Paulist, 1996), 88.

35. John of the Cross, *The Sayings of Light and Love* 158, in *The Collected Works of John of the Cross*, rev. ed. (Washington, D.C.: Institute of Carmelite Studies, 1964), 97.

36. See Frank C. Senn, ed., *Protestant Spiritual Traditions* (New York: Paulist, 1986); and Robin Maas, "A Simple Way to Pray: Luther's Instructions on the Devotional Use of the Catechism," in *Spiritual Traditions for the Contemporary Church*, ed. Robin Maas and Gabriel O'Donnell, O.P. (Nashville: Abingdon, 1990), 162-70.

37. See Walter Wink, *The Bible in Human Transformation* (Philadelphia: Fortress, 1973).

38. See Anthony C. Thistleton, *New Horizons in Hermeneutics: The Theory and Practice of Transforming Biblical Reading* (Grand Rapids, Mich.: Zondervan, 1992), 143.

39. This participation does not occur in an intellectual vacuum. "For this reason the symbol in biblical texts may remain *primary as a vehicle of power*, but always context-dependent and in this sense *derivative as a vehicle of truth*. It functions on the basis of traditions of interpretation which have been established in the light of critical reflection, including the use of communicative and didactic texts, and narrative texts which offer patterns of personal identification" (Thistleton, *New Horizons in Hermeneutics*, 578). See also Marjorie Hewitt Suchocki, *In God's Presence: Theological Reflections on Prayer* (St. Louis, Mo.: Chalice, 1996).

40. Dietrich Bonhoeffer, *The Way to Freedom* (New York: Harper & Row, 1966), 59.

41. See Martin L. Smith, *The Word is Very Near You: A Guide to Praying with Scripture* (Cambridge, Mass.: Cowley, 1989), 14-29.

42. See John S. Dunne, *The Way of All the Earth: Experiments in Truth and Religion* (New York: Macmillan, 1972), ix-xiii.

43. Ignatius Loyola counseled a person making the *Spiritual Exercises* to insert himself into a Gospel scene as an additional character, for example, as a servant to Joseph and Mary in the cave after the birth of Jesus: "I will make myself a poor, little, and unworthy slave, gazing at them, contemplating them, and serving them in their needs, just as if I were there, with all possible respect and reverence" ("The Spiritual Exercises," in *Ignatius of Loyola*, ed. George E. Ganss, S.J., Classics of Western Spirituality [New York: Paulist, 1991], §114, p. 150).

44. Ronald F. Thiemann uses the painting as an example of what George Lindbeck calls "intratextuality," whereby the believer enters participatively into the story of scripture. See Thiemann, *Revelation and Theology: The Gospel as Narrated Promise* (Notre Dame, Ind.: University of Notre Dame Press, 1985); also discussed in Elizabeth Barnes, *The Story of Discipleship: Christ, Humanity, and Church in Narrative Perspective* (Nashville: Abingdon, 1995), 17–19.

45. *Ignatius of Loyola*, ed. Ganss, §§121–26, p. 153; Paul R. Noble, "Reason, Religion and the Passions" *Religious Studies* 32 (1996): 513–17.

46. Ibid., §327, p. 205.

47. Smith, *Word*, 10.

48. Karl Rahner, whose entire systematic theology of grace is based on God's self-communication, wrote devotional works about contemplation as silent entry into the mystery of God. See Rahner, *Encounters with Silence* (New York: Newman Press, 1960).

49. John of the Cross, *The Dark Night*, in *Collected Works*, trans. Kieran Kavanaugh, O.C.D., and Otilio Rodriguez, O.C.D. (Washington, D.C.: Institute of Carmelite Studies, 1973), 297–329.

Chapter 7: Dispositions and Discernment

1. See Luke Timothy Johnson, *Sharing Possessions: Mandate and Symbol of Faith* (Philadelphia: Fortress, 1981).

2. See "Rules for the Discernment of Spirits," in "Spiritual Exercises," in *Ignatius of Loyola*, ed. George E. Ganss, S.J., Classics of Western Spirituality (New York: Paulist, 1991), 201–14.

3. Jonathan Edwards, *Religious Affections*, ed. John E. Smith, in *The Works of Jonathan Edwards* (New Haven: Yale University Press, 1959), 2:344–45.

4. See Gustavo Gutiérrez, *We Drink from Our Own Wells: The Spiritual Journey of a People* (Maryknoll, N.Y.: Orbis, 1984), 91–135; Jon Sobrino endorses this work of Gutiérrez as the finest expression of Latin American liberation spirituality (*Spirituality of Liberation: Toward Political Holiness* [Maryknoll, N.Y.: Orbis, 1988], 50–79; see also Sobrino, *The Principle of Mercy: Taking the Crucified People from the Cross* [Maryknoll, N.Y.: Orbis, 1994]).

5. Gutiérrez, *We Drink*, 27.

6. Even the great historical theologian Ernst Troeltsch considered that Jesus' moral message was purely private and interpersonal. See Ernst Troeltsch, *The Social Teaching of the Christian Churches*, vol. 1, trans. Olive Wyon (Louisville, Ky.: Westminster/John Knox, 1992), 51–66.

7. See William C. Spohn, *What Are They Saying About Jesus and Ethics?* rev. ed. (New York: Paulist, 1994), 38–55.

8. Paul seems to have been aware of the oral traditions about Jesus and echoes some of their emphases. See James D. G. Dunn, *The Theology of Paul the Apostle* (Grand Rapids, Mich.: Eerdmans, 1998), 650–53.

9. N. T. Wright, *Jesus and the Victory of God*, vol. 2 of *Christian Origins and the Question of God* (Philadelphia: Fortress, 1996), 577. See Richard B. Hays, *The Moral Vision of the New Testament: A Contemporary Introduction to New Testament Ethics* (San Francisco: Harper, 1996), 84–85, 193–204.

10. Linda L. Belleville reviews the literature on this theme in "'Imitate Me, Just As I Imitate Christ': Discipleship in the Corinthian Correspondence," in *Patterns of Discipleship*, ed. Richard N. Longenecker (Grand Rapids, Mich.: Eerdmans, 1996), 120–42.

11. The relations are not reciprocal, since Christ does not imitate the community nor does Paul.

12. For this discussion, it does not matter whether the present New Testament document represents one letter or a compilation of three messages to the Philippians. The parallels between chapters 2 and 3 developed below indicate a unity of theology if not of composition. See Brendan Byrne, "The Letter to the Philippians," in *The New Jerome Biblical Commentary*, ed. Raymond E. Brown, S.S., Joseph A. Fitzmyer, S.J., and Roland E. Murphy, O.Carm. (Englewood Cliffs, N.J.: Prentice-Hall, 1990), 791–92.

13. The verb *politeuesthai* refers to a common pattern of life; it originally meant "to discharge your duties as a citizen." It was in Philippi that Paul was vindicated by disclosing that he was a Roman citizen. See also Phil. 3:20.

14. The contemporary concern over self-esteem was not part of Paul's thinking. Self-sacrifice makes no sense if there is no self in question. Paul presumed a rather robust sense of self in the contentious congregants at Philippi.

15. Dunn, *Theology of Paul*, 281.

16. There has been considerable debate over the question of the "preexistence" of the Christ in this passage. If it refers to an Adamic Christology, the issue of preexistence is moot. See James D. G. Dunn, *Christology in the Making: A New Testament Inquiry into the Origins of the Doctrine of the Incarnation*, 2nd ed. (Grand Rapids, Mich.: Eerdmans, 1989), 113–23; and Raymond E. Brown, *An Introduction to the New Testament*, Anchor Bible Reference Library (New York: Doubleday, 1997), 490–93.

17. "Throughout his whole life, Christ lived out perfectly the demands of human existence before God. Death was not simply the terminal point of his obedience; it was the inevitable consequence of being both fully human and totally obedient in a world alienated from God" (Byrne, "Philippians," in *New Jerome Biblical Commentary*, ed. Brown et al., 795). J. D. G. Dunn writes: "the theme of Christ's 'obedience' in the New Testament always occurs in reference to his suffering and death, and probably always contains an allusion to Adam's act of *disobedience* which brought death to the world" (*Christology in the Making*, 118).

18. Christ did not humble himself in order to be exalted. "In the divine economy of

things one receives by giving, one is served by serving, one finds life by losing one's life, one is exalted by taking the lowly place. The one follows the other as day follows night . . ." (Gerald F. Hawthrone, "The Imitation of Christ: Discipleship in Philippians," in *Patterns of Discipleship*, ed. Longenecker, 163–79). See William S. Kurz, "Kenotic Imitation of Paul and of Christ in Philippians 2 and 3," in *Discipleship in the New Testament*, ed. F. F. Segovia (Philadelphia: Fortress, 1985), 103–26.

19. For similar appeals to the basic pattern of Jesus' life, see 1 Corinthians 11, 2 Corinthians 8 and 9, and Romans 14.

20. Hays, *Moral Vision*, 46. Hays emphasizes Jesus' obedience to the Father to such an extent that the motive of love for fallen humanity is eclipsed in the paradigm of the cross. He argues that love does not figure prominently across the full range of New Testament writings (ibid., 200–203). This reading accords with Hays's implicit acceptance of a deontological model for ethics.

21. Eastern Christianity has paid more attention to the way in which grace unites believers to God. On the rich concept of "theosis," or divinization, see Mark O'Keefe, O.S.B., *Becoming Good, Becoming Holy: On the Relationship of Christian Ethics and Spirituality* (New York: Paulist, 1995), 59–72; also Stanley S. Harakas, *Toward Transfigured Life: The Theoria of Eastern Orthodox Ethics* (Minneapolis: Light and Life, 1983).

22. Karl Rahner, *Spiritual Exercises* (New York: Herder & Herder, 1965), 118. "Ontological" refers to the basic existential makeup of the person. The Christian is alive in Christ, so her very being participates in the reality of Christ.

23. Literally, "*we have grown (into union) with (him).*" The Greek participle is "*symphytoi*, 'grown together,'—as a young branch grafted onto a tree grows together with it and is nourished by it. This bold image expresses the communication of a Christ-life to the Christian" (Joseph A. Fitzmyer, S.J, "The Letter to the Romans," in *New Jerome Biblical Commentary*, ed. Brown et al., 847).

24. "For Christ was raised from the dead not merely to publicize his good news or to confirm his messianic character, but to introduce human beings into a new mode of life and give them a new principle of vital activity, the Spirit" (Fitzmyer, "Romans," 848).

25. Wolfgang Schrage writes that "the dialectic of indicative and imperative is not merely formal. It can be understood correctly only from the perspective of christology" (*The Ethics of the New Testament*, trans. David E. Green [Philadelphia: Fortress, 1988], 171). The imperative makes sense and draws its force from the prior assurance of salvation. See also Victor Paul Furnish, *Theology and Ethics in Paul* (Nashville: Abingdon, 1968), 242–79; Dunn, *Theology of Paul*, 626–31.

26. Dunn, *Theology of Paul*, 486.

27. Dunn argues that the gift of the Spirit was not always identical with the ritual of baptism for the early churches. See *Theology of Paul*, 455–57; idem, *Jesus and the Spirit: A Study of the Religious and Charismatic Experience of Jesus and the First Christians as Reflected in the New Testament* (Grand Rapids, Mich.: Eerdmans, 1997).

28. For the opposite position, see James M. Gustafson, *Ethics from a Theocentric Perspective* (Chicago: University of Chicago Press, 1981), 1:275–79. It seems to me that the

Jesus presented in the New Testament does more than exemplify theocentric piety; he defines it in a distinctive way. See Gustafson's further specification of naturalist piety in *A Sense of the Divine: The Natural Environment from a Theocentric Perspective* (Cleveland: Pilgrim, 1994).

29. See John Mahoney, *Seeking the Spirit: Essays in Moral and Pastoral Theology* (Denville, N.J.: Sheed & Ward, 1981), 63–134; also David Lonsdale, S.J., *Listening to the Music of the Spirit: The Art of Discernment* (Notre Dame, Ind.: Ave Maria, 1992); Jules Toner, *A Commentary on Saint Ignatius' Rules for the Discernment of Spirits: A Guide to the Principles and Practices* (St. Louis, Mo.: Institute of Jesuit Studies, 1982); and Thomas Dubay, *Authenticity: A Biblical Theology of Discernment* (Denville, N.J.: Dimension Books, 1977).

30. See Karl Rahner, "Principles and Prescriptions," in *The Dynamic Element in the Church* (New York: Herder & Herder, 1964), 13–41.

31. Aristotle, *Nicomachean Ethics*, trans. Martin Ostwald (New York: Bobbs-Merrill, 1962) 1106b 21–23, p. 43.

32. See John Henry Newman, *An Essay in Aid of Grammar of Assent* (New York: Doubleday, 1955), 276–83.

33. Edwards, *Religious Affections*, 282.

34. See ibid., 284.

35. Aristotle, *Nicomachean Ethics*, 167, also 285, 291, on practical wisdom. For an account of practical wisdom, virtue, and character in Aristotle, see Nancy Sherman, *The Fabric of Character: Aristotle's Theory of Virtue* (Oxford: Clarendon, 1989). See Thomas Aquinas, *Summa Theologiae* 1–2, 60, 1, reply to second objection; also Mahoney, *Seeking the Spirit*, 65–67, 78–84.

36. "Since this connatural wisdom 'is more excellent than wisdom as an intellectual virtue, [and] since it attains to God more intimately by a kind of union of soul with Him, it is able to direct us not only in contemplation, but also in action'" (Edward Collins Vacek, *Love, Human and Divine: The Heart of Christian Ethics* [Washington, D.C.: Georgetown University Press, 1994], 3). Citing Aquinas, *Summa Theologiae* II-II, 45,2-4: 28, 3: 180, 7; *De Caritate* 6.

37. "God's own Spirit dwelling in our hearts gently, and sometimes forcefully, impels us to desire what God desires, to intend what God intends" (William A. Barry, S.J., *Paying Attention to God: Discernment in Prayer* [Notre Dame, Ind.: Ave Maria, 1990], 59). See also Herbert Alphonso, S.J., "Docility to the Spirit: Discerning the Extraordinary in the Ordinary," in *Spirituality & Morality: Integrating Prayer & Action*, ed. Dennis J. Billy, C.SS.R., and Donna Lynn Orsuto (New York: Paulist, 1996), 112–26.

38. Philip Sheldrake, S.J., *Befriending Our Desires* (Notre Dame, Ind.: Ave Maria, 1994), 102.

39. Jonathan Edwards, *Miscellanies*, vol. 13 of *Works of Jonathan Edwards*, ed. Thomas A. Schafer (New Haven: Yale University Press, 1994), no. 141, pp. 297–98.

40. See O'Keefe, *Becoming Good*, 113–24.

41. See Ignatius, "Spiritual Exercises," in *Ignatius of Loyola*, §183, p. 164.

Chapter 8: Identity and the Lord's Supper

1. I am grateful to Martha Ellen Stortz for this insight. For an extended treatment of these themes, see James B. Nelson, *Moral Nexus: Ethics of Christian Identity and Community* (1971; Louisville, Ky.: Westminster John Knox, 1996).

2. A culture of individualism produces some interesting examples of this conviction, as was reported recently. A woman in Nebraska planned to "exchange vows with herself in front of a mirror and 200 friends and relatives at a ceremony where she will marry herself, in a celebration of the fact that she is 'happy with herself'" (*Newsweek*, June 29, 1998, p. 19).

3. James D. G. Dunn, *The Theology of Paul the Apostle* (Grand Rapids, Mich.: Eerdmans, 1998), 454; see also p. 194.

4. When asked in class by a seminary student whether she was a "Christian feminist," my wife responded that she thinks of herself as a "feminist Christian," since the noun specified the primary term and the adjective its modifier.

5. No theologian has probed the moral implications of the ritual of the Lord's Supper more fruitfully than Don E. Saliers. See his *Worship and Spirituality* (Philadelphia: Westminster, 1984). See also William R. Crockett, *Eucharist: Symbol of Transformation* (New York: Pueblo, 1989); and Monika K. Hellwig, *The Eucharist and the Hunger of the World* (New York: Paulist, 1976).

6. Ironically, this passage has usually been taken as a call to individual self-examination rather than a call to communal conversion. "Not recognizing the body" refers not to having an orthodox sacramental theology but to the dissensions and divisions that were destroying the community.

7. See N. T. Wright, *Jesus and the Victory of God*, vol. 2 of *Christian Origins and the Question of God* (Philadelphia: Fortress, 1996), 557.

8. See ibid., 398, 434.

9. This symbolism is obviously undercut when a single official presider distributes wafers to the laity in a ceremony that does not look remotely like a meal.

10. Erik H. Erikson, *Identity, Youth and Crisis* (New York: W. W. Norton, 1968), 17.

11. See ibid., 87, 89, 157.

12. Timothy E. O'Connell, *Making Disciples: A Handbook of Christian Moral Formation* (New York: Crossroad, 1998), 98.

13. On the historical importance of the Reformation's "affirmation of ordinary life" and Puritan notion of calling, see Charles Taylor, *Sources of the Self: The Making of the Modern Identity* (Cambridge, Mass.: Harvard University Press, 1989), 211–33.

14. According to Dean R. Hoge, 73 percent of American Catholics under the age of thirty-six hold that "one could be a good Catholic without going to Mass" ("Get Ready for the Post-Boomer Catholics," *America*, March 21, 1998, p. 9).

15. H. Frankfurt, *The Importance of What We Care About* (Cambridge: Cambridge University Press, 1988), 83.

16. See Taylor, *Sources of the Self*, 27.

17. On the constructive role of principles in Christian communities, see Stephen E.

Fowl and L. Gregory Jones, *Reading in Communion: Scripture and Ethics in Christian Life* (Grand Rapids, Mich.: Eerdmans, 1991).

18. "Without interpersonal existence of which faith—as exercised in the reciprocities of believing, trusting, and being loyal—is the bond, there might indeed be experience from given moment to given moment but the continuity of the self in its experience would be hard to define, if such continuity would be thinkable" (H. Richard Niebuhr, *Faith on Earth: An Inquiry into the Structure of Human Faith* [New Haven: Yale University Press, 1989], 83).

19. H. Richard Niebuhr develops Josiah Royce's notion that every relation of persons is triadic, involving a common cause (Niebuhr, *The Responsible Self: An Essay in Christian Moral Philosophy* [New York: Harper & Row, 1963]; idem, *Radical Monotheism and Western Culture* [New York: Harper, 1960]).

20. See Frank McConnell, ed., *The Bible and the Narrative Tradition* (New York: Oxford University Press, 1986); Ronald F. Thiemann, *Revelation and Theology: The Gospel as Narrated Promise* (Notre Dame, Ind.: University of Notre Dame Press, 1985); Paul Nelson, *Narrative and Morality: A Theological Inquiry* (University Park, Penn.: Pennsylvania State University Press, 1989); and Garrett Green, ed., *Scriptural Authority and Narrative Interpretation* (Philadelphia: Fortress, 1987).

21. See Mark Johnson, *Moral Imagination: Implications of Cognitive Science for Ethics* (Chicago: University of Chicago Press, 1993), 150–84; idem, *The Body in the Mind: The Bodily Basis of Meaning, Imagination, and Reason* (Chicago: University of Chicago Press, 1987), 170–72; Sidney Callahan, *In Good Conscience: Reason and Emotion in Moral Decision Making* (San Francisco: Harper, 1991), 206–8; Taylor, *Sources of the Self*, 46–52.

22. Johnson, *Moral Imagination*, 170.

23. Some Protestant denominations prefer weekly services of the Word, reserving the Lord's Supper to occasional celebration on the principal feasts. The regular order of service and familiar hymns have a similar ritual rhythm that forms the worshipers. See E. Byron Anderson, "'O for a heart to praise my God': Hymning the Self Before God," in *Liturgy and the Moral Self*, ed. E. Byron Anderson and Bruce T. Morrill (Collegeville, Minn.: Liturgical Press, 1998), 111–25.

24. Wayne A. Meeks, *The Origins of Christian Morality: The First Two Centuries* (New Haven: Yale University Press, 1993), 96, in a chapter fittingly entitled, "The Grammar of Christian Practice" (pp. 91–110).

25. The link between practices and religious identity becomes clear in Ari L. Goldman, *The Search for God at Harvard* (New York: Random House, 1991).

26. See John R. Donahue, S.J., *Speaking in Parable: Metaphor, Narrative, and Theology in the Synoptic Gospels* (Philadelphia: Fortress, 1988), 75.

27. L. Gregory Jones, *Embodying Forgiveness: A Theological Analysis* (Grand Rapids, Mich.: Eerdmans, 1995), 195.

28. See Donald W. Shriver, Jr., *An Ethic for Enemies: Forgiveness in Politics* (New York: Oxford University Press, 1995).

29. H. Richard Niebuhr, *The Meaning of Revelation* (New York: Macmillan, 1960), 72–78. When we confer ultimate loyalty upon finite objects, it leads to the fatal

parochialism which he described in a blend of Jonathan Edwards and Henri Bergson: "Responsive and responsible to each other in our closed societies, we are irresponsible in the larger world that includes us all" (Niebuhr, *Responsible Self*, 138).

30. See Donal Dorr, *Option for the Poor: A Hundred Years of Catholic Social Teaching*, rev. ed. (Maryknoll, N.Y.: Orbis, 1992), 303.

31. "Solidarity helps us to see the 'other'—whether a *person, people, or nation*—not just as some kind of instrument, with a work capacity or physical strength to be exploited at low cost and then discarded when no longer useful, but as our 'neighbor,' a 'helper,' (cf. Gen. 2:18–20) to be made a sharer, on a par with ourselves, in the banquet of life to which we all are equally invited by God" (John Paul II, *Solicitudo Rei Socialis (On Social Concern)*, in *Catholic Social Thought: The Documentary Heritage*, ed. David J. O'Brien and Thomas A. Shannon (Maryknoll, N.Y.: Orbis, 1992), §39, p. 422.

32. Ibid., §40, p. 423.

33. See Meeks, *Origins of Christian Morality*, 106–9.

34. Stephen A. Post argues that the love command aims not at universal treatment of all humans but at a special emphasis on those with whom one shares Christ's life. The obligations of justice that meet basic human needs apply to all persons. See Post, *Spheres of Love: Toward a New Ethics of the Family* (Dallas: Southern Methodist University Press, 1993), 109–28.

35. See Don E. Saliers, *Worship as Theology: Foretaste of Divine Glory* (Nashville: Abingdon, 1994), 126–36.

36. See Dana W. Wilbanks, *Re-Creating America: The Ethics of U.S. Immigration & Refugee Policy in a Christian Perspective* (Nashville: Abingdon, 1996).

37. Roberto Unger writes about such "experiments in vulnerability" that can prevent character from becoming "the frozen self" (*Passion: An Essay on Personality* [New York: Free Press, 1984], 109).

38. Is baptism a practice? Although an individual receives the sacrament of baptism only once, the repetition of the ritual in the life of the community in which the congregation is asked to renew their own baptismal commitments can provide some of the regularity and progressively deeper meaning over time that is required by a spiritual "practice."

Conclusion

1. See *Optatum Totius* in *The Sixteen Documents of Vatican II* (Boston, Mass.: St. Paul Editions, 1965), no. 16, p. 329.

Index of Scripture References

Genesis
2:18 — 71
2:18–20 — 216n. 31

Psalms
1 — 136
1:2 — 136
22:1 — 124
22:24 — 124
35:20 — 136
42 — 134
43:1–4 — 79
91 — 123
91:2–5 — 123
93:1–2 — 79
103:8 — 122

Isaiah
38:14 — 136
40–55 — 77
56 — 80
56:9–12 — 80
57:1–21 — 80

Jeremiah
4:18–19 — 84
7:3–15 — 80
8:13 — 81

Ezekiel
36:22–32 — 125

Matthew
4:17 — 76
4:23 — 76
5–7 — 121
5:23–24 — 177
5:25 — 177
5:39 — 128
5:44 — 179
6:9–13 — 124, 125
6:10 — 117
6:12 — 176
6:14–15 — 177
6:22 — 105
6:32 — 116
6:33 — 116
6:44–45 — 106
7:7–8 — 116
7:11 — 116
7:16–18 — 110
7:16–20 — 31
8:22 — 109
9:17 — 109
10:2–5 — 83
12:28 — 83
13 — 84
13:30 — 84
13:40–43 — 84
14:13 — 137
16:1–3 — 75
18 — 177
18:15–20 — 178
18:22 — 177
18:34 — 177
18:35 — 177
19:12 — 83
19:16–22 — 121, 143
19:27 — 103
19:30 — 103
20:1–16 — 103
20:4 — 104
20:8 — 104
20:14 — 105
20:15 — 105
20:16 — 103
21:12–27 — 80
21:33–45 — 84
22:1–10 — 84
22:1–14 — 84
24:45–51 — 117
25:1–12 — 117
26:31 — 101
26:31–35 — 168
27:46 — 124

Mark
1:14–15 — 76
1:21–28 — 83
1:27 — 132
2 — 82
2:6 — 82
2:7 — 82
2:10 — 82
2:15–17 — 168
3:7–12 — 83
4:1–20 — 80
4:26–29 — 117
5:1–20 — 83
5:24–34 — 132

Mark (*cont.*)

6:5	133
6:5–6	85
7:24–30	132
8:22–10:52	111
8:31	145
8:34	145
8:35	145
10:35–45	101
10:52	111
11	80
11:12–14	80
11:17	80
11:20–22	80
11:28	139
12:50	111
14:20	168

Luke

4:16	128
4:42–43	76
5	128
5:11–12	129
10:25–37	32
10:31–33	89
10:34–35	90
10:36–37	90
10:37	4, 61
11:2–4	124
11:9–13	116
11:20	133
15	67
15:20	204n. 23
15:25–32	135
17:11–19	133
18:1–8	118
19	81
19:9–10	82
19:45–48	80
22:31–32	169
22:48	168
24:13–32	101

John

2:13–22	80
3	83
3:19–21	86

13	51–54, 55, 91
13:1–3	52
13:7	52
13:8	52
13:34	61
13:34–35	52
14:1–11	101
15:4	139
15:15	45
15:17	116
16:23–24	116

Acts of the Apostles

2:44–45	182
16:11–40	
17:28	88

Romans

5:3–5	134
6	147, 149–52
6:4	25, 150
6:5	151
6:6	150
6:10–11	110
6:11	151
7:19	29
8:26–27	46
12:3–8	171
13	194n. 49
13:14	165
14	212n. 19
14:7–8	164
14:17	125

1 Corinthians

5	179
7:31	87
8:9	114
8:11–12	114
11	212n. 19
11:1	146
11:17	167
11:21–22	167
11:23	168
11:24–26	175
11:28–30	167
12	171

13	32
13:1–3	43

2 Corinthians   146

4:11–12	85
8	182, 212n. 19
8:9	32
9	182, 212n. 19

Galatians

2:8	166
2:12–13	166
5:22	30
6:10	182

Ephesians

4:7–16	171
5	70–71
5:21	70–71
6:12	134
6:12–13	195n. 12

Philippians

1:3–11	147
1:27	10, 25, 145, 147
2	57, 147–49
2–3	211n. 12
2:3–4	147
2:5	25, 30, 143, 147
2:6–11	148
3:5–6	24
3:7	24
3:8	148
3:12–14	24
3:17	149
3:20	211n. 13

1 Thessalonians

5:16–18	41

James

2:1–6	167

Revelation

13	194n. 49
14:4	146
19:14	146

Index of Names

Adams, Robert Merrihew, 196n. 28
Ahern, Barnabas, 20
Alphonso, Herbert, 213n. 37
Anderson, E. Byron, 215n. 23
Annas, Julia, 194n. 3
Aquinas, Thomas, 60, 160, 197n. 34, 198n. 37, 213nn. 35, 36
Aristotle, 93, 94, 98, 102, 198n. 42, 204nn. 28, 29, 30, 205n. 38, 213nn. 31, 35
Ashton, John, 207n. 11
Athanasius, 123, 207n. 7
Audi, Robert, 194n. 2
Augustine, 100, 109, 205n. 10
Averill, J., 206n. 1, 207n. 15

Bailey, Kenneth E., 193n. 45
Barnes, Elizabeth Story, 210n. 44
Barry, William A., 213n. 37
Barth, Karl, 60, 88, 203n. 21
Bass, Dorothy C., 198n. 40, 199nn. 48, 53
Beach, Waldo, 205n. 9
Bednar, Gerald J., 200n. 7
Belleville, Linda L., 211n. 10
Bergson, Henri, 216n. 29
Birch, Bruce C., 192n. 28
Blum, Lawrence A., 204nn. 31, 34, 36
Bockle, Franz, 189n. 2
Bondi, Roberta, 199n. 47
Bonhoeffer, Dietrich, 137, 207n. 7, 208n. 23, 209n. 40

Borg, Marcus J., 9, 21, 36, 190n. 1, 196n. 21, 203n. 18, 208n. 25
Brown, Raymond E., 19, 192nn. 30, 32, 194n. 48, 203n. 17, 208n. 24, 211n. 16
Bultmann, Rudolf, 21, 60, 193n. 40
Burrell, David B., 200n. 6
Byrne, Brendan, 211nn. 12, 17

Cahill, Lisa Sowle, 193n. 44, 202nn. 41, 44, 203n. 11
Callahan, Sidney, 204nn. 33, 35, 207n. 15, 208n. 16, 215n. 21
Casey, John, 194n. 4
Cates, Diana Fritz, 204n. 37
Charlesworth, James H., 193n. 35
Chilton, Bruce, 202nn. 5, 6, 38, 203n. 10
Cook, Martin L., 190n. 6
Crabtree, Harriet, 201n. 26
Crockett, William R., 214n. 5
Crossan, John Dominic, 19, 192n. 31, 193n. 37
Cunningham, Lawrence S., 197n. 36, 209n. 34

Damasio, Antonio, 126, 208n. 17
Day, Dorothy, 65
de Jonge, Marinus, 21, 193n. 39, 208n. 25
den Heyer, C. J., 192n. 30
Dodd, C. H., 203n. 17
Donahue, John R., 192n. 28, 193n. 34, 202n. 37, 204n. 23, 205n. 4, 206n. 13, 215n. 26

Dorr, Donal, 216n. 30
Downey, Michael, 195n. 16, 196n. 22
Dubay, Thomas, 213n. 29
Dunn, James D. G., 21, 193n. 39, 194n.
    54, 211nn. 8, 15, 16, 17, 212nn. 25, 26,
    27, 214n. 3
Dunne, John S., 209n. 42
Dykstra, Craig, 197n. 31, 198n. 43, 199nn.
    48, 53
Dyson, Freeman A., 202n. 40

Edwards, Jonathan, 144, 159, 161, 198n.
    39, 210n. 3, 213nn. 33, 34, 39, 216n.
    29
Egan, Keith J., 209n. 34
Einstein, Albert, 66
Emmet, Dorothy, 199n. 4
Erikson, Erik H., 170, 214nn. 10, 11
Esquivel, Julia, 187

Fitzmyer, Joseph A., 212nn. 23, 24
Flanagan, Owen, 196n. 26
Foster, Richard J., 197n. 32
Fowl, Stephen E., 193n. 44, 214n. 17
Frankfurt, H., 214n. 15
Freeman, Lawrence, 209n. 33
Freyne, Sean, 193n. 46
Friedman, Marilyn, 108, 205n. 7
Froelich, Karlfried, 191n. 19
Fuchs, Josef, 191n. 17
Funk, Robert W., 192n. 29
Furnish, Victor Paul, 212n. 25

Garcia, Jorge, 194n. 2
Gilkey, Langdon, 40
Gilman, James E., 208n. 19
Goetz, Ignacio, 196n. 19
Goldman, Ari L., 215n. 25
Grant, Robert M., 191n. 19
Green, Garret, 122, 201nn. 22, 26, 27,
    206n. 4, 215n. 20
Green, Joel B., 193n. 34
Gustafson, James M., 31, 195nn. 5, 9,
    202n. 2, 206nn. 6, 9, 209n. 32, 212n.
    28
Gutiérrez, Gustavo, 88, 144, 203n. 20,
    209nn. 4, 5

Haddorff, David W., 195n. 7
Hall, Pamela, 194n. 3
Happel, Stephen, 201n. 30
Harakas, Stanley S., 212n. 21
Hark, G. Simon, 197n. 34
Harrington, Daniel J., 202n. 7
Harvey, A. E., 109, 205n. 11
Hauerwas, Stanley, 128, 195n. 6, 208n. 19
Hawthorne, Gerald F., 212n. 18
Hays, Richard B., 23, 32, 149, 190n. 7,
    194nn. 49, 50, 195n. 10, 200n. 5,
    203n. 11, 211n. 9, 212n. 20
Heisenberg, W., 67
Hellwig, Monika K., 214n. 5
Hinze, Bradford E., 203n. 16
Hoffman, Michael, 206n. 3
Hoge, Dean R., 214n. 14
Hooren, Roy W., 192n. 29
Hurtado, Larry W., 206n. 13
Hutter, Reinhard, 198n. 45

Ignatius Loyola, 139, 156, 210nn. 2, 43,
    213n. 41

James, William, 88, 203n. 19
John of the Cross, 137, 139, 140, 209n. 35,
    210n. 49
John Paul II (pope), 52, 181, 190n. 2, 216n.
    31
Johnson, Luke Timothy, 192n. 29, 199n.
    54, 210n. 1
Johnson, Mark, 200n. 14, 201n. 34, 207n.
    15, 215nn. 21, 22
Jones, L. Gregory, 177, 193n. 44, 215nn.
    17, 27
Jonsen, Albert R., 201nn. 23, 24
Josephus, 21

Kaminer, Wendy, 195n. 14
Kant, Immanuel, 61
Karris, Robert J., 208n. 21
Keane, Philip S., 199n. 3
Kekes, John, 191n. 9, 194n. 2
Kelsey, David H., 193n. 47
Kierkegaard, Søren, 60
Kingsbury, Jack Dean, 206n. 14
Kloppenborg, John S., 193n. 46

Kuhn, Thomas, 201n. 35
Kurz, William S., 212n. 18
Kvalbein, Hans, 201n. 33

Lamb, Matthew, 198n. 46
Lattin, Don, 202n. 43
Lauritzen, Paul, 135, 209n. 31
Leclercq, Jean, 196n. 23
Lindbeck, George, 200n. 17, 210n. 44
Longenecker, Richard N., 206n. 15
Lonsdale, David, 213n. 29
Luther, Martin, 109
Lynch, William F., 56-60, 124, 200nn. 7, 8, 9, 10, 11, 12, 13, 15

Maas, Robin, 196n. 18, 209n. 36
MacIntyre, Alasdair, 43, 128, 194n. 4, 195n. 11, 198nn. 40, 41
Macnamara, Vincent, 191n. 18
Maguire, Daniel C., 197n. 30
Mahoney, John, 213nn. 29, 35
Marcel, Gabriel, 155
Martin, J. S., 200n. 6
Maurin, Peter, 65
McConnell, Frank, 215n. 20
McDonald, J. I. H., 191n. 13, 192n. 26, 193n. 42, 203n. 10
McFague, Sallie, 200n. 6
McGinn, Bernard, 36, 196nn. 23, 27
McKim, D. K., 191n. 19
Meeks, Wayne A., 175, 193n. 43, 206n. 2, 215n. 24, 216n. 33
Meier, John P., 19, 21, 189n. 1, 192n. 31, 203n. 14
Meilaender, Gilbert, 195n. 6
Merton, Thomas, 156
Meyendorff, John, 196n. 23
Meyer, Ben F., 21, 193n. 38
Miles, Margaret, 205n. 10
Miller, Patrick D., 207nn. 6, 8, 12
Murdoch, Iris, 92, 204n. 27
Murphy, Nancey, 197n. 31, 198n. 44
Myers, Ched, 193n. 44, 208n. 28

Nash, Ronald H., 205n. 10
Nelson, James B., 214n. 1
Nelson, Paul, 215n. 20

Newman, John Henry Cardinal, 33, 195n. 13, 213n. 32
Newton, Isaac, 66
Niebuhr, Gustav, 201n. 19
Niebuhr, H. Richard, 3, 190nn. 4, 8, 192n. 20, 201nn. 25, 28, 202nn. 39, 42, 205nn. 1, 9, 215nn. 18, 19, 29
Noble, Paul R., 206n. 3, 210n. 45
Nussbaum, Martha C., 92, 98, 107-8, 196n. 26, 204nn. 26, 34, 205nn. 5, 39, 40,

O'Connell, Gabriel, 196n. 18
O'Connell, Timothy E., 126, 171, 190n. 5, 197n. 34, 208n. 17, 214n. 12
O'Donovan, Oliver, 196n. 21
Ogletree, Thomas W., 102, 190n. 7, 205n. 2
O'Keefe, Mark, 192n. 21, 195n. 16, 212n. 21, 213n. 40
Orsuto, Donna L., 196n. 27

Pinches, Charles, 195n. 6
Plato, 93, 102
Pleins, J. David, 207n. 10
Post, Stephen, 204n. 24, 216n. 34
Principe, Walter H., 196n. 24

Quinn, Philip L., 195n. 6

Rahner, Karl, 60, 150, 210n. 48, 212n. 22, 213n. 30
Rawls, John B., 65, 201n. 32
Ricoeur, Paul, 15, 191nn. 14, 15, 201n. 31
Ringe, Sharon H., 203n. 15
Roberts, Robert C., 206n. 3
Roof, Wade Clark, 196n. 17
Rorty, Amelie Oksenberg, 196n. 29, 208n. 18
Royce, Josiah, 215n. 19

Saliers, Don E., 41, 47, 122, 191n. 10, 198nn. 38, 39, 199nn. 49, 51, 207nn. 5, 6, 214n. 5, 216n. 35
Sanders, E. P., 21, 193n. 36
Schillebeeckx, Edward, 208n. 25
Schlier, Heinrich, 209n. 30

Schneiders, Sandra M., 17, 191n. 13, 192nn. 21, 23, 196nn. 24, 25
Schrage, Wolfgang, 212n. 25
Schuller, Bruno, 189n. 3, 191n. 17
Schüssler Fiorenza, Elisabeth, 17, 192nn. 22, 26
Schweitzer, Albert, 21, 203n. 18
Senn, Frank C., 196n. 18, 209n. 36
Shea, William M., 206n. 3
Sheldrake, Philip, 161, 213n. 38
Shelton, Charles M., 203n. 22
Sherman, Nancy, 213n. 35
Shorto, Russell, 195n. 15
Shklar, Judith N., 196n. 27
Shriver, Donald W., Jr., 215n. 28
Sigerist, Henry, 204n. 24
Smith, Martin L., 209nn. 41, 47
Sobrino, Jon, 11, 61, 67, 108, 189n. 1, 190n. 3, 201n. 21, 202n. 36, 210n. 4
Soelle, Dorothee, 196n. 21
Solomon, Robert C., 207n. 15
Spohn, William C., 190n. 2, 191n. 11, 194n. 51, 195n. 4, 196n. 26, 211n. 7
Stortz, Martha Ellen, 194n. 52, 214n. 1
Suchocki, Marjorie Hewitt, 206n. 17, 209n. 39
Swartley, Willard M., 208n. 20

Talbert, Charles H., 206n. 15
Tallon, Andrew, 206n. 3
Tannehill, R. C., 206n. 13
Taylor, Charles, 204n. 32, 214nn. 13, 16, 215n. 21
Theissen, Gerd, 193n. 46
Thiemann, Ronald F., 210n. 44, 215n. 20
Thistleton, Anthony C., 191nn. 13, 15; 201n. 31, 209nn. 38, 39
Tillich, Paul, 60, 201n. 31
Toner, Jules, 213n. 29

Toulmin, Stephen, 201nn. 23, 24
Townes, Emilie, 196n. 21
Tracy, David, 56-60, 62, 191n. 19, 199n. 2, 200nn. 16, 17, 201nn. 18, 20
Trible, Phyllis, 202n. 44
Troeltsch, Ernst, 196n. 20, 210n. 6
Tutu, Bishop Desmond, 179

Unger, Roberto Mangabeira, 108, 205n. 6, 216n. 37

Vacek, Edward Collins, 191n. 18, 198n. 37, 213n. 36
van der Ven, Johannes, 207n. 15
Verhey, Allen D., 199n. 50, 202n. 1
Vetlesen, Arne Johan, 203n. 22, 204n. 32, 205n. 8
Viviano, Benedict T., 207n. 11

Walzer, Michael, 199n. 1
Wawrykow, Joseph P., 198n. 37
Weakland, Rembert G., 48, 199n. 52
Weiss, Johannes, 203n. 18
Wilbanks, Dana W., 183, 216n. 36
Wilkins, M. J., 206n. 14
Wimsatt, William, 189n. 4
Wink, Walter, 18, 191n. 16, 192n. 24, 203n. 13, 209nn. 29, 37
Witherington, Ben, III, 192nn. 27, 30
Wolf, Susan, 196n. 28
Wolff, Tobias, 17, 191n. 20
Wright, N. T., 21, 77, 130, 133, 192nn. 29, 30, 193nn. 33, 38, 40, 202nn. 3, 4, 203nn. 8, 9, 12, 208nn. 22, 25, 26, 27, 211n. 9, 214nn. 7, 8
Wuthnow, Robert, 91, 204n. 25

Yearly, Lee H., 194n. 1

Index of Subjects

affections, 198n. 39
  feelings and, 41
  spiritual practice and, 41
agapē, 32, 203n. 23
analogical imagination, 4, 50–71, 85, 91,
  96, 100, 119, 127, 129, 135, 142,
  144, 146, 164, 165, 174, 186
  Christian ethics and, 60–66
analogy, 54–56, 58, 102
  meaning of, 54–55
asceticism, 4
attention, 92

baptism, 150, 151
body of Christ, 86

canon of scripture, 60
Catholic Worker movement, 65
character, ethics of, 13, 14
Christian
  meaning of, 9
commitment, 160
community, 22
compassion, 96–97, 204n. 23
  Good Samaritan and, 89–91
  Jesus and, 87–91
  meaning of, 90
conscience, 96
contemplation, 137, 139, 140
conversion, religious, 67, 98, 100, 101,
  108–12, 160

Corinthians, 103
cross and resurrection of Jesus, 23, 24, 32,
  52, 61, 142, 145, 146, 148, 150
crucifixion, 101
crusaders, 69
cultural values, 22
  of Palestine, 22

Daniel, book of, 78
Decalogue, 121
dialectical imagination, 58–60, 85, 87, 100,
  108, 133
discernment, 141
  Christian moral, 143
  outcomes of, 162
  practice of, 152–62
disciples, 164
  call of, 128–30, 208n. 23
  misunderstanding and, 30, 31, 100,
    110–11
discipleship, 60, 71, 110, 121, 142, 146,
  150
  ethics and, 10–12
  footwashing and, 51–54
  friendship and, 45
  obedience and, 22
  prayer and, 47–48
dispositional representation, 126
dispositions, 33, 38–39, 120–41
  discernment and, 142–62
  encounter stories and, 134–36

dispositions (*cont.*)
  meaning of, 121
  spiritual practice and, 38, 42
  See also moral dispositions

education, 108
emotions, 95, 120–41, 207n. 15
  meaning of, 121
empathy, 90, 96–97
  meaning of, 90
encounter stories
  dispositions and, 134–36
eschatology, 21
  realized, 85–86, 203n. 17
  tension and, 151
Essenes, 78
ethics
  analogical imagination and, 60–66
  Jesus and, 1
  norms of, 29
  sources of, 194n. 51
Eucharist, 14, 103, 112–14, 165–69, 182
  practice of, 175–84
  See also Lord's Supper
evangelicals, 1
exodus, the, 102
exorcism, 133

fairness, 103–6
faith, Christian, 143
feelings, 159–60
  affections and, 41
  See also affections
feminist theologians
  Jesus and, 2
feminist theology, 60, 70
focal meaning, 58–59
footwashing, 61–62
  discipleship and, 51
forgiveness, 107, 125, 176–80
friendship, 44, 47
  Jesus and, 45
  as practice, 44
  prayer and, 47
fundamentalists, 1

generosity, 106

Gentiles, 105
good news, 10, 17, 76
Good Samaritan, 4, 32, 50, 61, 73, 87,
  89–91, 99
gospel
  as moral norm, 10
Gospel of John
  kingdom of God and, 86
Gospels, 11, 17, 20, 21, 23, 61
  Christology and, 1
  naturalist ethics and, 2
  Synoptic, 83
grace, 103–6, 212n. 21
  means of, 112–19

habits, 39
  of the heart, 14
  moral dispositions and, 39
  spiritual practices and, 39
healing encounters, 132–34
hermeneutics of appreciation, 5, 18
hermeneutics of suspicion, 5, 17–18
historical analysis, 18–23
  limits of, 18–20
  usefulness of, 20–23
historical-critical method, 18
history, 11, 17, 18
Holocaust, 37, 70
honor and shame, 22
human condition, 100
humanity
  alienation of, from God, 100
human nature
  Protestant Reformers and, 1
  Roman Catholic view of, 1

identification
  social, 170–72
identity, 2–3, 24, 33
  Christian, 164–65
  communal, 5
  identification and, 169–74
  individual, 5
  meaning of, 24
  prayer and, 48
images, 207n. 15
  dispositions and, 126–27

imagination
  functions of, 63
  meditation and, 138
  reproductive function of, 63
  vocabulary of, 63-64
  See also analogical imagination; dialectical imagination
imitation of Christ, 146-47, 150
  as disciple, 162
  virtue ethics and, 163
intuition, 159
irony, 104
Israel
  history of, 77-79

Jesus, 1, 12
  Christology and, 1
  as concrete universal, 4
  death and resurrection of, 110
  encounters with people, 4-5, 127-34
  eschatology and, 21
  ethics and, 9
  feminist theologians and, 2
  footwashing and, 51-52
  friendship and, 45
  historical, 19-20
  historical analysis and, 18
  kingdom of God and, 79-83
  life of, as moral norm, 10, 29
  as Messiah, 111
  New Testament and, 3
  as paradigm, 1, 2, 4
  passion predictions of, 111
  preexistence of, 211n. 16
  quest for historical, 19
  as revelation of God, 2
  as Western figure, 2
Jesus Seminar, 19, 21, 192n. 29
Judaism, Second Temple, 81

kingdom of God, 4, 66-71, 87-89
  early Christianity and, 83-87
  Jesus and, 79-83
  Jewish expectations of, 77-79
  as metaphor, 66-67
  rejection of, 130-32
  See also reign of God

language, religious, 197n. 29
lectio divina, 136
liberation theology, 15, 35, 51, 60, 65, 133, 134, 144, 181
Little Brothers of Charles de Foucauld, 65
Lord's Prayer, 46, 124-25
  See also Our Father; prayer, Christian
Lord's Supper, 38, 168-69
  forgiveness and, 164
  solidarity and, 164
  See also Eucharist
love, 91
Lubavitch movement, 35

Maccabean revolt, 77, 78
marriage, 70-71
medieval spirituality, 137
meditation, 5, 63, 136-41
Messiah, 101
metaphors, 106
moral dispositions, 2, 4, 62
moral formation, Christian, 3
morality
  natural law and, 2
moral perception, 2, 4, 96-99, 100-119
  character ethics and, 93-94
  meaning of, 92
  virtue ethics and, 92-99
moral reflection
  on scripture, 55
moral rules, 93-94
  perception and, 97-99
mysticism, 36

names of God, 121-22
narrative
  New Testament and, 28
neighbor, 90-91
New Moses, 84
New Testament, 12, 13, 16-26, 37
  character in, 29
  engaged reading of, 16-17
  ethics and, 3, 28-29
  identity and, 24
  meaning of, 16-17
  paradigms and, 32
  role of Jesus in, 29

nonviolence, 15

Our Father, 46
    See also Lord's Prayer; prayer, Christian

parables, 80, 88, 102-3
    of the kingdom, 67-69
paradigm, 64-66, 109
    biblical images as, 120
    cross and resurrection as, 146
    Good Samaritan as, 91-92
    healing encounters as, 132
    Jesus as, 10-11
    Lord's Supper as, 165-66
    moral, 10, 23, 31-33
passion narratives, 32, 145
Pauline theology, 23, 144-52
Pauline writings, 23-26, 194n. 53
    Corinthian community and, 113-14
    kingdom imagery and, 85-86 .
    Letter to the Philippians, 10, 23-26, 32
perception, 33, 38, 62, 75-99
    correcting of, 100-119
    defective, 106-8
    Jesus and, 76
    judgment and, 94-96
    meaning of, 75
    moral principles and, 97-99
    practices and, 112-19
Pontifical Biblical Commission, 193n. 34
practices, 198nn. 40, 46
    See also discernment; friendship; medita-
        tion; prayer, Christian; spiritual prac-
        tices
pragmatism, 102
praxis, 198n. 40
poor, 102
prayer, Christian
    discernment and, 161
    intercessory, 101, 112-13, 114-19
    pedagogy of, 46
    as practice, 45-49, 140
    Moses and, 122
    transformation and, 46-49
Prodigal Son, 65, 138
Protestant Reformers
    human nature and, 1

Psalter, 123-24
psychology
    cognitive, 120, 126-27
    moral, 26
    virtue ethics and, 31

"Q," 194n. 48
Qumran, 78

racism, 108
reconciliation, 169
Reformation, 109
Reformers, 100
    See also Protestant Reformers
reign of God, 29, 61, 76-78, 82, 83
    See also kingdom of God
religion, 33-34
    New Age, 34
repentance, 160
    call to, 88

scripture, 10, 12-14, 48-49
    engaged reading of, 16-18, 20
    meditation on, 136
    scholarly criticism and, 15
    virtue ethics and, 12, 29
    See also New Testament
Second Temple Judaism, 78, 133, 146
sentiments, 121
Sermon on the Mount, 30, 65, 110,
        115-16, 121
sexism, 108
sin, 29, 110
social science, 22
solidarity, 180-84
Southern Baptist Convention, 71
spirituality, 3, 10, 12, 13-15, 22, 33-42
    Christian, 43
    lived, 36-37
    meaning of, 13, 36-37
    reflective, 37
spiritual practices, 3, 13, 37-49, 62, 63,
        126
    affections and, 41
    habits and, 39
    pedagogical, 38-40
    transformational, 40-42

symbol, 201n. 29
Synoptic Gospels, 110

techniques, 43
    practice and, 43-44
Temple, cleansing of, 80, 81
    Sadducees and, 81
    Second, 80
Ten Commandments, 10
Torah, 78, 82
transformation, 108, 197n. 32, 36
    continuous, 110-12
    radical, 109-10

unity and disunity, 165-69

Vatican II, 2

virtue ethics and, 3, 10, 12, 13-14, 15,
    27-33, 37, 92-99, 101, 112-13, 120,
    126-27, 164, 186, 205n. 12
    character and, 28-30
    forms of, 28
    human heart and, 30-31
    identity and, 163
    scripture and, 12, 13, 22, 28
virtues, 13, 92, 198n. 37
    definition of, 28, 32-33
    dispositions and, 39

Workers in the Vineyard
    parable of, 103-6
worship
    community and, 113-14
    contemporary tensions in, 175-76